FOR MORE VOCATIONS

FOR MORE
VOCATIONS

GODFREY POAGE, C.P.

THE BRUCE PUBLISHING COMPANY
MILWAUKEE

IMPRIMI POTEST:

Neil Parsons, C.P.
Provincial of Holy Cross Province
November 8, 1954

NIHIL OBSTAT:

Kenneth Ward, C.P., S.T.L.
Gregory Joseph Staniszewski, C.P., S.T.D.

IMPRIMATUR:

✠ Samuel Cardinal Stritch, D.D.
Archbishop of Chicago
November 21, 1954

Rosary College Dewey Classification Number: 271

Library of Congress Catalog Card Number: 55–7868

COPYRIGHT, 1955, GODFREY POAGE, C.P.
MADE IN THE UNITED STATES OF AMERICA

DEDICATED TO
THE MOST SACRED HEARTS OF JESUS AND MARY
IN THE HOPE THAT IT MAY BRING OTHERS
TO THEIR SERVICE

Introduction

AT THE Eighth Annual Vocation Institute a group of us were discussing the subject of vocations and what could be done to get more boys and girls interested in the service of God. There was general agreement that more should be done, but we could not agree on what that should be. Many suggestions were offered.

I remember one recruiter stanchly maintaining that the only way to get more vocations was to spend more money in advertising. "Boys and girls cannot love and desire what they do not know," he said, "and it is a plain fact that most of our youths are ignorant of the priesthood, brotherhood, and sisterhood. We have to instruct them. Therefore, the only solution I see is to put on an advertising campaign."

Someone cut in with an objection that it is not *information* that youth needs. It is *persuasion*.

That brought up the subject of personal example, and one recruiter, a sister, recalled a girl telling her, "I should like to be a sister, but I don't know any I'd like to be like. The holy ones are so cold, and the nice ones are so worldly."

Naturally we all wanted to know how she handled that problem, and the discussion almost got off on a retreat theme as various individuals helped her with suggestions and observations on the Sacred Humanity and how Christ was the only One who is completely imitable.

One old sister made the wry comment, "Just as a community seems to get the kind of superiors it deserves, so, I think, it gets the kind of postulants it deserves."

SENSE OF VOCATION

We might have digressed here had not Father John Wilson, C.S.C., reminded us of the point that Archbishop Richard J. Cushing of Boston made in his keynote address at the previous Institute. He said that our embarrassment about vocations was due not so much to a lack of inspiration on the part of recruiters or a lack of seriousness on the part of youth, but rather to a decline of the very *sense of vocation* . . .

"People are aware," he said, "of what it is to be summoned by a draft board. They are acquainted with application forms for the Civil Service. They read the 'Help Wanted' ads in the paper and go over the business opportunity listings. But the old idea of a call from God, a *vocation* in the spiritual, profound, and serious sense, has been lost in the shuffle of our materialistic, competitive civilization. Everyone is looking for a 'chance' or a 'break.' Few are on their knees listening for a *vocation*, a *call from God Himself!*"

This led very naturally into a discussion of the place of prayer in fostering vocations. One priest claimed that we could find our answer in a careful reading of the ninth chapter of St. Matthew's Gospel from the thirty-fifth verse to the end: "So Jesus went about all their cities and villages, teaching in their synagogues, preaching the gospel of the kingdom, and curing every kind of disease and infirmity. Yet still, when he looked at the multitudes, he was moved with pity for them, seeing them bewildered and dejected, like sheep without a shepherd. Then he said to his disciples: 'The harvest indeed is abundant, but the laborers are few. Pray, therefore, to the Lord of the harvest that he send more laborers into his harvest.'

"Careful reflection," he said, "upon those inspired verses in their full context will show how closely prayer and work must be bound together in any genuine and effective effort to recruit more laborers for the harvest. We must pray," he continued, "as though everything depended upon God, and work as though everything depended upon ourselves. . . ."

"That is exactly what the late Bishop William A. Griffin of Trenton said," another recruiter cut in. "His idea was that we should make the whole vocation movement an apostolate of prayer, reaching down to the smallest child, praying as if everything depended on God, for 'Without Me you can do nothing.' At the same time we should put on a promotion campaign as if everything depended on ourselves. In this constant prayer with untiring labor," he said, "lies the real secret of increasing vocations everywhere."

Listening to these many splendid suggestions I reflected upon the wisdom and experience that prompted them. Each statement seemed to bring into sharp focus one facet of the great problem before us. But still there was more to be said.

There was, for example, the consideration of what we must do to deepen the supernatural life of the youths with whom we come in contact. For only then will they be more responsive to the workings of grace within their souls. Only when we have developed in them habits of piety and devotion will they be more disposed to hear Christ's call to follow Him.

At the same time we must evaluate the lessons of experience. What other recruiters have done can help us. There is also a great deal to be said about the power of example . . . the avails of natural psychology . . . the effect of advertising.

As I reflected upon these things, the outlines of this present book took shape. My only hope is that in trying to crowd all that I have seen and observed about these subjects into such a small compass, I shall not skip much that is important.

TREMENDOUS INCREASE OF VOCATIONS

For example, I would not want to overlook the fact that, despite the pessimism of some recruiters, there has been a tremendous increase in vocations to the priesthood, brother-hood, and sisterhood in the past few years. A survey, con-ducted by the *Register* in March of 1954, showed that the number of vocations in the United States has gone up 109 per cent, while the Catholic population has increased only 70 per cent in the same length of time. The conclusion of this study was that the impression that vocations are decreas-ing in proportion to eligible young men and women is a statistical illusion.

Such a "point of view" has an important bearing on the problem. Another study on the number of baptisms from 1940 to 1950 shows that we have had a 75 per cent increase in the number of Catholic youngsters between the ages of one and five. When those children reach high school or col-lege around 1960 and 1970, we can predict an equal increase in vocations.

But right now we find practically every diocese and reli-gious institute in need of more recruits. A poll taken in 1953 of all the major dioceses and religious communities revealed that only one diocese and four religious groups had a supply of candidates equaling their needs. The rest claimed that they were from 20 per cent to 60 per cent behind in the number of vocations they needed to maintain their works and have normal expansion. How can we recon-cile this condition with the increase of vocations?

It is simply that the increase in the number of candidates has not been proportionate to the expansion of the Church in recent years. Shifting populations and the trend toward suburban living have forced many bishops to double the number of their suburban parishes. School enrollments have gone up over a million pupils in the past ten years, and in most places released-time programs have been worked out for the public school children. Hospitals and social service agencies have been increased and the number of foreign missionaries has doubled since the war. All these commit-ments make increasing demands on personnel.

In my own contacts with religious superiors I have often inquired about these increases in membership and how their recruiting programs are going. Most of them have been enthusiastic over the increase and said that their own efforts in getting vocations were "much improved" . . . that their candidates were "more numerous" . . . that the number of prospects today was "beyond comparison" with what it was ten years ago. Only one group said that they were merely "holding their own," and five claimed that they were only "slightly better."

A look at the statistics in the *Catholic Directory* confirms this over-all picture. Each year we have an increase of almost fourteen hundred priests, two hundred brothers, and thirty-two hundred sisters. This does not include the number of replacements necessary for deaths in our ranks. Thus the actual number of ordinations and professions each year is yet more impressive.

WHAT WE SHOULD PRODUCE

But when we break down the figures into parishes and schools, we see that many places are not fulfilling their quota. Some do not even replace the priests and religious they use.

Consider, for instance, the average parish with two priests and eight sisters in the grade school. The work expectancy of the priests is approximately twenty years and that of the sisters is close to twenty-five years. Thus in a hundred-year period it uses the lives of ten priests and thirty-two sisters.

This figure does not take into consideration the extra-parochial needs: the chancery office, the seminary, retreat houses, hospitals, orphanages, homes for the aged, high schools, colleges, and foreign missions. In these activities almost the same number of vocations is needed.

Such computations are not completely accurate, but they do give a graphic estimate of the situation. The average parish in our country, therefore, is falling behind in vocational promotion if it does not produce one priestly vocation for the diocese and one for a religious community every two years, one vocation for the brotherhood every five years, and one vocation for the sisterhood every year!

Happily many parishes go far beyond this quota. Monsignor Martin E. Muzik of St. Eulalia's parish, Maywood, Illinois, averages over three times that number of vocations each year.

In San Francisco Monsignor Harold Collins of St. Cecilia parish reports that he has twenty-four boys now studying for the diocesan priesthood, eleven for the religious priesthood, three for the brotherhood, and twenty-two for the sisterhood.

The Cathedral parish in Omaha practically ties this record. Monsignor E. G. Graham, the pastor, has nineteen boys studying for the diocesan priesthood, sixteen preparing in religious orders, and nineteen girls entering the convent.

Many other places, I know, have equaled or surpassed these records. But the sad truth is all too evident. Most parishes and schools cannot boast anywhere near this number of vocations, and statistics show that only 1 out of every 97 Catholic girls between the ages of fifteen and twenty-four becomes a sister. Only 1 out of every 132 boys in the same age bracket becomes a priest, and only 1 out of 1214 boys in the same group becomes a brother!

A CHALLENGE TO ALL OF US

These facts are a challenge to all of us. We must do something positive to increase vocations. God's grace, we know, is never wanting. Until the end of time He will be blessing individuals with the endowments of nature and grace that will enable them to accomplish His works. There will always be potential priests, brothers, and sisters, *but you and I must find them!*

If we sit back and wait for them to ring the front doorbell, we may wait forever! God will not ordinarily work miracles to ease our obligations, and too many of us seem to think that our recruiting can be done by a prayercard. That is not enough. We have to get out and work. We must speak! Write! Contact! Interview!

As Bishop Thomas J. McDonnell of Wheeling reminisced one day at a vocational meeting: "I was preparing to go to medical school when a priest said to me, 'Tom, have you thought seriously of the priesthood? If not, wait awhile and pray to see if you have a vocation.' I followed his advice, and, thank God, I ended up in a seminary. But I doubt if I would be a priest today, if it hadn't been put directly to me."

In Father George Kane's delightful book, *Why I Entered the Convent,* several sisters speak of the influence of a priest or religious on their making a choice for the service of God.

Sister Mary Adolorata, O.S.M., for example, says: "At this point I was given another grace from Almighty God, the grace of direction. A young priest, Father Monahan (now Msgr. Emmett A. Monahan, Director of the Propagation of the Faith in Trenton) had taken up his duties as assistant in the Church of this small New Jersey town. He told me that I should enter the convent. But I had given up the idea, if I ever really had it — so I thought!"

Sister M. Madeleva, C.S.C., says that the thought was put to her a little more subtly, but nonetheless directly, by one of her teachers at St. Mary's College, while she was musing about what the future held for her.

"If you thought you might be a sister, I suppose you would be indignant," her teacher commented.

"No, I would be the happiest girl in the world. But I know I could never be a nun," was her answer. "I would do anything God wanted me to do, if I only knew what it was."

"That is all one needs for a vocation," the teacher replied, and Sister Madeleva says that was the turning point in her reflection.

Father James Keller, M.M., confirms this idea by saying:

INTRODUCTION

"I owe my interest in the priesthood to a priest in St. Francis de Sales parish in Oakland, California, who came into my Sunday school class when I was six years old. Although that was forty-eight years ago, I can still see him standing before us children and making a very brief remark to me: 'You may be a priest some day. You may do some good for the world.'"

Such examples could be multiplied many times over, but there would be no purpose in that. The conviction we must make our own is that while many boys and girls are given the grace of a priestly or religious vocation, often they fail to recognize or carelessly reject the divine call. So if we want more vocations to our seminaries or convents we must get busy and help such favored individuals.

Too long has there been a "hands-off" attitude among certain priests and religious! These individuals have been pleased enough when aspirants came to them, but they themselves did nothing to promote vocations. They have said, "I'll let God take care of vocations" . . . or "If God wants vocations, He'll see that they come." . . .

These presumptive persons seem to have forgotten that God in His ordinary providence accomplishes His purposes through human means. They want miracles of grace and assume that vocations are ordinarily the product of revelation or inspiration.

Others have taken a defeatist attitude. They have tried once or twice to do something about vocations, but obtained no results. Now they say, "What's the use?"

These individuals forget that such an attitude is absolutely fatal in promotion work. No one wants to join a dying organization, and by their pessimism they are failing in more ways than one!

Still others seem to be afraid of the responsibility in directing vocations. That is the reason they do nothing. I have even heard the quotation of St. Paul to the Hebrews, "No one takes this honor to himself, but he that is called by God, as Aaron was," used by them in vindication of their position. "Vocations," they claim, "are a manifestation of the Holy Spirit's predilection for certain individual souls and it ill-behooves us to meddle in the workings of the Holy Spirit!"

With these individuals I can only plead that they review their theology and study the pronouncements of the Holy See. Particularly enlightening for them should be the polemical work of St. Thomas Aquinas, *Contra Pestiferam Doctrinam Retrahentium Homines a Religionis Ingressu.* Also interesting should be his *Summa Theologica,* IIa IIae, Q. 189, where he answers the question, "Should one *induce* others to enter Religion?" by saying, "Those who induce others to enter Religion not only do not sin, but they merit a very great reward."

But why argue the point? Surely we are unanimous in wanting to see an increase of priests, brothers, and sisters. The saints who have gone before us have left a great example of recruitment. Look at the records of SS. Benedict . . . Augustine . . . Dominic . . . Francis . . . Ursula . . . Ignatius . . . Vincent de Paul . . . John Baptist de La Salle . . . John Bosco . . . Teresa . . . Paul of the Cross!

FOR MORE VOCATIONS

It is in an effort to imitate these saints — at least to the extent of getting one more worker for Christ — that this book is written. In a way it is a sequel to *Recruiting for Christ.** But in another sense it stands alone.

For in the present volume the role of the recruiter is developed. There is pointed out the responsibility each one of us has of deepening the supernatural life of the boys and girls with whom we come in contact. Then follow clear and proven directives on how interest in the priesthood and religious life should be stimulated . . . how aspirants should

---

* The first book on vocational guidance by Father Poage, released in 1950 by The Bruce Publishing Company.

be interviewed . . . how candidates should be judged for acceptance or rejection. Finally, there is a treatment of the problems of environment, parental opposition, and age.

Much of the matter is not my own. I would like to be considered an amanuensis for wiser and better heads. The inspiration, I trust, comes from God. The rest belongs to the wonderful bishops, religious superiors, priests, brothers, sisters, parents, and youths with whom I have been associated from one end of this country to the other. I have only kept my eyes and ears open and laid hold of their wisdom.

But here we are digressing. This is only an introduction — an opening of the subject on what is needed

FOR MORE VOCATIONS!

Contents

FOR MORE VOCATIONS

CHAPTER I

Role of the Recruiter

THROUGH the years the *Divine Comedy* of Dante Alighieri has made the minds of men a little brighter and their hearts a little lighter with its sincere and wholesome message.

In rereading that great masterpiece I thought I saw prefigured the role of a recruiter. For Dante tells how he was taken on a long journey of purgation . . . then purification . . . and finally union. His guide the most important part of the way was the incomparable Beatrice, and the closer he approached to Divine Union, the brighter and more beautiful became the face of his guide.

What has this to do with a recruiter? Simply that those of us who are called upon to lead souls, even as Beatrice led Dante, must remember that we have no easy journey. For we, in truth, must take our protégés through a period of purgation and trial. Then we must develop in them habits of virtue and purify them for their roles as "Other Christs" and "Other Marys." Finally, we must bring them to the threshold of the priesthood or religious life and there say, as did Beatrice, "Turn now and look, for thou hast found Paradise!"

INFLUENCE OF PERSONALITY

But to be such a guide, we must show forth in our own lives the joy and happiness we have found. We must give experimental proof that the life we lead as priests or religious is greater than any other. Our vocation has more to offer than all the world.

As Clare Boothe Luce once remarked, "Converts are won by apologists, not apologetics." So I repeat, "Vocations are won by recruiters, not recruiting techniques." No amount of talking about the nobility and grandeur of our life will impress youth unless they see those advantages reflected in our conduct.

At the Quincy College Vocational Institute in 1950 Father Pacific Hug, O.F.M., put this point very succinctly: "Our desire to win many young people to the priesthood and religious life will be genuine and efficacious only insofar as we become saints ourselves, while remaining completely lovable and sincerely human."

Selfless and dedicated, we may then hope to move about among our boys and girls with a little of that sanctified personal power which, as G. K. Chesterton observed in his *Life of St. Francis,* so distinguished the Saint of Assisi: "He only saw the image of God multiplied but never monotonous. To him a man was always a man and did not disappear in a dense crowd any more than in a desert. He honored all men; that is, he not only loved but respected them all.

"What gave St. Francis (*who is said to have recruited over 2000 followers in his lifetime*) his extraordinary personal power was this: that from the Pope to the beggar, from the Sultan in his pavilion to the ragged robbers crawling out of the wood, there was never a man who looked into those brown burning eyes without being certain that Francis Bernadone was really interested in him; in his own inner individual life from the cradle to the grave; that he himself was being valued and taken seriously, and not merely added to the spoils of some social policy or the names in some clerical document."

We, too, have to love and respect those with whom we come in contact if we expect our vocational endeavors to be fruitful. Our personality will influence youths far more than our words.

The late Father Daniel A. Lord, S.J., says in his *Guidance of Youth,* "Eloquence never fools the young. Actions are what count. They want a leader who asks of others only those ideals and heroisms which he himself exemplifies in his life."

Not only in our lectures and public appearances do we reveal ourselves, but also in the most insignificant actions of our day. There is an old adage that says, "What you are talks so loudly, I cannot hear what you say." We cannot talk convincingly of the religious spirit, unless we are deeply in love with the religious life. If we are Christlike in all our thoughts, words, and actions, we will unconsciously draw souls, like a magnet, to the love and service of God.

Surely the noticeable increase of G.I. vocations immediately after the past war is proof of this. Many of them attributed their vocation to the example of the courageous and self-sacrificing chaplains, priests, brothers, and sisters they had met on the missions.

Accordingly, what we are as true priests and religious will mean a great deal, under God, in finding and fostering vocations. Our endeavor, therefore, should be to make ourselves attractive to youth. We should radiate joy and gladness. Our personal cheerfulness will be one of our strongest arguments for religion's importance. Our enthusiasm for and love of the life that we have chosen will be our conclusive proof of sincerity.

This means that we will try to smile as often as possible. We will have a kind and cheery word for all with whom we come in contact. When opportunity offers, we will slip in a word of praise. All this pleases youths and makes them happy to have us around.

I remember Father Pius Barth, O.F.M., stressing this point in an excellent address he gave on "Teaching Through Teaching." "I think it wise," he said, "to let our pupils know that we appreciate them. Many of us are teachers today because we were attracted by a glittering star. Stars we must all be or become, for 'those who instruct others unto justice shall shine as stars for all eternity.' No one is attracted to religious teaching or nursing in the abstract. We ourselves, if we examine our vocation, will find that we wanted to imitate some priest, brother, or sister who enjoyed working for God, who was happy, and who sought thereby to make others happy. No Gloomy Gus or Sad Susie ever attracted vocations!

"While we trust in the Holy Spirit, we must try to promote vocations in others through a socially expansive personality. We must radiate the happiness which we feel. We must meditate frequently on the importance and the inspiration of being happy in teaching.

"You do your best work for vocations," he concluded, "not through words, but through your friendly actions. You should never be considered by youth as a natural-born enemy. They should rather look upon you as their guide, and guidance is nothing more than a person to person relationship. It is the impact of one personality upon the other. So smile even though you would rather foam at the mouth. Smile! It is all-important! For boys and girls, at a time when they do not understand themselves and are misunderstood by others, need a cheerful guide at their side. They need someone who will understand them and walk with them until they can walk alone."

These observations were confirmed by a graduate thesis, submitted to the Catholic University of Washington by Father Glenn Holdbrook. After studying the attitude toward the sisters of 1200 girls, in eight high schools of northeastern Ohio taught by six religious communities, he discovered that many of the girls gave up the idea of entering religion because they failed to see the interior life and holiness of the sisters. They looked upon them only as instructors, paper correctors, and disciplinarians, not persons who are happily in love with God.

This was the case because it is always easier to understand a person than an ideal. Youths watch us and judge more from our conduct than our words. They are shocked, as a result, when they discover petty jealousy in us or notice that we are competing with one another for personal popularity.

Also for both youngsters and their parents it is sometimes hard to harmonize the idea of religious poverty and the way we go after money. They are confused when we show favoritism toward the rich. They find it rather revolting to see one of us, who professes to follow the meek and humble Christ, insist on personal dignity and wear an air of pompous authority.

I remember being embarrassed once by a high school senior who asked what was wrong with his pastor. The boy had phoned the rectory and asked to see him about going to the diocesan seminary. The priest answered haughtily, "Don't bother me with such trivialities. Take the matter to one of the assistants!"

You cannot blame youths either for suspecting that our vow of chastity is a kind of frustration should one of us be so foolish as to make slurring remarks about courtship or marriage. Likewise, when we go around with a frown or scowl, it is natural for them to think of it as sort of a religious hang-over.

Whenever any of us are so imprudent as to air complaints, boys and girls cannot help but doubt the genuine happiness of our life. Youths today are not attracted by sad faces, eyes tainted with envy, tongues sharp with criticism, or personalities that are proud and selfish. They like to think that Christ meant it when He said, "If you will be perfect, come, follow me."

Such good impressions and pleasing personalities, though, are not developed overnight. Often it takes years of patient effort and self-examination. But nothing will ever be developed, unless at rock bottom there is a real liking for boys and girls. Our interest in them must be so sincere and so genuine that they cannot help feeling it and liking us in return.

When young people sense interest and sympathetic understanding in a person, words are unnecessary. They know
their friend, and on their own initiative they seek the help
they need.

Sister Maura, S.L., put it this way, "We have to love
our students more and more. I do not mean with a sentimental love, but with one that is deep and consistent and
interested in everything they do. Then we don't have to
tell them that we love them. They just know it!

"Also," she continued, "I am growing more convinced
that this real love cannot reach our students until it first
reaches out to our own in the community. Through them
it is reflected on to the students, nurses, orphans, or whom-
ever we happen to be working with. We have to strive first
to be consistently gracious and helpful and uncritical of
our own — whether priests or religious — before our love can
reach even the Heart of Christ!"

At this point I am reminded of the practice of the early
Scripture copyists of inserting the word *"Selah,"* meaning
"Stop," whenever they came to a passage on which they
thought the reader ought to reflect. For here, certainly, we
need a *"Selah"* that you might ponder on the importance
of personality and appreciate its tremendous influence in
recruiting for Christ.

DEEPENING THEIR SPIRITUAL LIFE

Besides attracting boys and girls, the real recruiter must
also deepen their spiritual life. This is no easy task. Yet
it is absolutely necessary if we are to sign up the right kind
of candidates.

What we are looking for in a prospect for the priesthood,
brotherhood, or sisterhood is an integral Christian life with
a special readiness, stemming from the virtue of religion, to
consecrate his or her self to the service of God. We want
individuals who have this over-all goodness of life, coupled
with a great generosity for the things of God.

When we find individuals with these characteristics, we have found good prospects for the seminary or convent. But when these characteristics are not too evident, the recruiter must do all he or she can to deepen the spiritual life of those at hand and develop in them the virtue of religion by encouraging those acts proper to the virtue.

This means that the priest or religious who hopes to increase vocations must first inculcate habits of meditation and prayer in the youths with whom he or she comes in contact. For only after a boy or girl has learned to study the life and personality of Christ, as revealed in the Gospel, will it be possible for such a one to develop a great love for Him. After they know and love Christ, then it is but a step for them to follow Him "Who is the Way, the Truth, and the Life."

The great St. Teresa of Ávila once exclaimed, "Jesus Christ is my all. Without Him all is nothing to me!" But she did not come to that realization until she had first learned to meditate. In like manner, if we want our young men and women to echo those same sentiments in their own hearts and turn from the world to Christ, we must teach them to reflect upon the life of Christ and the lessons of the Gospel.

Such reflection, though, must be kept intelligible to them. Here it might be helpful to take an example from what our young people see around them to point out what love for God can mean in their lives.

Bill, for instance, who works at the corner grocery, meets Betty, the filing clerk — and their worlds are suddenly changed! In his eyes she is the most wonderful girl there is, and to her he seems the prince for whom she has been waiting. Going for a walk or to the movies, which used to be dull or only mildly interesting to both of them, now becomes high adventure.

The reason for this change is their love for one another, and by drawing out the parallel it is easy to show how a love for Christ will work a similar marvel in the life of one who becomes a priest or religious.

Abbot M. James Fox, O.C.S.O., of Gethsemani, in his address on the contemplative life at the First National Congress of Religious at Notre Dame University in 1952, gave two examples of the effects of this love on young men who have come to him.

One was an ex-major of the Marine Air Force, who had an office on Wall Street and was a member of the New York Stock Exchange, drawing a salary of about $20,000 a year, though he was not yet thirty. Father Abbot said he talked very plainly to him and said, "Before you decide on being a Trappist, let me tell you something of our life.

"There will never again," he said, "be any baseball, tennis, swimming, bowling, or cards. There will never be any meat, fish, or eggs, unless you are sick. There will never be newspapers, magazines, radios, television programs, smokes, drinks, or recreations. There will never be vacations to Florida, California, or Maine, or permission to visit home again — even at the death of father or mother. You will not even get to sing your First Mass in your home parish, if you persevere that long.

"There will be no possibility of a brilliant career of preaching or teaching. Your family can come only once a year to see you, but outside of that no other visits. After the first month you can write home only four times a year and receive mail only four times a year, apart from some emergency of charity or business. There will never be hope of a change from one Trappist monastery to another, and nothing but relentless regularity, whether it is Easter, Christmas, or the Fourth of July."

Then looking the young man straight in the eye Father Abbot asked, "Do you want to come now?"

Without blinking an eyelash he replied, "I do. I want to give all to Jesus."

Another case was that of a young man still in his twenties, who had been a captain in the Army, was a graduate of Fordham Business School, and had already risen to a high position with General Motors. He had come to Gethsemani to make a retreat and nothing more.

The first day, after seeing something of the community life, he remarked to a fellow retreatant, "This certainly isn't the life for me!"

The second day he remarked to the same individual, "I guess it's not so bad after all," and on the third day, "Perhaps I'll go down and see the Abbot."

"On the fourth day," Father Abbot said, "he came to me and I explained our life as best I could. I told him how we sleep at night on a straw mattress. We go to bed at seven, and we are up at two in the morning. As choir monks we spend some six or seven hours a day in choir, singing the Office and the Conventual Mass. Besides the Canonical Office there is also the Little Office of the Blessed Virgin every day, and on the average of every third day there is the Office of the Dead. There is also spiritual reading and private prayer. Finally, there is the manual labor each day — even for priests — in the hayfields, cornfields, swamps, forests, and shops. In other words it is a complete holocaust of self for Jesus."

The young man replied, "Jesus gave all for me. I will give all for Him."

"It is not a question," Father Abbot warned, "of giving 95 per cent, or 99 per cent, or even 99½ per cent — but of giving 100 per cent!"

"That's what I want to do! I want to give 100 per cent. I want to give all. That is what is burning me up. I will be back in six months."

"He was back in three months," Father Abbot concluded.

Where did these young men get such clearness of vision and strength of will in the midst of luxury, worldly success, power, pleasure, and popularity? Where did they find such ardent love for God? Surely it was in their prayer and meditation.

Accordingly, all recruiters should realize that many more young men and women will follow their example, if they are taught how to make meditation . . . if they are encouraged to take up spiritual reading . . . if they are given time and opportunity to make retreats.

Mother M. Walburga, S.S.J., said that after one such vocational retreat, which they had for ninety-six picked girls from their schools and their graduates, ten entered novitiates of five communities that fall, and eleven more entered the following year.

The Christian Brothers told me that vocations increased as much as 17 per cent in some of their schools after they introduced the practice of having Benildus Club members make meditation each day. This was particularly effective where time was so apportioned over each week that at least two members were constantly at prayer while classes were in session.

ADVANTAGE OF FREQUENT CONFESSION

In his treatment in the *Summa Theologica* of the virtue of religion, St. Thomas Aquinas points out that both moral and intellectual cleanness are absolutely necessary for the preservation and development of this virtue. In other words, there must be not only the avoidance of sin but also freedom of the mind from error.

The reason for this is obvious. Religion demands that we focus clearly on the excellence of our Divine Lover. The consequent act of devotion prompts us to honor and serve Him. But if we allow ourselves to become immersed in the things of sense, our minds become more and more incapable of considering the things of the spirit. If we have the misfortune to fall into sin, the order is destroyed entirely.

Accordingly, when the recruiter finds that the youths

with whom he is dealing are completely engrossed in the things of sense, his task is to wean them away from these created goods and direct their attention to God as their Infinite Good. When he finds that they have fallen into sin, he must urge them to rectify the disorder immediately.

An inestimable help in this matter is the Sacrament of Confession. Father Alfred Wilson, C.P., in his excellent book, *Pardon and Peace,* lists nine reasons why this is so:

1. The Sacrament deletes sin.

2. It remits the temporal punishment due to sin, and does this more effectively than ordinary acts of virtue, because of the sacramental efficiency.

3. It heals the soul from the evil effects of sin.

4. It has an incomparable power of restoring peace of soul. Making a clean breast of things gives one the maximum relief of mind and powerfully restores the resolution.

5. It gains a right to actual graces for future combats and supernaturally strengthens one's purpose of amendment.

6. It is a powerful moral and educational force, which fosters self-knowledge and self-control, gives insight into human nature, and makes one more sympathetic and understanding and therefore more helpful to others.

7. Confession to another human being helps to knock the conceit out of a person.

8. It enables one to get useful advice and surer guidance.

9. It increases sanctifying grace and the fervor of charity.

These reasons only bring out in detail what was summed up admirably by Pope Pius XII in his encyclical, *Mystici Corporis.* "To hasten daily progress along the path of virtue," the Holy Father wrote, "We wish the pious practice of frequent confession to be earnestly advocated. Not without the inspiration of the Holy Spirit was this practice introduced into the Church. By it genuine self-knowledge is increased, Christian humility grows, bad habits are corrected, spiritual neglect and tepidity are countered, the conscience is purified, the will strengthened, a salutary self-control is attained, and grace is increased in virtue of the Sacrament itself."

Such help should be received as often as possible, and this is why most recruiters recommend that a prospect for the seminary or convent get into the practice of weekly confession.

Father John P. Kennelly, Vocational Director in the Archdiocese of Chicago, stressed this point in his talk at the Vocation Institute of Notre Dame in 1948. He also brought out the fact that a recruiter should not only encourage boys and girls to a frequent and regular use of this Sacrament, but also keep alert for those who are using the Sacrament but not yet evidencing an interest in the priesthood or religious life.

To the priests he said, "There isn't a Saturday that goes by that we don't meet such boys and girls. To them we can say something like this: 'Is this your usual confession?' 'Yes.' 'Are you going to confession regularly?' 'Yes.' 'When was the last time you thought about the religious life?' (Always take it for granted that a good boy or girl has thought about it frequently.) 'Father, I've been thinking about it for some time; how did you know?' 'Well, when we find good boys and good girls like you, naturally we want you to attain the highest degree of sacrifice and sanctity and perfection possible. That is why I happened to mention this to you.'

" 'How often do you think about it? Do you ever pray for light to know God's will? What's your ambition? Do you dare to ask God to give you a vocation to His service?'

"If you have the time," he said, "you can probably go into more detail, stressing the supernatural motives, asking them something about their background to detect impediments or obstacles. Give them time in the course of their confessions. Saturday afternoons are not too busy generally. Even when we hear the confessions of these individuals for First Friday, we can ask, 'Are you praying for your vocation?

Do you ever ask God to make you a priest (brother or sister)?'

"Even though these youngsters are only in grade school, you will be surprised how much they are impressed by your questions and how much they have been thinking about the matter. Your questioning only confirms their half-articulate desires and brings the matter out into the open.

"Always add this," Father Kennelly urges: " 'Will you promise me one thing before this confession is over; namely, that you will talk to some priest about this? Whether you talk to me or somebody else makes no difference. But promise God that you will talk with a priest and clear up this question in your mind once and for all. Later on you will have no regrets. Never will you have to worry about whether you would have been better off in some other state of life.' "

I have quoted Father John P. Kennelly at some length, not only because of our long association in vocational work in the Archdiocese of Chicago, but also because I consider his techniques in the confessional or in private conference particularly effective. In the past twenty-five years he has helped over 300 girls to convents around the Midwest, and at a recent meeting he was challenged on the number that came to him voluntarily. His reply was, "Only 7 per cent came to me of their own accord or were sent by others. The rest I had to go after."

HELP FROM HOLY COMMUNION

Pursuing this theme of nurturing vocations by developing the virtue of religion in the young people with whom we come in contact, we cannot overlook that Sacrament which pre-eminently serves this purpose; namely, Holy Communion.

The encyclical *Mirae Caritatis* of St. Pius X expresses it: "By this Sacrament union with Christ is fostered, the spiritual life is more abundantly sustained, the soul is more richly endowed with virtues, and an ever surer pledge of everlasting happiness is bestowed on the recipient."

St. Thomas Aquinas in his treatise on this subject lists ten advantages from reception of Holy Communion.

1. The Sacrament of the Body of the Lord puts demons to flight.

2. It defends us against the incentives to vice and to concupiscence.

3. Venial sins are remitted, and the soul is strengthened against mortal sin.

4. There is a remission of the temporal punishment due to sin.

5. The understanding is enlightened to know God.

6. This Sacrament inflames the will and affections with the love of God.

7. It fills the memory with spiritual sweetness.

8. The whole man is confirmed in good, and merits are multiplied.

9. The soul is freed from eternal death.

10. Finally, the Sacrament leads us to our everlasting home and reanimates the body to eternal life.

St. Alphonsus Liguori, in detailing the advantages he had observed in recommending this Sacrament to souls under his direction, noted that it was particularly productive of a "readiness to accomplish the Divine Will joyfully and to support pain and trials with more patience and resignation."

In his pamphlet, *Frequent Communion,* Father John A. O'Brien brings out the added note that a "person who is strengthened by frequent Communion to resist temptation is by that very fact heartened to fight more courageously for virtue, honor, right, and manliness. One who knows he is free from sin and whose friendship with his Lord and Maker has been deepened and made more intimate through the Holy Eucharist throws himself into his undertakings with greater courage and abandon."

These are reasons why it is so important for a recruiter

to encourage frequent Communion. If we are to find many boys and girls interested in the seminary or convent, we must find them first at the Communion rail. Then as charity becomes inflamed in their souls, all the virtues flourish. The virtue of religion becomes increasingly evident and when we suggest that they give themselves to the service of God, there is an eager and prompt response.

A survey conducted by Father Ignatius Fabacher, S.J., in fourteen high schools of the Middle West and South reveals the effects of this Sacrament in the judgment of a teen-ager. In answer to the question, "What is your principal reason for receiving Holy Communion?" 43 per cent answered that it was "personal love for our Lord," and about 20 per cent said it was for "personal perfection" or "to decide my vocation."

One thing that is quite evident in this study is that our American youths are motivated by some immediate good in approaching Christ in the Eucharist, and when they have less motivation they receive less. Here you can play a very important role, for you can suggest innumerable reasons why this or that youngster should go frequently to the Altar.

If you really know the hearts of those with whom you work, you can propose excellent arguments for daily Communion. Once you have the individual receiving the Sacrament often, grace will take over.

Brother Peter, S.C., remarked after twenty-four years of counseling, "If I can get a boy to take his particular difficulty to the Master in Holy Communion, more than half the battle for him is won. One Communion made with great reverence and confidence will do more for a boy than all the advice I can give him in my private talks."

PARTICIPATING IN THE MASS

In his treatment of religion St. Thomas Aquinas explains how that virtue looks to God and seeks to pay something on the debt we owe Him. That payment is one of worship and service.

These facts are presented to our Catholic children in the very beginning of their Catechism. "Why did God make you?" the child is asked. And the answer is, "To know Him, love Him, *serve* Him in this life, and be happy with Him forever in the next."

It but remains for the recruiter to stress that this "service" and "worship" of God is given principally in the Holy Sacrifice of the Mass.

In *It's Your Mass Too,* Father Hugh Calkins, O.S.M., gives five excellent reasons for assisting at Mass:

1. Because we believe in God and wish to worship Him publicly.

2. Because we wish to offer sacrifice to God who has given us everything we are or have.

3. Because we wish to give ourselves to God whom we love, and the best way to give ourselves is through sacrifice.

4. But the greatest gift we can give God is His own Son, and when we offer Mass we offer Christ to God the Father.

5. And the best way to give ourselves to God is through Christ our Lord. We do that when we offer Jesus to His Father.

Once these truths are appreciated, it is easy to see why the Mass is so important in fostering vocations. In the Mass our young people are brought to a realization of how they can give Christ to God the Father and themselves to God through Christ.

However, before they come to such a realization they must understand the Mass and know how to participate in it. Four years ago in the *Faculty Advisor* a report was published from a questionnaire on "How do you follow the Mass?" Approximately fifteen hundred high school students answered this poll and their replies showed that 31 per cent read the Missal, 28 per cent made their own private prayer, 21 per cent said the Rosary, and 20 per cent had no plan or practice.

To make the Mass more intelligible to our youths, we have to take time out to explain and illustrate it. This should be done not only in the classroom but also in the pulpit, in the confessional, in private conference, on the playground, and any place we meet them.

We should make it clear to them that when they go to Mass they are actually visiting our Lord. There Jesus is offering Himself for us as He did on Calvary. The priest who officiates at the Holy Sacrifice represents Christ, and in His name and by His authority he offers the Sacrifice with the people and for the people. Then follow with an explanation of each step of the Mass, and instructions on the use of the Missal.

In many places the practice of the "Missa Recitata" has been instituted. This certainly gives the students a wonderful opportunity to follow the priest and helps them to maintain attention.

CONDITIONING CANDIDATES

Along with the encouragement to frequent prayer, attendance at Mass, and the use of the Sacraments, the recruiter must also condition his or her candidates.

So often we have seen the most promising young men and women go off to a seminary or religious institute. Then after a few weeks or months their enthusiasm has waned, they have grown tired of the religious life, and finally abandoned their ambition. If you ask them, "Why didn't you give the life a better try?" they will answer, "I didn't know it would be so hard," or, "It was so much different from what I expected."

Accordingly, the role of the recruiter should also be to initiate the candidates into what they can expect in the service of God. If they are prepared for the demands of

the seminary or juniorate, the percentage of perseverance
will be much higher. A vocation saved is a vocation gained.

Father John Kennelly, who claims that only eight have
returned of the three hundred he has directed to religion,
says very emphatically, "Train them as early as possible.
You must direct, prepare, and test them, so that when they
leave for the postulate or novitiate, there is no abrupt change
from their life in the world. With this preparation and
training, you will have more and stronger vocations. They
will not be at a loss trying to find themselves, seeking to
learn what it is all about. Also they will be more sincere
and better religious."

This period of preparation or formation should extend
over several months and during that time the director
should endeavor to see the candidates at least every two or
three weeks. Discussions at these times should take up the
subjects of the love of God, the necessity of sacrifice, purity of
intention, the nature of temptation, devotion to the Blessed
Mother, the indwelling of the Holy Spirit, and the like.

Life in the seminary or novitiate should be explained,
with emphasis on the problems of homesickness, dryness at
prayer, fear of studies, and difficulties with companions. At
the same time there should be an effort to deepen their awareness of how Christ has selected them above all others and
how much they can prove their love for Him.

Father Kennelly also urges the recruiter to have the boy
or girl disclose his or her doubts and fears. "Who put this
idea of a vocation in your mind? Where did it come from?
Did it come from the devil? No! Do you think the devil
wants you to be a leader in Christ's army? Of course not! The
inspiration, then, must be from God, and if He has chosen
you, He doesn't demand anything extraordinary. He simply
offers you an invitation. You can accept or reject. What will
it be?"

"Try especially," he says, "to develop this attitude: 'I am
presumptuous enough to think I have a vocation and I am

anxious enough to prepare myself as soon as possible so that I can lose no time in giving Him all the benefits of my capacities, my faculties, my love. I will keep that vocation until such time as He tells me, through an outsider, I have none.' "

At this point problems of a different nature often arise. Sometimes the prospect will say, "Gee, I never had any worry about purity until now. Just as I want to do something good and enter religious life, I start getting all kinds of temptations. I never realized I was so weak until now."

This is a particularly good cue to bring in a thorough explanation of the nature of temptation. Many boys and girls have the erroneous notion that the moment they put on a cassock or habit, they will become immune to any rebellion of the flesh. Point out that when the devil sees one entering religion he only renews his assaults the more fiercely. Mortification and prayer, however, will quickly rout him.

Constantly emphasize that *whatever* comes, it is but a test of one's love for God. It is a test of one's trust. It is a test of one's absolute abandonment to His wishes and desires.

Many of us would have given up the struggle years ago if we had not been schooled from the very beginning to ask ourselves, "What am I here for? Is it not for God? I expect to suffer like Christ. The more I can take for Him, the more generously I can give in return." With these same thoughts we must now school our prospects for the seminary or convent, lest they become disheartened in trial or temptation.

NO "COUNSELORS OF CONFUSION"

The theme of the 1951 Quincy College Vocational Institute was this important problem of prudent counsel and guidance before entrance. One very enlightening session was devoted to describing the "Counselors of Confusion." Two types were singled out for particular criticism. There were those who ignore or depreciate marriage, and those who are guilty of undue persuasion.

No recruiter can ever hope to go far by ridiculing marriage or ignoring it as a means of sanctification. We do not ask any boy or girl to give up marriage because it is bad, but precisely because it is so good. If it were bad, there would be no sacrifice involved, since we are obliged to give up evil in any case.

If we should ever induce a person to turn away from marriage in the belief that it is evil, we have achieved nothing. For such a one has not known what marriage is and so cannot surrender something unappreciated. What this person has rejected is a distorted monstrosity that we have painted in imagination, which is indeed a poor gesture to make to the Lord.

As for those who are guilty of undue persuasion, I can only say that their dearth of vocations must have distorted their perspective. When people are desperate, the means they use are sometimes extreme.

In this category fall all those cases of a boy being talked out of service to the diocese and signed up with some religious order, or vice versa. Or a girl interested in one community being solicited by another. Or a recruiter signing up an individual on his first contact, or stringing a prospect along with a so-called "scholarship."

I heard of one recruiter who offered free-tuition deals. After the boy was signed he reminded the parents that they were expected to pay $35 a month as "activities' fees."

The recruiter who has the interests of Christ and the Church at heart will never countenance such practices. He or she will be "big" and care not where the individual goes, so long as it is to the service of God. Such a recruiter will be catholic in the real sense and remain totally indifferent to the aspirant's choice. In the end God will not let such

a one suffer a loss of vocations but will bless abundantly the
diocese or community.

A good example of the right kind of recruiter is Father
George E. Ganss, S.J. It has been his job at Marquette
University, Milwaukee, Wisconsin, to keep his finger upon
the school's spiritual pulse. In the past six years he has
guided 250 students to over thirty-four different communities.

"One of the important reasons why large numbers of
Marquette students have chosen the priesthood or religious
life," he says, "is that they have not been annoyed by pressure
to do so. We realize and stress the God-given right of individuals to choose their own state of life."

MAKING A DECISION

To the inevitable and final question of youths, "Do you
advise me to enter?" most experienced directors think it
best to say, "You must make the decision. It is yourself
and your will that you are offering to Christ."

Others would go a little further and say, "I give my
approval to *your* decision to enter. You have shown a love
of Christ, a desire to please Him and live for Him, a spirit
of sacrifice, of humility, docility, and obedience. Why not
offer yourself to Christ saying, 'Here I am, if you can use
me'? Trust Him to give you the right answer through your
superiors, His representatives. Even if you should leave, your
doubts will be settled for all time. You will have gained
immensely by the spiritual training and Christ will bless
you always for having offered yourself."

At this point most recruiters have noticed that love
for God in the genuine aspirant has reached such an in-
tensity that the response is almost instantaneous. There is
a generosity that wants to sweep away all obstacles, a willingness that brooks no rival and needs no apology or de-
fense. It is something hard to define, and yet you can see
it filling the heart of the boy or girl with an eager desire to

do that which is so difficult to human nature. It prompts such a one to give up heroically all that the world offers that the divine life within the soul might be brought to a more complete perfection.

The phenomenon I have tried to describe, but it defies my efforts. For lack of a better explanation, I can say only that it is like a "light in their eyes." It is something found in every generous aspirant for the seminary or convent.

Your responsibility in all of this is very clear. You must encourage, nourish, and protect this manifestation of grace. For once you have said, "This boy or this girl has a vocation," then you mean that you have seen in such an individual an act of devotion in a degree which is superlative. You have found a soul in whom there are strong, firm habits of virtue, and that soul now shows a prompt, eager will to serve God.

It is true that there is much that is mysterious in a vocation. But that is not the field in which you are called to help. You are not asked to measure the divine love flowing into the individual's soul. You are not asked to tell the moment the divine invitation ignites a fire within the youngster's heart.

Your role is simply to detect these budding vocations and, as guide and guardian, conduct them to the threshold of the priesthood, brotherhood, or sisterhood.

CHAPTER II

How to Stimulate Interest
in Vocations

ONE of the old New England cookbooks, which specializes in recipes for wild fowl, instructs the user to "First catch the bird!"

With this same observation I begin the consideration of how to stimulate interest in the priesthood, brotherhood, and sisterhood.

It is all well and good to be imbued with the proper dispositions in the matter of vocations and to have a deep appreciation of your responsibilities to the souls you meet. But if you are to be considered successful as a recruiter for your diocese or community, you must "first get candidates!"

In the 1948 vocational campaign, conducted in the diocese of Pittsburgh, Pennsylvania, inquiry cards were passed out to 25,000 eligible youngsters through the schools and parish organizations. Thirty-five hundred answered that they would like to find out more about the priesthood, brotherhood, or sisterhood.

"That gave us our cue," Father Ferris Guay, the vocational director, told me. "We immediately started a publicity program to acquaint these youths with all aspects of the service of God. There were prayers and special devotions throughout the diocese, sermons in all the churches, talks in the schools, films, poster displays, vocational essay contests, and literature offers. Every medium was used in stimulating their interest."

CHRIST'S OWN METHOD

Christ Himself would probably have used the same means were He walking the earth today and recruiting the priests, brothers, and sisters necessary to carry on His work in the Church. In His own time He showed an interest in publicity media and used means that stimulated great interest and excitement.

For example, at His birth He announced the fact to the shepherds by a visit of angels, and to the Magi by a marvelous star. At His baptism He was the center of attention when a voice from heaven proclaimed, "This is my beloved Son in whom I am well pleased."

Frequently in His public ministry Jesus stimulated interest with miracles. Recall the excitement at the multiplication of the loaves and the drama at the raising of Lazarus. On Pentecost morning thousands were attracted to the Apostles by a mighty wind.

All of these things were terrific advertising techniques. While certainly we cannot expect to duplicate them, still we can be very "Christlike" in using the limited means at our disposal. We can use radio, movies, and television to proclaim our message. We can display our life and work through billboards and posters. We can confirm our words with colored films and reach thousands through the modern press.

AUDIENCE CONTACT

Another lesson we can learn from Christ is to adapt ourselves to our audience. When Jesus invited the Apostles to follow Him, He knew that they were interested in fishing. Accordingly, He promised to make them "fishers of men." We, in turn, must get the interests of our audience and develop them.

For example, the appeal for a fourteen-year-old boy is far different from that for an ex-G.I. The boy may want to be a flying missionary to the Arctic, and the former soldier is looking for a way to build a lasting peace. A teen-age girl may dream of "running off with God" and living out her days is a convent garden replete with rambling roses. Her older sister is probably more concerned with what it takes to be a good grade-school teacher.

In his study, *Environmental Factors Influencing Vocations,* Father Thomas S. Bowdern, S.J., discovered that the majority of boys started thinking seriously of the priesthood or brotherhood around the ages of fourteen to sixteen. The majority of girls, on the other hand, reach some kind of decision around the ages of sixteen to eighteen. Thus the most impressionable years for a boy are at the end of his eighth grade and beginning of high school. For a girl the best time is the last two years of high school and the beginning of college.

A recent survey conducted by the Catholic Students Mission Crusade in 94 of the 146 major seminaries in the United States confirms these boys' findings. After questioning 6314 clerics as to when they entered the seminary to become a priest,

47 per cent replied that it was between the ages of 13–16;
30 per cent said it was between the ages of 17–19;
23 per cent said it was at 20 or later.

As for the statistics on girls, there has been no attempt at a complete survey of all postulants and novices now preparing for the sisterhood. However, there are studies limited to individual communities that confirm these findings. For instance, Sister Mary Paul, O.P., Vocational Directress for the Maryknoll Sisters, after interviewing 112 recently received candidates, reports that "the most decisive years for these girls were between fifteen and eighteen. The highest number of candidates in our group decided on the sisterhood at seventeen."

Another point brought out by these surveys and interviews is that in the beginning, both for boys and girls, the appeal of the apostolate is strongest. Up to about fifteen years of age youngsters are more concerned with the type of work they will do in the service of God. They want to be missionaries to darkest Africa . . . or teach the First Communion class in the parish school . . . or become chaplains in the Navy. As they pass through adolescence, there is a tendency to romanticize, especially among girls. They are inclined to daydream about converting the world to Christ or picture themselves as another "Little Flower." As they mature, their ideas become more definite. Older youths are attracted to the religious life because it offers them the best chance to do most for God, themselves, and others.

These things you have to keep in mind in framing your appeal. It is also well to remember that surveys have shown that 66 per cent of today's religious have come from homes of four or more children. Eighty per cent of them considered their families "middle class." By taking your examples from this background and the life the youngsters know, you can make your explanations more appealing and intelligible.

HOW TO GIVE A GOOD VOCATIONAL TALK

All this brings us to a consideration of what makes a good vocational talk. If we are to stimulate interest in the priesthood, brotherhood, and sisterhood, we have to know how to talk effectively about them.

For five years, while teaching with the Sodality's Summer School of Catholic Action, I offered a course on "How to Make the Vocational Appeal" to modern youth. Immediately after this class I had one for teen-agers on "Finding Your Place in God's Service." Invariably twice the number of priests and religious wanted to hear me actually talk to youngsters than to hear me tell how it was done.

This fact makes me wonder about the practicality of any written explanations. Yet for lack of a chance to demonstrate, I will have to rely on a few written remarks.

The first thing I want to say is that enthusiasm and manner are almost as important as matter. The way you handle a group of youths is almost as effective as the things you tell them.

A couple of years ago I watched Father Daniel A. Lord, S.J., come on stage for a Midwest youth rally. Noticing a piano nearby he slipped onto the bench and shouted, "Let's all sing!" while he proceeded to pound out state songs. When he finally got to the microphone he had the youngsters in a wonderful mood. He could have talked Latin for five minutes and they would still have thought he was great!

Whether you use such a novel approach or simply stand up on a platform, there must always be affability and as much charm as you can exhibit. Humor has a way of dispelling tension, but it can become dangerous. This is especially true if you let the laughter get out of hand or create the impression that you are playing the comedian.

You have not come to entertain. You have come to instruct and persuade. Accordingly, your talk must have purpose and form. It is tragic that so many otherwise good speakers are addicted to pious and flabby "fervorinos" on vocations. I have sat through many of these miserable talks, which have begun in platitudes, rambled aimlessly, and ended up without conviction.

The organization of a vocational talk follows the usual formula for giving any good address. If you want to get off to a good start, you have to kindle a quick flame of interest in your first sentence.

Too many recruiters, I think, picture their audience as waiting with eager eyes and bated breath for their message. Otherwise, how can you explain their initial statement that goes something like this, "It is indeed an honor to be invited to address you boys and girls this afternoon on a subject of such signal importance . . ."?

They should rather take things as they are. Anybody that knows the mind of modern youth realizes that when a vocation talk is announced or an assembly is called at school, the majority feel either antipathy or apathy — or both! Only a few are eager and anxious to hear what the speaker has to say. The others may be respectful, but they are thinking, "Here we go again!"

Accordingly, your opening words, like the Redskin that "bites the dust" in the opening sentence of a Western thriller, must crash through any antipathy or apathy. This, I admit, is easier explained than done.

One afternoon two years ago we had about eight hundred students for a vocational talk in the gym at the University of Detroit. It was a hot day and two priests had already talked for about twenty minutes each. The last man on the program was a young diocesan priest. My sympathy went out to him, for the audience was practically "gone."

Slowly he came up to the microphones and looked over the group. Then suddenly to the tune of "Mademoiselle from Armentières" he let go in a rich baritone:

"Oh, the Passionists were founded long ago,
    And the Jesuits were founded long before;
But I am of the Order of Peter and Paul,
    We were founded first of all!"

The audience was electrified and, when he concluded, their applause shook the rafters. They wanted him back for an encore.

GET AN EFFECTIVE OPENING

It cannot be stressed too much how important are these initial moments when you face a group of youngsters. If you do not win their interest and sympathy then, you may never do so.

So many religious seem to think that humility demands an abject introduction. They want to start off by saying, "Really, I'm not the person to be giving this kind of talk . . ." or "At the outset it must be admitted that there are others who could do so much better than I . . ."

These weasel words are foolish and only give wiseacres in the crowd a chance to make slurring remarks. Certainly the speaker cannot believe such an introduction, otherwise virtue would demand that such a one step aside and let somebody else give the address.

By condemning all false and trite introductions I do not imply that we should skip any conventional acknowledgments or neglect any of the courtesies of the pulpit or platform. I am merely saying that no effective speaker should waste time on self-depreciation, meaningless generalities, and vague platitudes.

Some vocational speakers plunge directly into the heart of the subject with a question. I once heard Monsignor Arthur Terlecke of Chicago, Illinois, begin in this manner. "What are you going to do with your life?" he asked a group of high school seniors. "I am not asking about what kind of work you will do in life. My question is more fundamental. What state of life are you going to choose — the married or the single state?"

Such an introduction avoids any dillydallying and generally gets immediate attention from the group.

Another effective opening is to tell a story. Youngsters from six to sixty will cock their ears as you say, "The other day I was talking with a group of soldiers who served in Korea. They told me that in one of the skirmishes with the Reds a number of the fellows were cut off from their company. The lieutenant in charge yelled, 'When I count three, make the break. One! . . . Two! . . . Three! . . . Charge ! ! !' Nobody moved, not even the lieutenant.

"Suddenly one of the soldiers jumped up and cried, 'Come on, guys, let's go!' Down the hill he plunged, and every infantryman was right at his heels. They would have followed a man like that, they said, right into the mouth of a machine gun."

Such a story commands attention. It is then quite easy to show how this example of leadership illustrates the way

Christ deals with His followers. He doesn't send them into something He wouldn't do Himself. Rather He shows them His life and says through one of His representatives, "Come, follow Me!"

It is also quite effective to open a vocational talk with a story on oneself. Father Hugh Calkins, O.S.M., does this admirably. He tells about the time he was giving a Mission in Detroit and gestured in his cape to the right. A little boy in the first row was quite fascinated by the sight. Then Father gestured to the left. Again the child's eyes popped. Finally, as he threw out his cape in a double-armed gesture, the child cried, "Look, Mom, superman!"

Regardless of what method you use, it is all-important that you get off to a good start. You must have the boys and girls on your side and interested in what you have to say.

WHY TALK TO ME?

Your next concern is to explain your purpose in giving the vocational appeal. The audience wants to know. "Why pick on us?" You have to answer their challenge.

Most of them may not know that the United States Bureau of Vital Statistics has records to prove that in the past twenty years 93 per cent of our youth has entered the married state, and the prospects are that the same figures will hold for the future. But they do realize that maybe only one in their group will end up in a seminary or convent. So they want to know why you make them all listen to the talk on the religious life.

The reason is that while only a small percentage end up in the service of God, all of them have to choose between marriage or the single state. There is nothing in between.

If they choose the married state, then with their partner they will seek to raise up children in the fear and love of God. The sacrifices they make for their family is the way they work out their salvation and achieve happiness.

If they choose the single state, it is to find a greater happiness there and do more for God, self, and fellow man.

Now when a person is qualified to choose either state and there is some doubt about the matter, it is never prudent to try marriage first. One cannot enter this state and later back out with a remark to one's spouse or children, "It was nice knowing you. I am not completely happy here, so I think I will now try the religious life."

If there is any experimenting to be done, it must always be in a seminary or novitiate. There one of two things shows up: either one is happy and qualified, or one is not. If one leaves, it is no disgrace. It is merely evidence that the individual is trying to learn the will of God and now knows that it leads him elsewhere. If one stays, it is because one is happy there and has found evidence of a genuine religious calling.

This type of appeal will get results. From 1948 to 1952 I conducted both classes, "Courtship and Marriage" and "Priesthood and Religious Life," at the Summer Schools of Catholic Action. It was significant that in each major city we visited, a larger group by actual count turned up for the classes on the religious state than on the married state.

At least one third of our Catholic youth are thinking very seriously of the service of God, but they don't want us to "put the hooks in them" or "throw out a dragnet." The candid and reasoned approach is what they want.

Once the subject is opened, you will find that teen-agers want to talk about vocations. They want to know about the single state in the world. How does it fit in? What about those who cannot get married? What if one doesn't find a partner? Is it possible to get into the religious life and later become unhappy?

There is much that needs to be explained and developed. Many of our schools are now introducing obligatory courses on marriage. Where this is done I have always contended there should also be instructions on the religious life. Simply because the majority end up in marriage is no reason to give twelve talks on the married state and only one on the religious state!

It is certainly good to give all the marriage guidance possible. But it is also good to acquaint our boys and girls just as thoroughly with the religious life, for only when the two vocations are presented equally to the student is it possible to make a fair choice!

THE BODY OF THE TALK

We come now to the informative part of the talk. If it is a general vocational appeal, most speakers come right to the point and give the signs of a vocation. They then point out how an individual can recognize them.

Father Andrew Ansboro, C.P., one of the Passionist recruiters, likes to remind boys that practically every one of them has what it takes. "You are intelligent," he says, "and blessed with good health. Certainly most of you look well fed and able to live the life of a priest." As the boys laugh appreciatively, he goes on to explain that if they go to the Sacraments regularly they are also spiritually qualified. The only thing they lack is a desire for the religious life.

Perhaps you could make this same observation about the youths you meet. Certainly there will not be too many in the crowd whom you will have to exclude because of feeble intelligence or poor health. Nor will there be too many who have been away from the Sacraments or are spiritually weak. But there will be a very high percentage without any definite inclination or desire for the religious life.

Years ago these same youths may have dreamed of being priests or religious. Perhaps the boys in oversized coats played at saying Mass, and the girls with towels over their heads pretended they were nuns. But all that has changed now, and they rarely mention the subject. What has happened?

You know the answers as well as I. Perhaps in grade

school they developed a dislike for one of their teachers. Or maybe they had to endure ridicule from their classmates. Again they may have begun to feel an attraction for the opposite sex. Or possibly parents at home mocked their dreams or came right out and opposed them. Any one of a thousand things could have arisen to dull their enthusiasm and check their aspirations.

Accordingly, some vocational talks are built around these objections. The speaker endeavors to show how natural these problems are and tries to rekindle the youngster's enthusiasm. Examples are often worked in on how others have overcome these troubles. The theme is, "If they could do it, why can't you?"

Another effective mode of developing a vocational talk is to picture what would happen if you put a cassock or habit on everyone in your audience. This approach goes over very well with high school students, particularly if you work in a little pantomime with the explanations. In imagination you take them out to the seminary or convent and describe the place. You show them their quarters . . . you meet their new companions . . . you eat dinner . . . you go to recreation and finally say night prayers.

As the greater silence begins you show how a change comes over the new recruits. By now they have had enough of the religious life and want to get out. Windows creak open and knotted sheets are thrown out. As the youths prepare to clamber down, you plead with them, "Why don't you want to stay here? Aren't you happy in the life?"

"We're not the type," they answer. "This life doesn't appeal to us. It is only nine o'clock and already we are supposed to go to bed. We are taking off for where there is excitement . . . music . . . romance!"

Most boys and girls will howl in sympathy with this situation. You then have the group in the palm of your hand and it takes only a deft twist to show them that individuals who run away don't know what the life is all about. They are passing up a great chance for happiness without giving it a fair trial. Christ promised the hundredfold "not only in the life to come, but even in this present time!"

Still another approach is to take a heroic example from the life of a saint or some good human-interest story from the religious of today. Once the youths are interested in the account, you begin to analyze the matter. Why did the saint do so much for God? What motivated the religious to such heroism?

Naturally the audience will answer that it was love for God. As you develop the theme, they will see that there is a parallel between the love for a person and love for God. When we love a person, we will sacrifice for such a one. The more we love, the more we want to give. It is the same with God.

Older students, naturally, understand this better than younger ones. It is not that those who give their heart to God could not love a partner in marriage. It is only that they do not find another human being who is capable of eliciting their fullest generosity. No other person seems quite so worthy of all they want to do. So instead of finding a human lover, they fall "head over heels" in love with Christ.

It is particularly effective when you show how in the reception of a religious this idea is brought out in symbolic ritual. This is why a boy is said "to have given his heart to Christ" or a girl "has become the bride of Christ."

A similar theme can be built on illustrations taken from the world that youth admires. For example, you could tell the boys about young men like George Kerr, who made All-American while playing football at Boston College. He turned down a wonderful contract to play pro ball in order to go to the seminary. Or Jose Mojica, who gave up a promising operatic career to become a Franciscan. At his First Mass police had to hold back the crowds that came to hear him sing.

You might tell the girls about young women like Helen Horton, who gave up a very successful career as a night-club singer to become a Sister of Charity. They would also be interested in Stella Consili, who left the Ice Follies to become a Dominican nun; and Olga Hanchar, who quit the Rochester Girls' Basketball team to become a Sister of Notre Dame.

Indeed, there are any number of ways you can develop this matter. To date I have written seventeen pamphlets and one book on the subject, but this has hardly scratched the surface. In *Follow Me,* for instance, the appeal is taken from the analogy of God's Army and the way young men can serve in it. The companion booklet for girls, *Follow Him,* has a theme taken from the example of Mary and Martha.

In *Catholic Religious Vocations,* a book I wrote for the Vocational Guidance Manuals Corporation of New York City for use with Catholics in the public schools, there is a theme developed from each of the different apostolates that are open to Catholic youths.

Some of these ideas may be of help to you, but probably your own experience and the circumstances of the talk will suggest better material.

Finally, if you have taken the matter to prayer, you can expect the wonderful help of the Holy Spirit. For in recruiting for Christ He never fails. Rather you will notice an abundance of those lights and special inspirations which are so helpful in putting the appeal across!

THE GRAND FINALE

The conclusion of your vocational talk must be more than a graceful leave-taking. It must be more than a review of the examples covered in the body of the address. It must be more than a reminder of the subject's importance. It must answer the thought uppermost in the audience's mind, "What do you want us to do about it?"

Accordingly, always suggest some action response. This is why so many recruiters conclude by passing out cards and having the youngsters indicate whether or not they would like more information.

Archbishop Richard Cushing of Boston sometimes ends his vocational appeals with a request that all stand up who want to be priests or religious. The Archbishop then invites the audience to give them a big hand. "You'd be surprised," he said, "how that gets results."

Another dynamic youth leader is Father Erwin A. Juraschek of San Antonio. He, too, ends his talks with an appeal for action. They are to put up their hands . . . go to the principal . . . or do something within their power.

I once heard him conclude a rousing appeal for recruits by saying, "Those that stand will be 'heads' and those that sit will be 'tails,' and we all know that with 'heads' the Church wins, and with 'tails' it loses! Now which will it be?"

If you haven't an appeal like this for action, there will be little response. Always, then, work in something for the youths to do. Have them see their pastor . . . talk to their teacher . . . write for literature . . . investigate further!

THE WRITTEN APPEAL

We come now to the consideration of vocational literature. In one way it is supplementary to the personal contact and the vocational talk. In another way it stands alone.

Speaking on the subject at the 1954 Convention of the National Catholic Educational Association, Father Charles F. McCarthy, M.M., Publicity Director for Maryknoll, gave statistics to prove that their magazine and vocational literature pulled two to one over all other modes of contacting youths.

Each student coming to Maryknoll is questioned as to what first interested him in the community. He is also asked what kept alive his vocation. To date almost 64 per cent of them have answered by saying that it was a vocational booklet that stimulated their interest and mission literature that kept that interest alive.

Over twenty million comic books are sold every month to our American youths. This fact not only proves that there is a tremendous reading public among our boys and girls, but also that they want something to fire their imaginations.

Here is where vocational literature should come in with a stirring appeal to follow Christ. Taking examples from the modern day or the lives of the saints, it should picture Him as a teen-age Hero and build up the greatness and glory of His apostolate.

When Bing Crosby wrote "In My Book These Are the Stars," he was using this appeal. He shows that real teen-age heroes must be more than actors and actresses. They must be people who have given all to Christ. Priests and religious fit into this category.

In presenting such appeals we must remember that the reading level for most vocational pieces should be set at the sixth grade. Various surveys and exhaustive studies by advertising and magazine consultants have established that the average education in the United States is nine years of schooling. Even more surprising is that they have proof that the *preferred* reading of our people is at the seventh grade level. Teen-age preferred reading is one grade below.

Now in order to make the vocational literature read as easily as material for sixth grade students, you will have to develop a prose style as simple as the Bible.

The average sentence length should not go over fourteen words. Long sentences should be broken up. The syllable count should be about 140 per hundred words. Ten per cent of the vocabulary should be personal words. The verbs should be active, and there should not be more than one passive verb per hundred words.

Whether or not you like such a simple style, the fact remains. The simpler the prose, the more effective is the appeal and the greater is the number reached.

Before my entrance into the Passionist novitiate I spent the summers of 1937 and 1938 writing for the Sunday magazine section of the Des Moines *Register and Tribune*. Constantly the editors were drumming into my ears, "Keep your sentences short; the shorter, the better. Keep your paragraphs short; the shorter, the better. Use plenty of periods!"

Such advice keeps your thought from bogging down in the middle of a sentence. Any time you have to read a line twice to get the meaning, the author has misfired.

I am talking here about the wording and punctuation of a popular appeal. This is a recommendation for vocational literature, not an explanation of great prose. My sole concern is that you use the simple language of youth and be communicative rather than oracular. This does not mean that your phraseology should be racy or casual. Nor should it include slang or jive talk. It is simply that your vocabulary should be one that is familiar and specific.

One of the best writers of this type is Father Leo Wobido, S.J. Often in his writing classes at Summer School he used to insist, "Everybody prefers to read that your monastery or convent 'is set in a stately grove of blue spruce' rather than that 'there are trees around the place.' The phraseology that all readers like, young and old, is one that has color. People want words to paint a picture in their imagination."

Above all, keep the thought clear. The purpose of your writing is to reveal the religious life, not conceal it.

One pathetic example of what not to do was sent to me the other day. "Daily striving to become a champion of Christ," this recruiter wrote, "empties the soul that God may fill it at every moment with grace to cultivate a right sense of values, which convinces you that the more you give yourself to God as a religious, the more He gives Himself to you, and in turn brings happiness greater than anything the world can give."

This is only one sentence of a four-page folder. But for whom was the author writing? Certainly it wasn't for us!

And if he was addressing himself to teen-agers, how much would they grasp on first reading? Even after rereading that first sentence a couple of times I am not sure I got everything the writer intended to convey.

A SUBJECT AND POINT OF VIEW

The subject matter of vocational literature is almost limitless. Any aspect of the life and work of priests, brothers, and sisters can be treated. Preference should be given to inspirational and informative pieces, but historical and narrative works are also needed.

About once a year I arrange to spend some time with at least one Public Relations officer for the Army, Navy, Marine, and Air Forces. These men are charged with appealing to American youth through patriotism. They are out to instruct and inspire young men and women and thus gain new recruits for the Armed Services.

Since patriotism and piety can be considered two different aspects of the same virtue of religion, I think there is a great deal that can be learned from their experience. Accordingly, we go over each new piece of literature they have and analyze its contents.

One thing they have shown me is that boys and girls want a challenge. They want to prove their love right here and now. They also want to know what happens as soon as they sign up. What is the training program?

All this is good to remember in wording our vocational appeals. We must challenge youth to ever greater heroism. We must show them how they can prove their love for Christ even in a seminary or novitiate. We must explain very thoroughly the training program they go through and the reason for the years of study.

Once you have picked the subject you must find the focus, the perspective, the angle of vision that will make your reader see clearly the thing you are describing. This is most important, and it is the point where many vocational writers fail.

If you are going to write effectively, you must not only put the reader in the right frame of mind, but you must keep him interested. A cursory check, though, of current vocational literature will probably prove that most vocational appeals have a very routine development.

Before me as I write are ten samples pulled at random from my files on this year's vocational articles and pamphlets. Seven are stale and humdrum. One of them starts off with the question, "Have you ever wondered about Catholic nuns?" and the rest of the article could have been quoted from the *Catholic Encyclopedia*. Only three are clever, interesting treatments of the subject. That is a very poor score for such important matter!

It might help to remember that the best and most popular form of writing is the narrative. If we put a little more of this type in vocational publications, it would make our appeals much more interesting. This is what made *Seven Storey Mountain* so popular. Thomas Merton has made thousands of readers sympathetic to the contemplative vocation by detailing his own personal confusion in approaching Catholicism and the religious life.

Another secret of popular writing is to quote snatches of conversation and bits of direct quotation from what is said about the subject. To interest your readers you must turn a good deal of your matter into narrative. Then enliven the narrative with dialogue. All exposition needs some story; and all story needs some drama.

Finally, the conclusion of the vocational article, like the end of a vocational talk, must make some appeal to the reader. This is why so many vocational folders and brochures conclude with a coupon. The reader is asked to clip the coupon and mail it in for more information.

It is very good to have some kind of follow-up. We know that if St. Ignatius Loyola had not repeated his question several times to Francis Xavier, there would not have been that great apostle to the Indies. Many recruiters, therefore, send monthly bulletins or mimeographed letters to all prospects requesting them.

One excellent practice along this line is to send out a vocation-toned greeting at Christmas and Easter. Sister Mary de Paul of the Nursing Sisters of the Sick Poor has a whole letter worked out on the Christmas theme with a lithographed picture of the Nativity. She shows how every generous girl at this time of year wants to show Jesus in a special way how much she loves Him . . . how much she appreciates all He has given.

"Why not give a special gift this Christmas?" Sister Mary de Paul asks. "Why not give the *gift of yourself?* Have you ever thought of that? Jesus is waiting for you. In the person of His sick and needy He longs for your care and sympathy."

This kind of vocational literature keeps contact with the prospects and elicits letters in return. Such correspondence produces a sort of bond that becomes increasingly persuasive as the months roll by.

PICTURES AND POSTERS

In February of 1949 the editors of *Parade* pulled a good stunt on three of the top artists in the country. They commissioned them to draw the animal, which the *Encyclopaedia Britannica* thus describes: "Its body is stout, with arched back; the limbs are short and stout, armed with strong, blunt claws; the ears long; the tail thick at the base and tapering gradually. The elongated head is set on a short thick neck, and at the extremity of the snout is a disc in which the nostrils open. The mouth is small and tubular, furnished with a long extensile tongue. A large individual measures 6 feet 8 inches. In color it is pale sandy or yellow, the hair being scanty and allowing the skin to show."

The artists were not told that this animal was an aardvark, but were simply to draw it as best they could from the very accurate description of the encyclopedia. Though all later admitted they had often seen one of these African anteaters in zoos, not one of them came anywhere near portraying it.

This incident shows how even the most precise words do not convey an idea so graphically as a single picture. Photographers have long contended that "A picture is worth a thousand words." Many times in vocational work a picture can say more than 10,000 words!

Youngsters, for example, want to know what it is like at the seminary or convent. Where do you sleep? What do you wear? How much do you have to study? How are the eats? Can you play games? Do you get to see your family and friends? These and many more questions can be answered by good pictures.

For example, a scene of the seminarians starting dinner — with action — not only tells about the amount and kind of food, but the surroundings and the dispositions of the boys. A postulant entertaining her family in the convent parlor tells a great deal about the community's attitude toward the family and the spirit of the girl.

In an article entitled, "Religious Life Must Be Publicized," John McMahon of the Mellon Institute tells how one steaming day in August he was crossing the campus at Notre Dame University with his two sons. As they neared St. Mary's Lake they saw the boys from Moreau Seminary swimming off a float.

"The reaction on my sons," he said, "was electrical, especially on the older one, aged eleven. Who are those boys? What are they doing over there? The questions came in a stream. The next day the older youngster announced to me that when he grows up he is going to Notre Dame to become a priest.

"All the words in Webster's dictionary," Mr. McMahon concluded, "could not have conveyed the impression to the youngsters that they got from seeing the seminarians in swimming."

This power of pictures, therefore, must never be overlooked. You should use plenty of them to illustrate your life and work, and the better ones could be utilized for poster displays. The Seraphic Society for Vocations at Westmont, Illinois, publishes many excellent suggestions for such promotion.

VOCATIONS COST MONEY

As soon as we bring up the subject of printing and advertising displays, somebody is bound to ask, "How much is it going to cost?"

Father Peter Miller, S.C.J., answered this question very well in the article, "Vocations Cost Money," published in the January, 1949, *Review for Religious.*

He quotes a superior as saying that each of his candidates for the brotherhood had cost him $1,000 in advertising. "Yet the religious who uttered that statement," Father Miller said, "discovered that he is leading noble young men to the service of Christ and that monastery work is being accomplished without spending thousands of dollars annually for outside salaries. Within six months each brother candidate paid off penny for penny the cost of the whole advertising program."

In the same theme Father Charles McCarthy, M.M., adds, "None of us would be so foolhardy as to measure vocations in dollars and cents, yet looking back we can say that on one occasion Maryknoll obtained more than a hundred seminarians and brothers by investing $1,000 in vocational literature.

"During World War II," Father McCarthy explained, "a priest in the office of the National Catholic Welfare Conference requested 50,000 copies of our vocational booklets for distribution to the Armed Forces. In this booklet we ran a page of suggestions to servicemen about correspondence courses in Latin. More than one hundred ex-servicemen, who entered Maryknoll as aspirants for the priesthood or brotherhood since 1945, have persevered. The net cost, if one can dare to put it that way, was less than $10 per candidate."

Sister Berchmans of Mary, noticing that postulants for the Sisters of Notre Dame de Namur were falling off, decided to spend $1,200 on a new community vocational booklet. 20,000 were distributed and the order received seventeen additional postulants. The following year they put out another 20,000 and found eleven more interested girls.

These examples illustrate a fundamental principle in vocational advertising; namely, that distribution is basic to success. The best vocational pamphlet gathers dust on a shelf. You will recruit nothing in an old folks' home.

Distribution means getting the booklet to many individuals and to the right kind of people. In this matter we can turn for advice to the professionals. For businessmen are much wiser in this matter than we are.

Dennis J. O'Neill, an advertising executive, told a group of us at the Vocation Institute in 1949, "Your *product* is the religious life. Your *brand* is the particular community to which you belong. In the commercial field it is axiomatic that there can be no outstanding *brand* success in advertising unless there is a big, broad base of acceptance for the *product*. And it is competitive *brand* advertising that creates this widespread *product* consciousness and acceptance.

"Therefore," he said, "your community's decision to make use of effective advertising is not a matter of community self-interest alone. It is a matter of playing a part, no matter how small, in helping to create a better, more widespread acceptance for the whole idea of the religious life among the youth and parents of America."

Such advertising is of two kinds. There is the *direct appeal* for candidates, and there is the *public-relations* type. The former is concerned with newspaper and magazine ads; blurbs, brochures, pamphlets, and books; posters and displays. The latter has to do with creating a good impression on the public and keeping the community's name before clergy and laity through news releases and feature stories.

PAID ADVERTISEMENTS

Some groups of priests, brothers, and sisters have found that ads in the Catholic press are a worth-while source of vocations. Others claim they get no response.

For instance, at the National Conference of Brother Directors of Vocations, held at Christian Brothers College in St. Louis in January, 1954, a report was made on all the paid advertisements run by brothers. Of the ten communities reporting, four said it was a waste of money for they received no answers. The other six claimed a response varying from 5 per cent with the Xaverian Brothers to 90 per cent with the Alexians. These latter are exclusively devoted to hospital work and find that the best way to get into homes and schools is through newspaper and magazine ads.

Reports from sisters vary from 1 per cent response to 55 per cent for their advertisements. A California community placed one ad in *Our Sunday Visitor* and got from Michigan a candidate who had never before heard of them.

Practically every community in the country has invested in folders, pamphlets, and other printed pieces. Some have simply a little brochure telling of their life and work. Others have a whole array of different style pieces for different age levels and different types of distribution. They range from inserts in community mailings to colorful jubilee books.

The most important pieces are the two-color folders and the sixteen-page booklets. The folder is a come-on and is distributed widely. In schools and parishes one is given to every eligible youngster. When the individual writes in for more information, the sixteen-page booklet is sent. This explains by way of text and picture the whole life and work of the community and makes an appeal to the youth's generosity.

It is very important that the address be shown near the front of all pieces of literature and that there be only one address to which prospects write. The address should be repeated on the back in a box format or coupon. This latter form is the best way to obtain replies. It also lets you know which vocational piece of literature is making the biggest impression, if several kinds are in circulation.

PUBLIC RELATIONS

The second type of advertising, called "public relations," is simply living up to our Lord's test for one of His own: "By this shall all men know that you are my disciples, if you have love for one another."

Too often we forget some of the aspects of our life that greatly influence the laity. Take, for example, the answering of the telephone. I wonder how many people are convinced that the monastery or convent is filled with joy when they hear one of us take the call with a grunt or sigh?

The courtesy and attentiveness of the porter also mean a lot. First impressions are made as the person steps through the front door. I have heard of more than one case of people ringing at a religious house for fifteen minutes and nobody bothering to answer. A young lady told me that she announced herself one Sunday afternoon at the convent parlor and asked for Reverend Mother. The sister at the door had a sour personality and left her standing in the vestibule until one of the rooms was empty. Naturally the girl wasn't interested in joining that group.

Public relations also concern the cleanliness of the house, the promptness in answering letters, the friendliness of religious with children and strangers. The Lord alone knows how many vocations are due to the treats which religious cooks have given from the kitchen door to neighborhood children!

Mother M. Killian, C.S.J., in an excellent address before the delegates to the First National Congress of Religious in the United States, stressed this point. "Sincere interest in *people* as people and not only as potential subjects," she insisted, "willingness to take trouble, to spend time, to change a schedule, if need be — these qualities, community-wide, will win friends and vocations."

Through such consideration we try to interpret our life and work to others. "It is, therefore, very important," Father McCarthy, M.M., explains, "that particular attention be given to the parish priest. He is the one responsible for cultivating and developing vocations.

"It is important, too, to co-operate with the teacher in the classroom. She has the respect and confidence of the children. You can lecture to the youngsters for an hour and convince them of the value of a priestly or religious vocation. But if you do not win the teacher's respect, she can undo your work in one remark.

"Lastly," he says, "you have to use good public relations with parents. They have to be convinced that their children will be happy in the seminary or novitiate. Discussion and explanations do not convince them. A visit to a seminary or convent where they can visit the students or young religious does more to change their minds than anything else. When they visit your house, be sure that they associate with the younger members, who are earnest, refreshing, warm, genuine, and have time for them. Don't push them off on the older ones in the community."

Another kind of public relations, which is very beneficial to the cause of vocations, is to make friends with local editors and reporters. Once a year it is good to invite them out to the religious institute and entertain them along with the doctors, lawyers, and other benefactors. In return they will be delighted to run a feature story on your life and work and give you a break in the news whenever possible.

There is also a great deal of human interest in some of the activities of individual members of the religious group. An alert promoter will write up some of these stories and send them in to the N.C.W.C. News Service, to Catholic magazines, and to the diocesan paper. The resulting newspaper and magazine articles will keep the community's name in the public eye.

GETTING RESULTS

In preparing this chapter I have gone over the reports of 117 recruiters and vocational promoters. Most of their ideas I have tried to pass on to you. But it is almost impossible to evaluate the individual results without getting extremely repetitious. I think it best, therefore, to take one and let it speak for the rest.

Thus Sister Mary Ronald, O.S.F., says that their campaign was quite successful, because the Mother General was very vocation-minded and didn't worry about the cost of materials for publicity. Also, over 300 sisters in her community pledged a holy hour a week for the success of the work. There was a good public-relations program in the schools visited and the teachers gave 100 per cent co-operation.

"Totaling the score," Sister says, "I find that I gave thirty-five talks in twelve schools to 982 students. Two hundred and eight of these were high school seniors and 231 were eighth graders. The rest were in between. Of the seniors twenty-three wanted to have private interviews with me about their vocation and seven of them signed up for our novitiate. Eighty eighth graders wanted private interviews and twenty of them are entering our Prep School in September."

Reading between the lines of this and other reports, we know that it takes hard work to get such results. It also takes a great deal of personal ingenuity with plenty of prayer and sacrifice.

But in this as in all vocation work, Christ's words are our directive: "You are the light of the world . . . So let your light shine before men that they may see your Father who is in heaven."

We must, therefore, speak . . . write . . . and advertise as best we can in obedience to His command. Only then will we really be stimulating interest in vocations!

CHAPTER III

Recruiting From Special Groups

ONE of the favorite stories of Sister Mary Augustine, S.M.S.M., concerns an American G.I. in the past war. He had wandered into a Marist Leprosarium in the Solomon Islands and watched dumfoundedly while a sister dressed the nauseous sores of a native.

"I wouldn't do that for a million bucks!" he exclaimed.

"Neither would I!" Sister replied. Then, as the soldier became even more amazed, she smiled and tried to explain that it was not love for money or anything of this world that brought her to the South Pacific and such sacrifice. Rather it was love for Christ and because she was willing to serve Him in the person of His sick and poor.

This same explanation of a vocation we try to give to all of our Catholic youths. But it is obvious that we must adapt ourselves to different age levels. A college youth will understand the matter differently than a youngster in grade school. We do not talk to girls in bobby sox the same way we appeal to nurses.

In taking up the subject of recruiting various groups, therefore, I intend to distinguish their age levels. By showing the best approach and techniques for each age group, this chapter will be more practical.

PRIMARY GRADES

There are many priests and religious who hold that talking on the priesthood and religious life to children in the primary grades is a waste of time. They do not mind talking to eighth graders or high school students, but not the lower grades.

In a way such an attitude is understandable. Older children can grasp so much more of the idea of a vocation that it is easier to talk to them. They are also so much more like adults in their judgments that it is easier to gauge their response. But a child in the primary grades has to be dealt with in a different way. There is practically no previous knowledge of what the service of God entails to help us, so it is our duty with these little ones to lay the foundations on which others may build.

Speaking before the National Catholic Educational Convention in 1952, Sister Mary Isabel, S.S.J., presented a plan for fostering vocations in the elementary school. In speaking of these primary grade children she pointed out that we have a responsibility to lay the foundation of a vocation by:

1. Helping the children to become good boys and girls.

2. Establishing good work and study habits.

3. Holding up the ideal of the religious life as the "perfect" way to serve God.

In this third category youngsters are capable of a much deeper grasp of religious truth than most people realize. In this matter it is important not to confuse ability to express thoughts in words with actual knowledge acquired.

Children from five to eight years of age can understand even quite abstract religious ideas without any great difficulty, provided that they are explained in a simple way. These same youngsters are also capable of a very deep love for God, provided that this love is elicited in the same manner as their love for parents and home.

What we must do in the course of our instructions is to correlate the basic instincts of childhood with the youngsters' ideas and instincts with regard to God. Just as children know that they live, move, and have dependence on their parents, so they should be taught that their whole life is lived in union with and dependent upon God. Actually the dependence on their parents is a very minor thing, when compared with their dependence on God, who gave them their father and mother.

We can go on to explain to the children that in God's arms they are perfectly safe from all harm, and that they are loved by God so much that He came down on earth and suffered on the cross for them. This love is greater than anything else they have ever known, and it is so powerful that it will protect them from all dangers and bring them ultimately to heaven. As the children begin to grasp these ideas, they want to return this love.

Sister Mary Rosaria, S.S.N.D., told me that she was once telling the children the story of the Nativity and stressed how the Son of God came to us, even though it was very cold in the stable at Bethlehem. Then she asked the youngsters what they would have done for the Christ Child if they had been able to be present at His crib.

Most of the children gave the usual answers. One would have built a fire for Jesus; another would have brought some warm clothes for Him. But they finally decided that it would be best to take Him in their arms and hug Him to keep Him warm. Their own experience told them that such love and comfort would mean more to the Christ Child than anything else.

Sister Mary Blaise, S.S.N.D., told me that, when she takes the children through the study of creation, she develops the idea that God makes everything for a special purpose. Some boys and girls, whom He has made healthy and intelligent, He will select for His special helpers. All of them, therefore, should try to grow better day by day, so that they will be ready to do His will, regardless of what He wants them to do.

Sister Miriam David, S.S.N.D., added that she likes to focus attention on Mary and her preparation for her vocation. She tries to make the children realize that Mary was ready when God's messenger appeared to her. "From the time she was a little girl," Sister explains, "Mary did everything to please God. God chose Mary because when God chooses helpers, He looks for boys and girls who try to be like Mary — obedient, pure, humble, kind, unselfish, generous."

The recruiters who follow in the same pattern will certainly not be wasting time! By telling the children of incidents from the lives of the saints or stories about priests and religious who have done so much for God, they will create a profound impression.

After such an appeal I have seen practically every hand go up when I have concluded with the challenge: "Now, how many of you would like to be priests, brothers, or sisters?" Never for a moment have I expected all of the youngsters to persevere in their childish resolve. But I do know that the seed has been sown, and in the years to come it may bear fruit.

INTERMEDIATE GRADES

It used to be that when a person came to school to talk on vocations the children in the intermediate grades, like those in the primary grades, were skipped for the same reasons of immaturity. Nowadays, however, educational psychologists are pointing out that this was a serious oversight.

First of all, the years from nine to twelve manifest a great imaginative development, and the child begins to dream about the future. It is then that the ideals and ambitions planted in childhood begin to manifest themselves.

At this period the Catholic youngster takes quite naturally to the idea of an invisible world which cannot be sensed, but which is very definitely peopled with angels and saints. God is often more real to such a one than we ever imagine.

It is at this time, too, that youngsters tend to develop mistaken notions of the nature of the "call from God." They can so easily think of the divine invitation as a voice that comes to them in a dream . . . or an angel whispering in their ear. They need to be instructed, therefore, in exactly what a vocation is and how it can be recognized. Otherwise these ideas will carry over into adolescence; and because the youngster hasn't "heard" anything, he or she will no longer think of the matter.

Another serious mistake is to ignore the power of divine grace at this period of the youngster's growth. In school all the fundamental doctrines of the Catechism have now been covered and the infused virtues received in Baptism are helping the child assimilate that divine truth. The youngster not only believes what God has revealed and the Church teaches, but it has begun to transpose these truths from the intellectual level into effective practical action in daily life.

In a booklet entitled *How to Be an Instrument of Grace in Fostering Religious Vocations,* Sister M. Rose Agnes, O.S.F., makes many suggestions on how the teacher can help in this matter. She takes up not only the subject of religion, but also shows how vocational help can be worked into English, speech, and history classes.

Sister Mary Sarah, C.S.J., explained that with this age group she treats of how priests, brothers, and sisters bring Christ to people throughout the world. She starts with the diocese and explains the work of the pastor and assistants in the parish. Then she takes up the work of the sisters, caring for infants and orphans, teaching in the schools, and nursing the sick. As time permits Sister tells about the missionary vocation and what priests and religious are doing in South America, Asia, Africa, and Europe. In geography the youngsters try to find these mission fields and realize the extent of the Church's apostolate.

This is not pushing the child, for at this age many are inclined by nature and grace to make a decision regarding their lifework. Father Albert J. Nevins, M.M., made a survey several years ago among boys in the seminary. He asked them to put down on a questionnaire, as best they could remember,

the exact year in which they made their decision to give
themselves to God.

4.5 per cent stated it was at nine years of age.

8.1 per cent stated it was at ten years of age.

3.6 per cent stated it was at eleven years of age.

23.4 per cent stated it was at twelve years of age.

In all 39.6 per cent claimed they made the decision between the ages of nine and twelve, which are the intermediate
years. It is, therefore, very foolish for recruiters to overlook
the youngsters in these grades and neglect to speak to them
when visiting the school.

SEVENTH AND EIGHTH GRADES

Most youngsters in the seventh and eighth grades are
just beginning their teens. It is a period of rapid growth,
both physical and mental. Educators notice at this time a
development of the youngster's sense of observation, especially where details are concerned. There is also a development in the powers of attention and concentration, together
with a constructive imagination and sensitive memory.

Along with this mental growth is an increased moral
sense. Not only do the child's moral judgments grow in
force and extent, but also the sense of personal responsibility
for actions increases from day to day. Gradually the youngster becomes aware of the application of principles to the
solution of practical problems, and you often find such a
one "sitting down to figure things out."

This is why some recruiters find that Christ's promise
of a hundredfold to His followers makes a great appeal to
youngsters at this age level. They like to discuss the meaning
of that promise and apply it to themselves.

Youngsters at this age also have a strong tendency to
travel in groups. It is the "gang age" and through these group
experiences the boy and the girl develop a sense of social
responsibility and obedience to authority. At the same time
they are learning in the Catholic school about the Mystical

Body of Christ and their place in it. If rightly presented, this doctrine will make a strong appeal to them and influence greatly their vocational thinking.

Father Leslie Darnieder of Burlington, Wisconsin, brings out this theme very effectively in his religion classes. He explains the doctrine of the Mystical Body of Christ and then points out how priests, brothers, and sisters care for that Body of Christ by preaching, teaching, healing the sick, caring for orphans, and comforting the dying. He then inspires the youngsters to be "other Christs" in their daily life and urges them to try "to see Christ in others."

But perhaps the most notable characteristic of youngsters at this period is their sense of loyalty. They tend to despise the timid and cowardly and will try anything. Some have even been known to sign up for a seminary or convent on a dare.

This period also marks the beginning of high ideals, and from a guidance standpoint it is most important. If the recruiter fires the imagination of the youngsters with the example of heroes and heroines of the Church, they will have a goal for which to strive.

The reading, too, tends to books of adventure, travel, and excitement. Boys want action and stories about people they can imitate. Girls have a little more mature taste at this period. They like romantic stories and sentimental appeals. But while a boy will not read something written for girls, you will find that the girls can, and often do, find information and enjoyment in things written for boys. Accordingly, in vocational literature meant for both boys and girls there should be emphasis on the masculine appeal.

One danger in dealing with youngsters that have this strong idealism and tendency to hero worship is that they tend to put a priest or religious in the place of Christ. They pay less and less attention to their teacher's words and try more and more to imitate his or her actions. Their untried emotions run away with them, and they develop "crushes" on those they admire and want to imitate. This can be absolutely detrimental to a vocation, unless corrected immediately.

At such times we must make every effort to show the youngsters that Christ alone is the One they want. If it is upon ourselves that they have fixed their affections, we must point out that no human person can mean so much to them. Certainly their affection and devotion cannot be reciprocated, except insofar as it enables us to pass on their love and devotion to Christ.

This is hard for boys and girls to understand and sometimes the best solution to the problem is simply to force them to keep at a distance for a while. If they do not overcome this emotionalism and sentimentality, they will never persevere in a seminary or convent. Not finding the director of students or mistress of novices there as sweet and amiable as ourselves, they will quickly become disillusioned with the religious life and leave.

TECHNIQUES IN THE CLASSROOM

During their summer "vacation" I once asked some of the Sisters of Providence in Chicago to draw up a list of all the projects they had ever used or even heard about for the promotion of vocations among grade school children. Their report ran to fifty-two pages and included everything from explanations of how to set up a sand-table project to handling a vocational essay contest.

Many of the ideas, naturally, overlap, and some of the suggestions are limited to schools with special facilities. But there are many pointers that are applicable in all schools and these I pass on to you.

In regard to attending Mass and thereby coming to love Christ more, many of the sisters found that it helped to give the children a special intention. Many of them were willing to go to an extra Mass on a day like Saturday if it was for the reason "that God might bless one of the class with a vocation." Other sisters said they elicited a special interest in the Holy Sacrifice by having each pupil contribute a little toward a Mass stipend. Boys and girls, they found, had an added enthusiasm for Mass when they themselves requested it and the Mass was announced on Sunday for their intentions.

Another way these sisters unearthed some interesting ideas and provoked original thinking was a contest in which a prize was awarded to the student who suggested the best means of overcoming the difficulties of frequent Communion. The winner was generally chosen by a vote of the class.

Most of the sisters had a prayer for vocations written on the blackboard and recited daily before class. Where prayer cards were available, they were used and constantly checked by the teachers, lest they became lost or forgotten.

When encouraging private prayer there was a great emphasis on aspirations. The sisters felt that many of the youngsters had the erroneous idea that to pray meant to say the Rosary or Stations. So that they might not lose heart and quit altogether, they were encouraged to add to their morning and night prayers the simple prayer: "Dear Jesus, help me to become a priest (brother or sister), if it is your holy will."

There were also many suggestions about days of recollection, class novenas, grade school retreats, and the like.

One of the suggestions for creating a vocational atmosphere in the classroom was to invite the students to bring to school all the pictures they could find of priests, brothers, and sisters in action. These pictures were then pinned on the bulletin board, around the blackboard, on the window sills, everywhere. Smaller illustrations were pasted in groups and displayed on poster paper. The more pictures there were, the better it was. For they gave a distinctive tone to the room, aroused curiosity, and set the youngsters talking about the different exhibits.

Vocational literature and posters can be obtained gratis

from practically every religious institute in the country. It was, therefore, often recommended by the sisters that a supply of this reading matter be obtained and displayed in the classroom.

During English class and reading periods pertinent passages were often selected from such booklets, and individual students were told to read them aloud. At other times the teacher preferred to do the reading herself, and the pupils had to comment on the thought content of the passages, sentence structure, and the like. Some of the biographical pieces of literature were given for book reports.

The most zealous teachers said that they set aside some time, at least once a week, for a special talk on vocations. In the course of the school year they covered the whole subject from the qualifications of the individual for the religious life to the various apostolates there are in the Church.

Many suggestions were given for the effective use of "play-ways" to review the matter covered in these talks. Sometimes it would be in the form of a game; at other times it would be with a panel of "experts."

In using the game technique to review, the teacher, for example, would say that all the pupils on her right were one team and all those on her left were another. A score-keeper stood at the board. A list of review questions was drawn up, and team captains tossed to determine which side would answer first.

In the "football game" three questions correctly answered in succession by members of one team constituted three downs. The fourth question was much harder, but if answered correctly it was a touchdown. A fifth question correctly answered gave the point after touchdown, and the opposite side took over. Any question incorrectly answered gave the ball to the opposite team, and the game continued.

In the "basketball game" each question was a shot. If answered correctly, the team scored two points and retained possession. If missed, the opposite team took over. Prompting or talking nullified the "basket" and gave the opposition a "foul shot," or an easy question.

Another form of these review techniques was to select individuals from the class and prime them on all aspects of the life and work of some Order or Congregation. Then on appointed days one of these "experts" would be selected to stand before the class and answer any question their companions threw at them. The sisters felt that the eagerness of the class and the determination of the "experts" not to be stumped made for mental alertness all around. It also gave the youngsters valuable experience in arguing for a vocation.

In some larger schools, where there were two or more classrooms for the same grades, this idea was worked out at assemblies in the form of a "Quiz Program." The "experts" of each class were pitted against one another. The advantage of this program was that each youngster in the assembly mentally answered the questions tossed at the "experts" and was both surprised and delighted at knowing most of the answers. Also the "experts" were representing their class, and their companions in the audience were jubilant when they made a good showing.

In the upper grades, too, it was found that a "Question Box" was helpful. Some of the more serious youngsters like to ask questions of the teacher without embarrassing themselves, and when the real questions ran out, the teacher had a chance to slip in a few of her own. Answering these questions helped fill in a few minutes between class assignments or the intervals resulting from a lag in the schedule.

As the program drew to a close, many of the sisters recommended a paper on the subject: "Why I would (or would not) want to be a priest (brother or sister)." This was their way of finding out how much interest was aroused and how their explanations were received.

In many cases the sisters expressed surprise at the number

who were interested in the priesthood or religious life. Sometimes it was as high as 35 per cent of the class. When this happened, the sisters jumped to the conclusion that the pupils wrote merely to please them. But later experience proved them wrong. Vocational compositions are generally sincere. Especially is this true when the students are urged beforehand to be honest in their statements.

When the papers were in, the teachers corrected them as English or religion assignments. Then there was a follow-up on those who expressed an interest in the service of God. Papers from boys who said they were interested in the diocesan priesthood were referred to the pastor or the diocesan director of vocations. Those interested in religious communities were turned over to religious recruiters. Thus the youngsters obtained further information and had a chance to talk over their vocation if they were really interested.

IT CAN BE DONE

In the fall of 1953 Sister M. Sophronia, O.S.F., died of cancer, and the School Sisters of St. Francis lost one of their best recruiters. It was my good fortune to know Sister M. Sophronia for many years, and for every one of her years of teaching she guided at least one girl to the convent and one boy to the priesthood or brotherhood. The record was all the more amazing in that sister was working most of the time with small classes in little country schools.

Since Sister M. Sophronia was so practical, I recommended that she put her ideas in writing. In 1952 the Serra Club of La Crosse published the outline as one of its vocational services. In digest it is as follows:

"In September," she wrote, "starting the very first day of school, I set a definite time, 1:00 p.m., to pray for vocations About the third week of September I organize a class club having a Vocation Committee with a chairman, who, I feel, is interested in vocation work. Generally this is a prospective recruit.

"In October I start my weekly vocation talk. I set a time every Friday for this purpose, five to ten minutes. I close with some pertinent story clipped from some magazine and then have a five-minute discussion period.

"In November I start the Question Box. When there are no voluntary questions, I have all the pupils write one or more questions. This is my best way of reaching the individuals and their problems. Timid pupils would otherwise never receive help.

"We have a Vocation Day once a month, starting in October. The pupils select a certain feast day and on that day I give special instructions, tell a vocational story, and say special prayers before Mary's shrine in the classroom.

"Thus we go on, month by month, until March. Meanwhile I have spotted some recruits. Here is where the direct approach begins. I immediately encourage them to frequent Communion, then daily Communion. I suggest sacrifices they should make, and we make a novena together. From the moment I 'spot' a vocation in a child I begin to take time out for individual personal help and encouragement — a remark here and there, a fine book or pamphlet, a question as to how the vocation is coming along.

"Then comes March, Vocation Month, the culminating point. We have special activities all month and correlate these with every subject possible — posters, book reports, compositions, letters to their patron saints, novenas, and class plays.

"In April I have private interviews. I use a guidance card, a sort of questionnaire to which I add my own points. It takes thirty to sixty minutes for each child in these interviews, and when the youngster warms up during the talk and says definitely, 'I would like to be a priest (or sister),' I immediately have the boy write to the seminary or the girl to the convent. This requires the parents' approval, and if the youngsters haven't yet spoken to their mother and father, I coach them on how to do so. Then I

have the parents come to see me. I tell them how God
has privileged them and how He will also bless them for
the sacrifice of their child. As a rule the appeal succeeds.
The parents seem happy at the thought that I am so personally interested in their youngster.

"In May I continue instructions, stories, and question box
as usual. We select a feast of our Blessed Mother and make
an act of special consecration to her, adding that we recommend to her special care those of the class whom Jesus has
called to His special service. I also provide a day of recollection for the seventh and eighth grades.

"Finally, I keep in touch with my recruits during vacation. I encourage them to receive Holy Communion frequently, even daily. I urge them to recite daily prayers, and
invite them to drop over to see me for an occasional talk.
The boys I arrange to help with special Latin lessons, so
they will not have too much difficulty during their first
weeks in the seminary."

There were many more comments and suggestions that
Sister M. Sophronia made. But one thing is evident from
the little I have quoted. Sister was willing to sacrifice herself for vocations, and her efforts paid off. At her death she
could claim almost a hundred priests, brothers, and sisters
for whom she had been responsible.

If more teachers and religious followed her example,
there would not be so much need for instruction and
guidance when the youths enter high school.

HIGH SCHOOL STUDENTS

Any alert recruiter, in passing from grade school to high
school, notices a difference in the mental attitude of the
students. In grade school the youngsters are quick to respond
to suggestions. In high school there is a tendency to uncertainty.

It is both interesting and instructive to consider the causes
of this uncertainty. On the one hand, life is now making

increasing demands on the growing boy or girl. Not only are they expected to conform much more closely than before to adult standards of conduct, but also they are being called upon far more frequently to make decisions for themselves. At the same time, they are very conscious of an inward conviction that they are not capable of performing the tasks which confront them or of coping with the many and varied situations in which they find themselves.

In his "Christopher's Talks to Catholic Teachers," David L. Greenstock develops these ideas with keen insight into the mind of these youths. "Only too frequently," he says, "they are made aware of the instability of their mental and emotional reactions, which lead them to desire a thing with all their hearts one day, and hate the very sight of it the next. This is a period of violent ideals and ambitions, which are all too often laughed at or suppressed. The adolescent's behavior is, to the outsider, inconsistent and exaggerated; yet to the youth himself it is a normal reaction to present circumstances. All this leads to a natural and basic lack of confidence, not merely in himself, but also in others."

The responsibility of the recruiter now is to give understanding and sympathy. Boys and girls in high school are looking for someone who can help them reach mental and emotional stability. If we come to their help we will not only do a great deal for vocations but also perform a great charity.

At Immaculate Conception High School, Elmhurst, Illinois, during the time of the annual retreat in 1950 a religious vocation questionnaire was given to approximately 350 of the students. Ninety-two per cent of this group answered "Yes" when they were asked, "Do you feel you really understand what a religious vocation is?" But when they got down to answering, "Do you think that if one had a vocation, God would give him or her a special sign?" 72 per cent said "Yes" and 28 per cent said "No."

Right here we have proof of the common confusion in

the minds of so many high school students. They could quote the signs of a vocation and explain the qualifications necessary for the religious life. But when it came to deciding the matter personally, the majority were confused. Some thought there should be an "inward feeling." Others thought there should be a "disgust for material things" or "a leaning toward something special for God — like praying a lot." A few even thought there might be a manifestation of the divine will through an "accident" or "failure in everything else."

About 60 per cent of the students figured that the best way out of this doubt and confusion was to consult a priest or confessor." Twenty-seven per cent of the youths, mostly girls, thought it a good idea to "talk the matter over with Sister." The rest thought it well to seek guidance from parents, from prayer, or from reading.

Substantially the same conclusions were reached by a religious vocation survey conducted by the Sodality throughout the Wichita diocese in the spring of 1950. The study of over twelve hundred questionnaires was broader in number but less exact in its findings. Accordingly, I preferred to quote the more limited investigation at Immaculate Conception High School.

In a later chapter a great deal more will be said about interviewing and counseling. But here it is important to realize the basic reasons for such help and the mental attitude of these teen-agers.

THE CORRECT ATTITUDE

One of the most noticeable traits of students at this period of their development is a resentment toward any pressure. They don't want to be "talked into" anything and tend to shy away from vocational conferences.

The reason is simply that the youths at this age have become conscious of the fact that they have a mind of their own. Nobody is going to make any judgments for them.

In childhood the youngsters were concerned more with simply observing facts, and because of their immaturity and lack of experience they relied upon others for decisions as to what they should do. Now they are capable of seeing all angles of the problem, and they want to reason the matter out for themselves.

Some recruiters and counselors become discouraged in their dealings with these adolescents, for they think the youths are in revolt against discipline and authority. Most of the time this is not true. Resistance or opposition is only superficial.

In helping with diocesan vocational campaigns I have often visited two or three schools a day in company with the local vocational director. Many times — especially with high school boys — we have run into opposition. They have not wanted to quiet down for the assembly, or have openly grumbled at the idea of having to listen to a vocational appeal. This is only natural.

Adolescents, boys and girls, are reaching a point of mental development where they need reasons and motives for their conduct. Mere authority, whether of the teacher or anybody else, is not enough to hold them to a course of action. In childhood it was customary for youngsters at the sound of a bell or order of the teacher to take a special place and listen respectfully to whatever the speaker had to say. But all that is over now.

To get such a response once more the youths must know the reason why such talks are important and how they can be helped personally. It is foolish to think that one need only tighten the discipline and get a better response.

At the 1952 National Catholic Educational Convention, Brother Frederick, F.S.C., gave an excellent paper entitled "Promoting Vocations in the High School." He pointed out that for any recruiting program to be successful, the teachers must be "enlightened with these proper attitudes."

"It is important," he said, "that the faculty give the impression of sincere interest in the vocation of everyone in the high school. It makes no difference whether he decides to serve God in the married state or the single state. The teachers want only to help the individual make the right choice. This is the only way to get students to approach their teachers for guidance."

In the classroom Brother Frederick urges that the students be given a thorough indoctrination on the reasons for choosing either marriage or the service of God. He listed three topics of prime importance:

1. Explanation of the Christian concepts of living;
2. Explanation of the obligation of striving for perfection;
3. Explanation of the married state and the single state lived for God.

Once the youths have grasped these ideas they will realize that there is no forcing of their judgments. They may choose either marriage or the single state in religion. In either case they will be trying to do most for God, themselves, and others. If they choose marriage, they have courtship as a period of preparation. They must use it well. If they choose the service of God, they have a preparatory course in a seminary or convent. They must use that time well.

Brother Frederick concludes with the exhortation: "No teacher should say, 'I'm not the type for vocational counseling.' You don't have to be a personality type to counsel. Just be interested. God will use your good will and will bless your efforts to further His kingdom in the souls of youth."

PROMOTIONAL TECHNIQUES

Much of what has already been said about deepening the supernatural life of the students through frequent reception of the Sacraments is applicable to those in high school as well as grade school. The same holds for creating a vocational atmosphere in the classroom.

Only when it comes to the actual techniques of putting

the informative matter across will you make allowance for the added maturity of the students.

In a talk before the Vocation Institute in 1949, Father Louis E. Riedel stressed the importance in high school of having an "office available to all, so that students can see you freely and without delay. An opportunity for personal interviews is appreciated especially by these older students."

Father Riedel also pointed out that it is good in a high school to have a religious bulletin with vocational talks and comments appearing regularly. He also urged constant contact with the religious alumni, publishing from time to time their whereabouts and work in the school paper. Where possible these same religious alumni should be invited back to the school at special times to speak to the students. "One of their own," he said, "making good as a religious makes an indelible impression on the whole school."

Much the same idea was worked out at Rosary Academy, Watertown, South Dakota. Because it was not possible to bring back all forty-six of the alumnae who had entered religious life, the senior class put on a poster project. A picture of each religious was mounted on a poster and displayed with interesting data about the individual's vocation.

The Vocational Congress, held by the Christian Brothers at La Salle Institute, Glencoe, Missouri, in January of 1953, gave a report of the activities in all the high schools of their five districts. All the foregoing suggestions were listed, together with the suggestion that the homeroom teacher visit the home of a likely prospect with the school's vocational director. This made the contact much more personal and helped check any parental opposition.

The Brothers also reported that in the New Orleans and Santa Fe districts they had had a great deal of success with a special vocational night for the parents of the students. Sometimes there were panel discussions given; at other times there were explanatory talks and simple dramatizations of various aspects of the religious life.

Various communities of sisters, too, have sent me lists of suggestions for the promotion of vocations in girls' high schools and academies. At the moment I have before me twenty-seven pages of suggestions, ranging from how to word daily vocational telegrams for the bulletin board to directing a vocational verse choir. Some of the suggestions have a very limited appeal. Others are but a repetition of ideas already suggested for the grade school level, like having a question box, posters, vocational service flag, dioramas, vocational plaques, and the like.

Vocational forums and open discussions, or even vocational debates, are much more practical and helpful for these older students. These youths are also capable of staging effective vocational pageants and religious tableaux.

Several schools have also pointed out how important it is to have a vocational reading section in the library. A clever display of pamphlets and books is always interesting, and if easily accessible, the youths will read them.

PUBLIC SCHOOLS

With over 5,000,000 Catholic students in the present public school system, it is quite natural to expect that there are vocational prospects in such schools. All of us have known many priests and religious who never had the advantage of a parochial school education. It is reasonable, therefore, to expect that more will come from this source.

One very good means of contacting these eligible boys and girls is to get their names through the parish files and send them vocational literature through the mail. Then invite them by letter to come to see you. Many who are priests and religious today were contacted that way.

Another good means of contacting them is to arrange through the pastor for them to make one of the vocational retreats that are becoming increasingly popular. Most lay-retreat houses now have one or more sessions that are devoted to vocations and to helping young men or women make up their minds regarding the service of God.

Several religious communities also invite interested prospects to "Be a Seminarian for a Weekend" or "Be a Sister for a Day." Eighth grade or high school students may come to the religious institute on the designated date to spend a little time just like a seminarian or postulant. It gives them a good insight into the life and quickly makes up for any lack of instruction they may have had regarding the service of God.

The vocational magazine, *Contact,* published by the Archdiocese of Boston, noted in its February, 1950, issue, "Many of our Catholics in the public school are at a loss as to how to act upon their desire to serve God in the religious life." To solve this problem a committee of Catholic teachers in the public schools of the archdiocese was organized to inform Catholics in each school about vocational rallies and programs in which they might be interested.

Sister M. Bertrande of Marillac House, Chicago, Illinois, put an invitation in *Novena Notes* for any girls interested in the religious life to "come and live with us for a month or two." There was to be no charge for room and board because the girls made up for the expense by working in the Institution. Only those who had completed at least two years of high school were eligible.

In two weeks she had received thirty-one replies, and after a limited correspondence twenty of the girls arrived at Marillac House. Their daily routine of prayer, work, and play was much the same as that of the sisters. The morning spiritual exercises were somewhat shortened, but the girls observed silence, periods of spiritual reading, and mental prayer. They worked right with the sisters and performed practically the same duties. Within six weeks most of these girls made up their minds, and eight of them joined the community.

COLLEGE STUDENTS

At this period of their development our Catholic youths are to be considered in many respects as adults. However, they lack experience, and in this regard vocational counselors are expected to help them.

They want to talk out their problems with a sympathetic listener. Rarely, though, do they want you to make any decision for them. Nor do they want you to appeal to your age or experience as an argument for what they ought to do.

When recruiters and counselors have tried to fall back on this argument from maturity and experience, they have found that it does not convince a college student. Most young men and women who will seek advice are too sharp to be taken in by such an approach. They know that it is not experience that is important, but the lessons learned from such experience. Many people have lived a long time and had many experiences, but they are none the wiser. Also youths have a tendency to peg everybody over twenty years older than themselves as belonging to another generation and "quite old-fashioned."

Your responsibility with this group of young men and women is to win their confidence. This cannot be done so much by group talks as by informal sessions with them in private. At St. Mary's College, Winona, Minnesota, for example, Brother Ambrose, F.S.C., has arranged for the past four years to have Guidance Weeks. A priest visits each classroom during ethics period and explains the decision these young men have to reach regarding their state of life. He then is available for private interviews.

Often these affairs have been exhausting sessions. In my own experience I have found that about one fourth of the students want to come around during the day for private conferences. In the evenings there are informal get-togethers and "smokers" with as high as a hundred students. Invariably some of the seniors have insisted on continuing these discussions far into the night. They want to talk interminably about their ideals and their future.

Among these students there is a great enthusiasm and high idealism on which the clever recruiter can capitalize. Nothing seems impossible to these young men and women; therefore, if they are given sufficient motivation, there is nothing they will not attempt.

With them there is still a tendency to hero worship, but it is not so pronounced as it was in adolescence. However, by having Christ portrayed as One to love and imitate, many of them can be inspired to follow Him. With such youths there is no problem in the thought of giving up the world if only their generosity is stirred.

In a paper entitled "Vocations in Colleges," Sister M. Bernice, O.S.B., told the Vocation Institute in 1949 about how the sisters had tried at the College of St. Scholastica, Duluth, Minnesota, to acquaint their girls with the different types of work undertaken by the community and thus arouse their interest.

"One practical scheme," she said, "was to give a Christmas party for about ninety youngsters from St. James Orphanage. The names and ages of the children were sent to the college beforehand, and each girl picked out one of them. They then purchased a gift for their child, and on the afternoon of the party entertained the youngster. The happiness of these orphans seemed to give the students a new sense of values. Over and over again they expressed their appreciation of the self-sacrifice of the sisters who give their lives to this work."

Bishop William T. Mulloy, in one of his excellent vocational appeals to college students, pointed out, "Today they are too apt to plan their whole life as *they* think it should be and too little inclined to ask: 'Lord, what wilt Thou have me to do?' "

We can be very influential in guiding the thinking of

college students in that direction when they come to us.
It is not always necessary to mention a vocation, but we
can emphasize the importance of talking their future over
with God in prayer and meditation in order to discover
the divine plan in their regard.

NURSING STUDENTS

Our final consideration will be with the nursing students. At present there are approximately 3500 of these
Catholic girls in some 380 schools around the country.

To evaluate the recruiting problem with this group Sister
Miriam Dolores, C.S.C., sent a questionnaire to approximately twenty-five religious communities operating 110
schools of nursing. She asked them to give the number of
candidates who had entered their community over a period
of ten years from their own school or other nursing schools.

There was 100 per cent response on the questionnaire,
and it was learned that 297 girls had entered from these
twenty-five schools over a ten-year period. The Daughters
of Charity of St. Vincent de Paul had 120 girls, by far
the largest number, entering from their own schools.

Breaking these figures down, we find that there are
scarcely thirty girls a year coming from 110 schools. Then
if you eliminate the 120 candidates of the Daughters of
Charity, there are not many left for the other twenty-four
communities! What is wrong?

Again it seems to be a question of guidance and motivation. Father Gerald R. Sheahan, S.J., made a study of this
problem through the Sodality nurses in Kansas in 1951. He
concluded that the drop-off in vocations arises from the
fact that the girls live too close to the sisters and see them
only as instructors and disciplinarians. They see the hardship
of their life, but do not realize the motive behind it.

As one nurse expressed it in the survey: "I believe there
are so few vocations from our school because so many girls
see the human weaknesses of sisters. We go on duty with

someone we have always admired and find out that the sweet nun isn't everything we expected her to be! Some sisters are wonderful, and we want to do all we can for them. But others are impatient, businesslike, and hard on those under them."

Another girl explained: "The sisters keep us under such an iron discipline with a whole series of 'do's' and 'don'ts' that most of us compare the life of a sister with that of a nurse. If the sisters would be a little nicer and let us talk over our troubles, the feeling would probably change and we would see the religious vocation in its true light."

A third nurse said that most of the students in her class had an uneasy feeling when sister was present. Invariably sister would try to show them how to do things better, but her manner was that of a reprimand. She somehow seemed to be scolding them.

In all of these criticisms very few girls were vindictive. They were not complaining about injustices, but simply giving the reasons why they were not personally interested in joining a nursing sisterhood.

Accordingly, since understanding and example are such powerful factors in youth guidance, it would be well for those who are not very successful in recruiting nurses to watch others who have been successful. They will see how the successful directresses smile, laugh, and give themselves to their students. One of the surest ways of winning others to oneself is to do things for others — things that require time, energy, and thoughtfulness.

One of the Daughters of Charity, who averaged two girls a year over the ten-year period checked in the Sodality survey, did not always have large classes. One year she had only eleven girls in the senior group. But her time was their time, and she was always arranging things for them. The last time I called on her she was decorating the hall for a student dance. The time before she was straightening up the office after a little birthday party. The secret of her success is that all the nurses admire her and feel indebted to her. There is not a student in the school but would like to imitate her.

Because of this admiration and friendship, I am sure, there are many times Sister can show these girls how her life is not a love for a job, but love for a Person. The hard thing about her life is not the privation of human comfort but the fact that she cannot see face-to-face the One to whom she has given her heart.

This type of instruction is very necessary. In counseling nurses privately on retreats I have found that they stress particularly the dullness of routine in the hospital, lack of interest in the work, and example of the sisters as reasons why they are not interested in that vocation.

One girl put it, "I think that most of the Catholic girls who enter nursing have at one time or another thought about being a sister. But they give up the idea very soon after entering, for they realize they can serve God by helping His sick and find greater happiness for themselves by getting married."

Another girl, a graduate nurse, told me that neither she nor her friends would ever consider the nursing sisterhood. "It is not a natural life," she said. "The sisters are deprived of fresh air and sunshine because they have no time to get out during the day. If they go outside, it is usually in the evening after sundown, when they are completely exhausted from ten or twelve hours of duty. We want a chance to relax, to enjoy our friends, and to lead a normal life in a home."

A third-year student added that she had come into nurses' training with the idea of becoming a sister but quickly changed her mind. "The sisters were always talking vocation to me, but didn't seem to be happy in their own."

Now such mistaken notions of the religious life are traceable, in part, to ignorance, which should be combated by friendly gab sessions with Sister. The other cause is that these girls have not been introduced to the exciting aspects of their religion. They have not been inspired with the high ideals of their Faith. Otherwise they would not so readily confuse their working conditions in hospitals with the nursing vocation.

This is where those of us on the outside can help. We know so well that no time is more satisfying than that which is spent with Jesus, and no work is more rewarding than that which serves Him in the person of His sick. These truths have inspired us, but they are unknown to most of the girls.

Students in our nursing schools need inspiration more than recruiting appeals. When Mass and Holy Communion seem routine to them, it is not because religion is that way. It is rather that they have failed to grasp the romance and transformation that takes place in every life given to God.

For example, we should teach them to live in the consciousness of what Holy Communion means. Jesus gives Himself to us totally in the very Body with which He suffered on Calvary. He loves us so much that He gives Himself entirely to us. We, then, should give ourselves entirely to Him, and we can deepen this realization in a hospital by repeating after Holy Communion: "Dear Jesus, you have been so good to give Yourself to me. I will give myself to You and serve You in the person of the sick all day long. In being kind and helpful to them, I will prove my love for You."

Such aspirations are the easiest kind of prayer for nurses. The round of study and work in a hospital is so exhausting that most of the girls feel they have no time for an extra rosary or a five-minute visit to chapel. But they can learn to say hundreds of aspirations during their work. "All for Thee, O Jesus" or "Jesus, help me" are wonderful ways of purifying one's motives in dealing with the sick.

One old Alexian Brother, Director of Nurses for many years, used to stop students coming out of a patient's room with the question: "Did you remember in that room that you were serving someone who is dear to Jesus . . . and did you offer it all to Jesus?"

Thus through instruction, prayer, and the use of Holy Communion we can instill into nurses an awareness of the Mystical Body of Christ and a great personal love for Jesus. Then it will be easier for them to understand what the sisterhood really is, and monotonous or menial tasks of a religious will take on a new meaning through the light of Faith.

CHAPTER IV

Vocational Clubs

GILBERT KEITH CHESTERTON, in his book, *The Common Man,* devotes a chapter to what he would talk about if he had only one sermon to preach. You may recall that his topic would be the evils of pride and the value of humility.

Thinking along the same lines, I was intrigued by the thought of what I would write about if I had only one chapter in this book.

Several things suggested themselves, but since my whole theme is "how to find more vocations," it seemed that such a chapter would have to be on vocational clubs. They are the most practical means I know of finding suitable prospects and fostering in them the seeds of a divine vocation.

NATURE OF THE CLUBS

In most places our Catholic youths lack the proper encouragement and guidance to the service of God. Some may object to this opinion, in that there are so many appeals for vocations and so many dioceses and religious communities are conducting recruiting programs.

But taking things as they are, we know that God constantly gives the vocations necessary for the growth and development of His Church. On all sides we see Catholic boys and girls with every blessing of nature and grace as will qualify them for the service of God. Dioceses and religious communities are desperately in need of new recruits. What, then, is wrong?

It can only be that there has been a failure to show these qualified boys and girls how they can recognize the divine invitation and use the blessings they have for God's greater glory.

If you have worked with any number of these youths, you know what I am talking about. They have health, intelligence, and moral fitness. They come from fine Catholic families, and their characters are above reproach. Many of them may be daily communicants, and their spiritual generosity is most heartening. But the moment you suggest the possibility of a vocation to the priesthood or religious life, they shy away.

In your heart you know that any aversion the boy or girl may feel springs from ignorance or prejudice. If you had time and opportunity, you could probably overcome it. But you know you cannot call the youngster in for repeated conferences without arousing opposition. If the youngster doesn't rebel personally, you can be sure his or her companions will want to know "what it's all about," and parents will think you are "talking their child into something."

It was at this point that the club idea presented itself. Why not have qualified boys and girls meet in some kind of organization? There they could get systematic instruction on what a vocation is and how they can respond to it. Thus instead of spending time on only one or two prospects, it would be possible for an interested priest or religious to help all of them.

ORIGIN OF THE CLUBS

These ideas were experimented with by Fathers Henry and Matthew Vetter, C.P., in 1938. They started with eight altar boys from Holy Cross Church, Cincinnati, Ohio. They called their little group the "Bosco Club," after the great patron of youth and promoter of vocations, St. John Bosco.

By the end of the year they had thirty-three members in the club, and eleven of them went to seminaries.

During the following October Brother John Joseph, C.F.X., decided to try the Bosco Club technique with high school students at St. Xavier's, Louisville, Kentucky. Twenty-six boys were present for the first meeting, and a second get-together brought the membership to thirty-four. By the end of the year they had sixty-one members, of whom nine went to seminaries or juniorates.

Simultaneously the Sisters of Charity of Nazareth attempted to establish a vocational club for girls at Nazareth College, Louisville. They named the group in honor of Our Lady of Good Counsel. The idea was also taken up by the Ursuline nuns, the Mercy Sisters, and the Sisters of Loretto. In all, about 200 girls joined these Good Counsel Clubs and twenty-six entered the convent.

In 1940 there was a variation of the Good Counsel Club attempted by the Mission Helpers of the Sacred Heart, Towson, Maryland. They used the organization as a technique for interesting working girls in the religious life. Meetings were taken out of the school and put into the convent parlor. Members met there on Sunday afternoons for a religious discussion, followed by outdoor Stations and Benediction in the convent chapel. The meeting concluded with refreshments and an informal visit. As many as seventy-five girls attended these meetings and five of them joined the community.

During these years I kept in touch with these programs and experimented with two vocational clubs myself at the Passionist Seminary in St. Louis, Missouri, and St. Paul's Monastery, Detroit, Michigan. My instructions to the youngsters in these clubs were published in the pamphlets *Follow Me* for boys and *Follow Him* for girls.

The Provincial of the Passionists, Very Rev. Fr. Herman Stier, C.P., was interested in all that contributed to the promotion of vocations, and he thought it would be a good idea to publish a handbook for these different clubs. Accordingly, the *Bosco Club Handbook* and *Good Counsel Club Handbook* were written and 5000 copies distributed in 1943. Since then the clubs have expanded tremendously, the handbooks have been revised, and many variations on the club technique have been worked out.

As of July, 1954, there are 964 units of the Bosco Club in the United States. There are also units organized in Canada, Argentina, Uruguay, Australia, Japan, India, Africa, Spain, France, England, and Ireland. The Club of Our Lady of Good Counsel numbers 1172 units in the United States, and branches have been started in other countries along with the Bosco Club.

JUNIOR CLUBS

The club originated with seventh and eighth grade youngsters, and there it finds its most enthusiastic following. Boys and girls are then at the "gang age" and readily sign up when an appeal is made for membership. Some units have reported that as high as 35 per cent of the youngsters approached have responded to their invitation to join.

Prudent recruiters know that this does not represent another "Pentecost." It is just youthful enthusiasm. But it is possible to sift out the more promising prospects, and that should be the aim of every club moderator.

A unit is started by a moderator, who visits the seventh and eighth grade classrooms of one or more parochial schools in a given area. This moderator can be a priest in the parish, a teacher in the school, or any interested religious.

In the recruiting talk the boys are told that they have a chance to join a wonderful organization that will acquaint them with all aspects of the priesthood and brotherhood. It is the St. John Bosco Club. The girls are told about their club, which is that of Our Lady of Good Counsel. It will open up to them all the wonderful things about the life of a sister. The youngsters are reminded that they do not have to become priests, brothers, or sisters, but they must have an interest in finding out more about these vocations.

Naturally "study" about the service of God does not appeal to them. So the club utilizes films and visits to religious communities as its method of indoctrination. There are trips for the boys' club members to seminaries, where they tour the buildings, see how the young men live, and sometimes even play ball with the future priests. The girls' club visits different convents and members see how the sisters live. Sometimes they play games with the aspirants and postulants. At other times they have a picnic in the convent garden.

This appeal is followed by the announcement of when and where the club meeting will be held. Boys' and girls' groups *always* meet separately, and there is always a sister moderator for the girls' clubs. Age groups, too, are kept distinct.

If the junior club is formed of members of one school, it generally meets in the school or parish hall. Sometimes it is possible to schedule these meetings during school hours; at other times the youngsters meet on Saturday mornings or Sunday afternoons. The latter time is the most popular.

When the members come from several schools in the area, a centrally located hall or auditorium is generally picked. When the youngsters have to travel too far for the meetings, attendance is always poor.

When an interested group has been assembled, the meeting opens with a prayer to Mary, Queen of Vocations. Then follows a rousing talk by the club moderator on the importance of the club. In the course of the talk the rules are explained:

1. To say a prayer daily to know and fulfill God's holy will in regard to one's vocation;

2. To receive Holy Communion once a week, and more frequently if possible;

3. To offer Mass and Holy Communion for all the club members on the first Sunday of each month.

No official ritual has been formulated for the admission of members, but in many places the club moderator makes a little ceremony out of the affair. Those who wish to join the club fill out an application card, then individually they come up before the moderator and promise to keep the rules. A little solemnity of this sort makes a deeper impression on the youngsters, and they remember their pledge longer.

In some of the junior clubs initiation ceremonies are quite popular. It seems the younger boys, especially, like the idea of going through an initiation, and several stunts have been worked out for them. The main advantage of these things is that it gives them something to talk about with their companions.

One form of such initiations is a peanut race. Each candidate lines up with a peanut, and at a given signal all run a race to see which one can push it across the finish line with the nose. The first three winners are considered initiated, while the losers must enter another contest.

Girls' groups have sometimes preferred an egg race. Each contestant brings a hard-boiled egg to the meeting. Entries line up with spoons in their mouths. At a given signal they are to put the egg into the bowl of the spoon, and without touching the spoon or egg, negotiate the distance to the finish line. The first three winners are initiated; the others must do something else.

In the orange-eating contest, entries are paired off in groups of two. Each has an orange and is allowed to puncture it at one end with a knife. At a signal each must feed the orange to his partner. This is very popular with boys, for they invariably end up squirting the juice in one another's faces.

A walnut hunt consists in digging with one's mouth for

walnuts in a panful of flour. It is a gagging job, and any boy or girl who does it is worthily initiated.

A whistling contest is staged by giving each entrant five soda crackers. At the signal he or she must eat the crackers and then whistle. The first three winners are initiated. The rest must try again.

Often the moderator will prolong these initiations over several meetings and vary the program each time. However, the stunt is always the last thing on the agenda, for the boys and girls are then less disposed for serious reflection. After such affairs they are dismissed for games on the playground or home.

THE CLUB PROGRAM

In subsequent meetings a definite program is inaugurated. There is always a selected prayer to open the meetings and another to conclude.

Since the whole purpose of the organization is to bring the youngsters under the influence of a zealous and capable moderator, who will intensify their spiritual life and give them adequate instruction, no meeting should neglect these two purposes. Accordingly, there should be at the beginning at least a five-minute meditation on some religious truth or example from the Gospel. This should be followed by a brief recommendation for the practice of some virtue.

The instructions should cover all the signs of a vocation and the requirements for the service of God. As opportunity permits, outside speakers are brought in to explain their life and work. Slides and movies are used to supplement this instruction and, since so many films are available from the Propagation of the Faith and various seminaries and religious institutes, there is no lack of this visual aid material.

Meetings are held at least every month in the junior clubs, and for every third meeting an outing or trip to some religious house is arranged. This consists of a visit first to the chapel and the regular club prayers and meditation. Then follow a tour of the buildings and an explanation of the particular community by one of the members. Afterward there are refreshments and a chance to visit with the younger religious. Sometimes there is a ball game or some other entertainment.

With the boys' clubs there are a minimum of nine meetings in the course of a school year, and the following subjects are covered thoroughly with talks, films, and trips:

1. The signs of a vocation and how to detect God's call.

2. The training of a seminarian. (Many of the clubs supplement this instruction with the showing of the film "Captains in His Army," produced by the Serra Club, St. Louis, Missouri.)

3. The difference between diocesan and religious priests.

4. The life of a brother and the different communities of these religious. (Often there is a visit to one of these groups.)

5. The vows of religion and the reason for them.

6. The kinds of work on the home and foreign missions. (Often a missionary is invited to tell his experiences.)

7. The teaching and nursing orders. (A film or visit to one of the communities is arranged.)

8. The qualities of an aspirant and method of preparation.

9. The way to make application and answers to objections that might be occasioned by parents, poverty, or the like.

Variety is always sought in the matter of instruction, with quizzes, occasional contests, and raffles to sustain interest. The program for the girls' clubs follows the same general theme. Sometimes the sister moderators arrange for members to have meetings every two weeks, but there should be a minimum of at least one meeting a month. The subjects should cover:

1. The signs of a vocation and how to detect God's call.

2. The training a girl receives in the convent. (Many of the clubs supplement this instruction with the film "God's

Career Women," produced by the Serra Club, St. Louis, Missouri.)

3. The vows of religion and the reason for them.

4. The communities that devote themselves to the care of children. (Often a trip is arranged to visit some nursery or orphanage.)

5. The teaching vocation. (Generally a film from one of the teaching communities is used to supplement the instruction.)

6. The nursing vocation. (Sometimes a visit is arranged to one of the local hospitals. It is not just a tour of the institution, but an explanation by one of the sisters of all the things a religious does in the care of the sick.)

7. The missionary vocation. (Often the moderator invites a missionary sister to tell the girls her experiences, either in the home or foreign field.)

8. The qualities of an aspirant and how a girl can prepare herself.

9. The way to make application and to answer objections from parents or friends.

Most priests and religious welcome a chance to address such a select group as the Bosco or Good Counsel Club, so there is rarely any difficulty in getting speakers. However, no money is offered for this service, and all are informed beforehand of the *no treasury but lots of treasure* policy of the clubs.

At all meetings there is always a supply of vocational literature from at least the communities in the area. Some clubs appoint committees to request this literature from seminaries and religious houses. They then display it at each meeting and save all the pieces that are not taken by the members.

With these junior clubs the greatest danger is in loss of club morale from the enrolling of too many who come only for the diversion or excitement. The moderator must remember that these organizations are not Catholic youth clubs but *vocational* clubs. Accordingly, all who do not have a serious purpose or conform to the club rules and discipline should be dismissed.

Most moderators will always insist that when a youngster is dropped, it is not an indication that he or she has no vocation. It is merely that the individual is not cooperating with the system of formation and instruction.

HIGH SCHOOL CLUBS

As soon as a vocational club is suggested for high school students, there are always priests and religious who exclaim most emphatically, "It won't work!" They have not tried the program themselves, but they feel they know youth well enough to predict the result.

"If I were a girl," one sister told me, "I'd never join such a club!"

"A real vocation," a priest warned, "is something sacred and deep. You can't expect boys that have a vocation to talk up. The only ones you'll get are those who are misfits."

A brother assured me that he had been counseling boys for twenty-seven years. In all that time he had never known a genuine candidate for the priesthood or brotherhood who wanted to broadcast his aspirations.

Another sister just laughed at the thought of the girls signing up for a club that offered only instruction on the religious life. "The moment a girl joined such a group she would be out of luck in getting dates. Also she would be in for a lot of teasing from her friends."

Commenting on these mistaken notions about youth and trying to explain the seeming ambiguity of their behavior in such matters, Doctor Rudolph Allers remarked: "Many have wondered at the fact that the same young people who so much resent authority, restrictions, discipline, and order, are quite ready to join organizations which demand the strictest obedience and discipline. But the contradiction is only apparent.

"Youth," he insisted, "longs for guidance and authority, but the persons or groups providing these must be either freely chosen or at least be to the liking of the youthful mind.

"Many difficulties which the existing authorities encounter, be they of the home or the school, or society or the Church, are due to the fact that their way of approach is no longer adequate to the mentality of the younger generation. Sometimes," Doctor Allers concluded, "one feels inclined to apply to these persons or groups, entrusted with the care of youth, a slightly modified adage: 'Times change, but they do not change with them.'"

It has never been my purpose to enter into controversy with either group of these modern educators. All I ask is that they look at the club records and observe the success of those who have tried the technique in their schools.

Some of the misunderstanding, I am sure, has arisen from the assumption that high school clubs are run the same way as grade school ones. This is not true. The objectives are the same, but the methods are different.

Anyone who has worked with high school students knows that there are pronounced emotional and psychological changes taking place at this age. These youths are quite different from boys and girls in grade school, and yet they are not adults.

The prudent vocational director accepts these differences and works with them. He or she also acknowledges that there is a distinction between freshmen and sophomores, and juniors and seniors. The younger ones go in more for play-ways of instruction, while the older ones prefer the discussion type.

Ordinarily neither group is mixed in a high school club, and all the avails of natural psychology are used in appealing to them. They are given every opportunity to bring to light the mysterious longings and secret ambitions hidden in their hearts. They have a chance to pick up as much information as they want, and they know that at any time they can seek personal help from a moderator of their own choosing.

This is what puts the club over and explains its popularity. At present there are 162 moderators of high school vocation clubs in the Midwest Vocation Association, and the majority of them claim that from one fourth to one third of their entire school enrollment is interested in the vocational club!

Speaking for the Good Counsel Club moderators on problems in forming a vocational club, Sister Hyacinth, O.S.F., principal of Alvernia High School, Chicago, Illinois, stated that the best thing the vocational club did in their school was "to bring the religious life out of the closets and into the open where all can see and analyze and understand its meaning. We have been keeping it tucked away long enough. Young America wants to know what it is all about. We have failed them so much in the past that they are now taking their problems on religious vocation to lay people. One lay woman, an authority on Catholic Action, made the statement recently that literally hundreds of young people have come to her with questions on the religious life. Within the last three years in England a group of laity organized a society for the sole purpose of fostering vocations to our communities! It is about time we let the world know what a sublime and breath-taking adventure a religious vocation is!

"In schools with a large enrollment," she continued, "it is a physical impossibility to reach students individually. You cannot afford to have many full-time counselors. You are grateful if you have enough teachers to go around. The vocational clubs, therefore, afford a wonderful opportunity for group counseling on the religious life."

ORGANIZING IN THE HIGH SCHOOL

The organizing of a vocational club in the high school ordinarily presents little or no difficulty. The subject should be proposed by the principal at one of the faculty meetings in the beginning of the school year. All aspects of the program are then discussed, and the teachers are asked to co-operate.

On the appointed day there is an assembly of the student body and a talk is given by a priest or religious who is able to elicit interest in the service of God and arouse the students' curiosity about what goes on in seminaries or convents. It is a poor talk if he or she does not get at least 20 per cent of the students interested!

At the point where interest is highest, the speaker explains that not all can be told in one talk. Neither can one film or a visit to some religious institute give the whole picture of the service of God. Therefore, it has been decided to have a special club at school whose particular purpose is to find out about all aspects of the religious state.

This club will not be just another study circle. It will be a live discussion group. There will be movies and slides. Club members will take special trips to the places they study to see at firsthand what they have been talking about.

Emphasis is placed on the fact that members of the club do not have to become religious. All they have to do is to want to find out about the religious life.

There is then a brief intermission. The teachers and those who are not at all interested in the vocational club are told to return to their homerooms. Those who want to know more about the club stay seated. The speaker then passes out application blanks and membership cards to the students who remain. The club rules of daily prayer to know their vocation and weekly Holy Communion are explained. If there are any questions, they are handled very informally, just as though a meeting were already in session.

The important business of this gathering is the selection of a moderator or moderators. In larger schools there should be at least one for each class. The students, accordingly, write down on a ballot sheet the individual they would like for moderator. All voting is kept secret, and a couple of the student officers are selected to act as scrutineers.

Every effort is made to record the votes accurately and where several moderators are chosen, the student is assigned to the one requested. It makes no difference whether in the same class one moderator should have twelve students and the other fifty. The important thing is that each student gets the vocational guide he or she wants.

The individual thus chosen by the students as their vocational director has a grave responsibility. He or she is to lead the group, stimulate their interest in the service of God, and help them solve any difficulties that arise. It would be foolish for anyone who did not enjoy being with youths to accept such a position. Neither should there be any moderators who cannot give their full attention to the work.

The moderator must also be very catholic in outlook. The club is not a scheme for getting vocations into any one order or community. It serves the needs of the diocese and the Church. Any narrowness or selfish concern on the part of the director will vitiate the whole program. In the end such a club always fails.

In many of the larger schools, where many moderators must be chosen, all the homeroom teachers have made themselves available as moderators. When meetings of the club are announced, each moderator stays in his or her classroom, while the club members are free to seek out their own group. The rest of the student body goes to the auditorium for a study period.

Once the moderators have been chosen by vote of the interested students, the date and time of the first meeting are announced. The vocational program has been launched and the club is on its own.

A great deal of the success or failure of the idea depends upon the rating it is given by the faculty in the school curriculum. At all times the vocational club must retain its identity. Never should it be merged with other activities, no matter how good or praiseworthy they may be.

The vocation club can never be an affiliate of the Sodality, the Catholic Students Mission Crusade, or any of the Catholic Action groups. The vocational club has its own goal, which is distinct from these other organizations. It meets for a very special purpose; namely, to study the priesthood, brotherhood, or sisterhood and find out how members can tell if they have a vocation.

HIGH SCHOOL MEETINGS

When a club is organized in the high school, generally one meeting a month is held on school time. It is worked in during an activities period. When other meetings or trips to some religious institute are had, they are arranged by the moderator at the request of the members. Monday or Wednesday evenings are the most popular times for the meetings; holidays and Sundays are best for the trips.

At these meetings, whether in school or outside, every effort is made to avoid a classroom atmosphere. There is no insistence on formality or discipline. It is simply a relaxed group that gathers for a friendly discussion of what they have observed about the priesthood or religious life.

The meetings, like those in the younger clubs, open with a prayer and a short consideration of some aspect of the life of our Lord or the life of a saint. A little resolution is suggested for each of them to practice until the next meeting.

In preparing for the meetings the moderator selects nine subjects for study and discussion, which he or she thinks is best suited to the particular club. Freshmen will generally be concerned with the signs of a vocation and the various apostolates. Sophomores are interested in the different kinds of work, but they also want to know about the training program in a seminary or convent. Juniors sometimes have problems and worries about making up their mind . . . "What will Mother or Dad say?" and the like. Seniors are more mature in their discussions and like to consider such questions as, "Are religious really happy?" "Why practice poverty?" or "What does it mean to imitate Christ?"

When there are several moderators holding meetings in the same school, often two or three of them volunteer to draw up the agenda which are used by the others.

Sometimes moderators will have the members list the topics they should like discussed. This is done at the first meeting and the group follows through on these topics throughout the year. In some of these groups a student leads the discussion; in others, the moderator takes over.

Recruiters of other communities are always welcomed at these club meetings, and sometimes there is a film or slide lecture. Occasionally there are trips planned to some religious house where the club members get firsthand information on the life and work of the particular group. It is sometimes arranged that they mix with the aspirants or novices.

SAMPLE DISCUSSION

As has already been stated, each moderator draws up the discussion material for his or her group. However, a sample of one of these discussions may be of help in understanding the matter.

Let us say that a junior-senior vocational club is interested in knowing whether or not religious are happy.

The moderator makes an introduction and asks each member to comment on the following points:

1. When is a person happy, or at least not too unhappy, in a natural way?

   A) What does work contribute? Must there be a sense of accomplishment? Must it be something worth doing in itself? Must the person be able to cope with it? Must it be an expression of love? Does there have to be in it a sense of newness or something different?

   B) People, we know, have to feel needed. They have to have affection. They want a chance to serve those they love. They don't want anybody cramping their style.

2. Are religious happy in this natural sort of way?

   A) Maybe yes. (Moderator checks with the members on each point discussed.)

   B) Maybe no. What about failure at work? How about difficult adjustments? What about incompatibility?

3. Religious should be happy.

   A) Not a mere absence of difficulties, moods.

   B) They must live either a supernatural life or face unhappiness.

     1) Their work is a participation in the mission of the Church. The service of God is a challenge to all their abilities and talents. It is also an expression of their love for Jesus.

     2) Religious are needed to help build up the Mystical Body of Christ. They dedicate themselves completely to God, and, while they cannot see the One they love, they are yet very close to Him.

The length of the discussion should be sufficient to attain the twofold purpose of the club. There should be some advance in vocational knowledge and some new incentive toward the practice of virtue. It should also be short enough to avoid anything like dullness or boredom. Ordinarily thirty minutes is sufficient. This with the spiritual exercises and a little recreation takes about fifty or sixty minutes in all. Meetings held outside of school time, naturally, are extended much longer. The length of the period is dependent upon the interest of the members.

CLUBS IN COLLEGES AND NURSING SCHOOLS

Vocational clubs in colleges and schools of nursing are not so numerous as those in the high schools. But this is true for the same reason that we have fewer clubs in high school than we have in grade school. There are not so many students available. There is no reason, though, why the club program cannot be utilized in any college or nursing school if the necessary adaptations in approach and program are made.

At present we have forty-two such groups, and the interest of the students attests the success of this technique.

Collegiate groups always open and close their meetings with a prayer. The first five minutes are used by the moderator to give the usual meditation and recommendation for some virtue for the coming month.

Meetings are generally divided into formal and informal sessions. The formal sessions are publicized and all interested individuals in the school or college are invited to attend. The subject matter is then presented through a formal lecture or a panel discussion.

Open forums are very popular, and discussion is sometimes stimulated by planting objections in the audience. The priest, brother, or sister will make statements and be challenged by some of the listeners. Some groups have even invited a parent or older person to give a talk on "Why I Would Not Want a Son or Daughter to Go to the Seminary or Convent." The audience is then challenged to refute the arguments. If the speaker is clever and forceful, a very stimulating session ensues!

VARIATIONS OF THE CLUB PROGRAM

From the very beginning of the Bosco and Good Counsel Clubs, other groups started under different titles. But since they were established for the promotion of interest in the priesthood and religious life, these clubs generally followed the plan that we have sketched.

It is impossible to list all of these groups or give accurate statistics on them. But it may be of interest to note the different types.

One of the first groups for boys from public high schools and working youths is the Catholic Center Club. Founded in 1944 by Father Andrew Ansbro, C.P., in Jamaica, Long

Island, the club has for its purpose to cultivate and guide the vocational interests of those young men who are not reached by a Catholic school club.

The director reports that nearly one hundred members are now studying in some twenty different minor and major seminaries, and two have already been ordained priests.

A similar group was founded at the same time by Father Ansbro for girls under the title of St. Jean Club. Catholic girls who want to find out more about the sisterhood join this group and regularly visit various communities of religious in the New York area. Most of the members are from public schools or are working in offices. What they see and study makes a profound influence on them, for to date eighty-two members have decided to enter the convent.

In Boston Archbishop Richard J. Cushing formed a vocational club for boys interested in the diocesan clergy. He named the group after the patron of Boston, St. Botolph. At present the club numbers over 300 high school students who meet regularly with either the Archbishop or one of the seminary professors. The various works of the priesthood are explained to them and they receive renewed inspiration to continue their high school studies until such time as they are able to enter the diocesan seminary.

In the Diocese of Pittsburgh Our Lady of Fatima Vocation Clubs were established by Father Ferris Guay in all the diocesan high schools. Moderators are elected by the students, and meetings are held during the activities period.

Similar clubs have been started by other communities and schools. Some have chosen the title, Sacred Heart. Others are named with one of our Blessed Mother's titles. A group in St. Luke's School, Waverly, Massachusetts, called themselves the Twifs, and I was at a loss to figure that one out. They explained that they hoped to increase vocations "Through Mary, With Mary, In Mary, and For Mary" — which made TWIF!

The Franciscans have the St. Anthony Clubs; the Dominicans, The Young Dominicans; and the Carmelites, The Young Carmelites. Some groups are named after a patron saint, like the St. Dominic Savio Vocational Clubs, the Mother Cabrini Vocational Clubs, and the St. Maria Goretti Vocational Clubs.

The Christian Brothers have a very successful program in their Benildus Clubs. These groups are named after their great recruiter, Blessed Brother Benildus, who is credited with getting 245 vocations in his lifetime.

Units of the Benildus Club are established in each of the Christian Brothers' schools, and membership is open to all their students. There are two degrees of membership, the "actives" and the "associates." "Active" members participate in all the purposes of the club, while the "associates" promise to pray for the success of the club. Meetings are held every two weeks and last for one hour. Officers are elected by the boys and much of the organization and matter for discussion is left in the hands of the members.

The Little Flower Circle, founded in 1925 by Father Joseph J. Strauss, C.SS.R., brings in another type of vocational club, which is nonetheless effective. Older girls and even belated vocations are invited to joint this group, and they function as a study circle. Members meet in one another's homes and discuss the subject of their vocation and the requirements of the sisterhood. Each circle has its own priest moderator, and members occasionally make days of recollection together. Their publication, *Come Follow Me,* is available through their club headquarters, 389 East 150th Street, Bronx 55, New York.

The Seraphic Society for Vocations is both a prayer crusade and a means of propagandizing the vocational apostolate. It is open to all men, women, and children who will promise to say three "Hail Marys" a day for vocations. It also offers to send literature on any community to boys or girls who are interested in the religious life and serves pastors and teachers with excellent posters and teaching aids.

For youngsters who can be contacted only by mail there are the Future Priest Club and the Future Sister Club. These groups were founded by Father Pung, S.V.D., five years ago and now number approximately 10,000 correspondents from fourth grade up through high school.

The boys in this group each receive regularly a copy of the club's magazine, *The Shepherd*. They are also encouraged to write about their vocation to one of the seminarians at St. Augustine's Seminary, Bay St. Louis, Mississippi, or Sacred Heart Seminary, Girard, Pennsylvania.

The girls each receive regularly a copy of their club's magazine, *The Handmaid,* and correspond with the Sisters of Mercy at St. Francis Xavier Academy, Vicksburg, Mississippi, regarding their vocation.

EFFECTS OF THESE CLUBS

This vocational program has in the past fifteen years developed and guided hundreds of those who are now priests, brothers, and sisters. Practically all who have had anything to do with the organization, either as members or moderators, are enthusiastic in its support, for the club attempts to give what the youths of today need: information, inspiration, and direction.

The whole secret of the program's effectiveness lies in the fact that it brings youngsters with every blessing of nature and grace under the influence of zealous vocation-minded directors. The club gives a moderator only an excuse to talk about vocations to the priesthood and religious life at any time. It makes the school or youth group vocation-conscious and brings the subject out in the open. It also dissipates much of the parental opposition, for there is so much talk about the club at home that the parents soon resume on their youngster's decision before he or she mentions it.

As Father Howard Ralenkotter, C.P., who organized over eighty Good Counsel Clubs in the Midwest, insists: "The club technique will always create an 'atmosphere' for vocations. It will banish all fear and mystery about what God's call really is.

"The club," he continues, "makes priests and sisters more vocation-minded, for they discover that many students want their help and will follow their direction in regard to the service of God. It also develops many vocation-minded teachers, who in turn will refer good prospects to zealous confessors and counselors. Lastly, we cannot overlook the effect on the members themselves. In years to come those who have not gone ahead to the priesthood or religious life will have a greater understanding and sympathy for the vocation. They will help their own children and thus become vocation promoters."

Thus the club idea is built on human nature. It is not a method of cramming vocational matter into boys and girls but rather a program that is interest-creating and encouraging. Only about 12 per cent of those who join do anything about entering a seminary or convent, but the 88 per cent are wiser and better for their training. For this, if no other reason, the clubs deserve investigation.

All branches of the two most popular clubs, the St. John Bosco Vocational Club for boys and the Our Lady of Good Counsel Club for girls, are completely autonomous. The national moderator of these clubs, 5700 North Harlem Avenue, Chicago, Illinois, acts as co-ordinator for the various groups. All necessary information regarding the establishing or furthering of the clubs is available from the national office. It is also the center for the exchange of club ideas and suggestions.

Individual clubs can be affiliated with the National Office on request. They then receive the club bulletins and profit by the experience and suggestions of other moderators. Thus, also, they share in the prayers of the whole club, and priest directors offer Mass on the first Sunday of each month for all the members.

A final word must be said about the lay organizations which are doing such a splendid work in helping to prepare young men and women for the service of God and in creating a better understanding of a religious vocation among the laity.

The most prominent of these groups is the Serra International, named after Father Junipero Serra, the noted Spanish Franciscan missionary, who played a leading role in the early missionary efforts of the West.

Starting in 1935 in Seattle, Washington, the Serra Club has, by July, 1954, spread to over one hundred cities of the United States, Canada, Alaska, Puerto Rico, and Peru. In all they number some 5600 members.

Each member of the Serra Club is a business or professional man and his objectives are:

1. To foster vocations and assist in the education of young men for the priesthood;
2. To further Catholicism through enduring friendship among Catholic men.

In the beginning their efforts were confined mainly to discussing the subject of vocations at luncheon meetings and contributing each year to the education of a boy in the diocesan seminary. But as one of their outstanding leaders, Dr. John P. Treacy of Marquette University, Milwaukee, Wisconsin, stated in an address at their national convention in 1947: "Suppose that a rector of a seminary had his choice between receiving from the Serra Club each year a thousand dollar contribution or having the Serra Club discover and send him *one* boy with a real vocation for the priesthood. Which do you think he would choose? Which would he choose if the club helped send him five such boys?"

This appeal made a great impression on the club members and from then on there was increased emphasis on what Serrans could do to help guide boys toward the priesthood and religious life. Various projects were worked out. Now many of the Serra Clubs:

1. Send out lay speakers for Holy Name breakfasts, Cana meetings, and similar lay gatherings;
2. Distribute the vocational films, "Captains in His Army" for boys and "God's Career Women" for girls;
3. Hold vocational essay contests;
4. Conduct nocturnal adoration groups and similar activities for the cause of vocations;
5. Entertain seminarians and newly ordained priests;
6. Invite boys out to the diocesan seminary;
7. Obtain employment for seminarians during the summer vacation.

Another group, founded recently in Washington, D. C., is called the Regina Cleri Society. It is organized on parish lines and is made up of men and women who promote vocations by contributions of prayer and money.

The members of this group fall into three groups. There are the "promoters," who divide the parish among themselves and make a house-to-house visit of the "ordinary" members. These latter are individuals who have promised monthly to make either an offering of prayers or money, or both, for the cause of vocations. Finally, there are the "honorary" members, who live outside the parish and contribute either spiritually or financially to the society's activity.

A similar organization, founded in Pittsburgh, Pennsylvania, is known as the Friends of Our Lady. This society started among parents of priests and religious and includes those who promise to say a prayer daily for vocations and try to interest others in praying for this intention. The group also sponsors vocational triduums and novenas.

Members of the Friends of Our Lady study about vocations at their meetings and then make positive efforts to enlighten misinformed parents on the subject. They distribute vocational literature, and act as "scouts" by keeping an eye open for likely candidates. When such a boy or girl is found, the member mentions the fact to the pastor. Also if anyone in the parish needs financial help in going to the seminary or convent, the Friends of Our Lady help.

Thus these and many other excellent lay clubs are also aiding in the promotion and cultivation of priestly and religious vocations. What they have done should inspire other groups!

CHAPTER V

Interviewing Prospects

PAGING through some back issues of the *Readers Digest,* I came across an article about a person who became impatient to see the first rose in the garden. For days there had been a bud quite conspicuous on one of the bushes. However, it had seemed too slow in opening.

In an effort to help nature the overeager gardener tried to unfold the petals. That seemed to be the best and quickest way to enjoy the flower's beauty and color.

But after the petals were opened, there was not the gorgeous bloom that had been expected. Because nature had been forced, the rose's beauty had been destroyed. Within a day the flower withered and died.

Reflecting upon this parable from nature, I realized how perfectly it illustrates one of the dangers in vocational guidance. Too many recruiters become overeager for results and try to force the budding vocations they find. They cannot wait for the individual to open up and manifest the beauty of God's grace. They rush the matter, and the boy or girl turns away in frustration. Or they jump to conclusions with insufficient data.

GETTING THE FACTS

Apart from a special revelation or inspiration from God, every recruiter should remember that it is impossible to decide immediately whether or not an individual has a genuine priestly or religious vocation. It is possible to detect right away a lack of aptitude or an impediment that will keep the individual out of the seminary or convent. But one cannot tell at the very first interview what God wants of the individual.

Accordingly, at your first meeting with any boy or girl who expresses interest in the priesthood, brotherhood, or sisterhood, you should seek information. Later on it may be necessary to make a judgment on this or that point. But at the first interview you should go after the facts. You should find out about the person's fitness for the service of God. You should discover his or her physical, mental, and moral qualifications. You should inquire into the reasons for this person's choice of the religious life and find out if there are any impediments.

Some time ago I was told how a girl, after four years of encouragement in high school, was abruptly turned down by a certain community. All along her teachers had been building up her hopes for the convent. They had picked on her because she was so different from the rest in the class. She was quiet and retiring and never went out on dates. At the last minute it came as a shock to them to discover that her "religious" disposition proceeded not so much from virtue as from an anemic condition!

The youngster was heartbroken at her rejection, and the sisters at school were embarrassed. All this could have been avoided if the one who first contacted the girl had waited until it was learned whether or not the youngster had all the qualifications for the religious life.

Only when you have all the information are you in a position to give clear and confident direction regarding an individual's vocation. This chapter, therefore, is an attempt to show you how to set up the interview . . . how to draw out the prospect . . . and how to get the necessary information.

ARRANGING THE INTERVIEW

After you have stimulated interest in vocations through a talk, distribution of literature, a vocational club, or any other technique, there inevitably follows a personal interview.

You make yourself available in the rectory or convent parlor, or, better still, in some neutral place — like a school office. It is hard to predict when the youngster will decide to talk about his or her vocation. But when the decision is made, you must be accessible. Your time must be their time, and whenever you are forced to interrupt the interview, always arrange to continue the matter at the very first opportunity.

The place where you talk must be absolutely private. If it is in school, it should be arranged that the other students do not see those who are coming in or going out of the vocational director's room. Above all, there should be no danger of others nearby hearing what is discussed. Youngsters are very sensitive on this point and want no betrayal of their secret.

It almost goes without saying that the matter discussed in this interview should be kept private and personal. In his book, *Counseling in Catholic Life and Education,* Charles A. Curran states: "Once it becomes known that a counselor violates confidences even in a small way, his effectiveness will be seriously impaired. This must be particularly emphasized in interviews with children. When adults express confidences people generally consider them seriously and do not readily violate them. They are not aways so conscientiously aware of their obligations to children. But the confidences of children are equally important.

"A child," he continues, "who feels he has been betrayed in a confidential relationship with an adult may be deeply hurt and may even become bitter as he broods over it. Consequently, if, for any reason, the counselor intends to use the information children give him, he should state this openly to the child before the interview begins. If the counselor does not make this clear, then the child has a right to assume a state of confidence for private relations."

Often you may know that a boy or girl wants to see you before he or she actually comes in for the interview. When this happens it would be well to brief yourself beforehand on the individual's background. Consult the parish records or the school office files and ask for whatever data on the youngster there is available.

Many schools have regular testing programs. Some of this material may be of great help to you in evaluating a situation and saying the proper thing. It is also well to talk with the youth's teachers and friends. Often they can tell you more about the individual's character and disposition in five minutes than you would otherwise learn in five hours of interviewing.

Some vocational directors recommend that you get this information on the individual by handing him or her a questionnaire and asking that it be filled out. From a psychological standpoint this would seem to be a very poor approach, since there would then be danger of starting the interview under tension.

The ideal situation is a friendly and relaxed atmosphere. When the boy or girl comes in to talk, you should rise and smile. Priests or brothers generally shake hands with a boy and invite him to sit down. Sisters often do the same with girls, but the important thing is to make the individual feel welcome.

There are a few manuals on counseling that make a great deal out of the handshake. If the hand is moist, he or she is supposed to be nervous. If it is "fishy," then the person is either not interested in seeing you or on guard as to what you will say. A hand that is strong and purposeful represents either a wholesome individual or a youth who is trying to compensate for an inferiority complex. Much of this matter, as you can see, becomes quite ridiculous, for a person can read into it almost anything desired.

All you should be interested in is getting the prospect into the room and seated for the interview. Most recruiters start the discussion very casually with a comment about how glad they are that the individual has come around.

Often I have found that it helps when I smile encouragingly and say, "Before we start, I am quite curious as to whether you came in voluntarily or because somebody sent you." In some places you will find that a very zealous teacher is shoving everybody in for interviews. The youngster might not be disposed to talk, and it is well to find it out immediately. If the youngster has come in voluntarily, he or she will quickly admit it and feel better for letting you know.

At this point it is sometimes well to launch right into the matter of the interview. However, if the youngster is nervous, it is always better to spend a little time putting him or her at ease. This may be done by discussing some neutral subject, like sports, schoolwork, hobbies, or the like. Then as the youngster relaxes and opens up, you judiciously bring the interview to the point you want to discuss.

QUALIFICATIONS FOR THE LIFE

Since the individual has come in to talk over the question of a vocation to the priesthood or religious life, you should first explain the obvious qualifications for the life and then find out if he or she has what it takes.

Often by looking at a person you can tell whether or not he is blessed with good health. You can generally notice, too, if he has any deformity or noticeable physical defect.

At the outset it is not necessary to question a person at any length on these points. The medical examination which the individual will later undergo will bring out the details of his medical history and present physical condition. Now you are looking for the obvious weaknesses, such as:

1. Undue nervousness in any part of the body that might indicate some serious disorder;
2. Record of heart disease or tuberculosis;
3. History of insanity or epilepsy in the individual or family.

These are the things a recruiter should find out in the very beginning, for they can pose a serious obstacle to any further consideration of the priesthood or religious life. Some recruiters also hold that you should find out immediately if the individual has any difficult allergies, trouble with asthma, or the like. This matter, though, would seem to belong to the more thorough investigation that you make when there is a judgment to be made. In the following chapter that subject will be treated at greater length.

In regard to intelligence you generally ask the individual how much education he or she has had and what are the school reports. You inquire about the person's scholastic average and ask the individual how he or she rates in class. Would it be in the upper, middle, or lower third of the class? Usually the individual will be very honest in this appraisal.

If he or she claims to be in the lower third of the class, it is always well to ask if the schoolwork represents the person's best effort. Sometimes boys or girls are working after school and have to cram in homework while riding on a bus or late at night. If they had more regular hours, they could do much better work.

The majority of genuine prospects for the priesthood or religious life will be in the upper third of the class. This is particularly true of youngsters from the eighth grade. Those who are struggling along in the lower third of the class are generally poor risks intellectually.

In 1953 Father Jude Senieur, O.F.M.Cap., conducted a survey among minor seminaries of the United States to determine the reasons why boys leave. His findings were reported at the Seventh Annual Vocation Institute and lack of talent led the list. In some places the defection for this reason was as high as 53 per cent. The same point was brought up in private discussion among the seminary rectors at the Catholic Educational Convention in 1949, and the prevailing opinion was that any boy under a 100 I.Q. could not be expected to persevere.

Superiors of brothers and sisters have hastened to add that they, too, cannot accept any dull or weak-minded individuals. Unless an individual has sufficient intelligence to grasp the nature of the religious life and to fit into community living, he is not qualified to join.

On the subject of moral fitness you can generally determine if the person has been living habitually in the state of grace by asking how often he or she has been going to Holy Communion.

Most youngsters will answer that they receive weekly or daily. It is then helpful to ask quite casually if they are accustomed to go with their parents to Mass and Communion on Sunday. If the answer is "no" you might ask if the parents go to an earlier or later Mass. If you have a doubt, ask the boy or girl if the parents ever go to Communion. This is generally a subtle way of determining whether or not the youth comes from a good Catholic family.

If the parents have not been going to the Sacraments, it is well to determine immediately if they are validly married. This should be asked indirectly and without embarrassing the boy or girl or even arousing suspicions as to what you are investigating.

DESIRE FOR THE RELIGIOUS LIFE

Fortunately it takes much longer to explain the way to conduct such an interview than it takes actually to do it. Once you have determined that the youngster has no impediment and that he or she has the fitness of nature and grace for such a life, the next thing to investigate is the desire. Why does he want to be a priest or brother? Why does she want to be a sister?

Sometimes it helps to start in a chronological way. The recruiter asks the persons being interviewed when the thought first came to them and how they have thought about it since then. Some will say they have thought about it from earliest childhood. They are the "born" vocations. The great majority will tell how the idea took shape during the beginning of adolescence. A few will mention that it came later. They and older individuals who have been impeded from going earlier to a seminary or convent are the "belated" vocations.

In the course of this recital various contradictions will appear. It is not good, as a rule, to point out these discrepancies immediately. The youngster is probably having difficulty with the interview. There is much he or she wants to say, and the right words do not seem to come.

Seeing an interested and sympathetic attitude in you will be a great help to this boy or girl. Some recruiters nod approvingly at everything that is said. Others simply insist with the youngster that the problem is quite normal. But never do they laugh at anything that he or she tries to confide.

This is sometimes very hard. I recall how a teen-age girl once told me of her great perplexity about the sisterhood. In the winter she wanted to be a nun. But when summer came around she couldn't stand the thought of the religious life. What should she do?

It was on the tip of my tongue to exclaim: "Join an Alaskan community where you can have the feeling the year round!" But I repressed the urge and seriously probed her attitude toward swimming, riding in convertibles, dancing under the stars, and other teen-age delights. Finally, she realized that her conflicting feelings arose from the fact that she did not have a supernatural outlook. She had never tried to understand the real nature of the religious life.

USING THE HORNS OF A DILEMMA

Let us say, for example, that a boy has told you about how when he was in eighth grade he wanted to be a priest. Then during high school the idea faded. He went out for sports, dated girls, and worked evenings in a grocery store. He did not think any more about the priesthood, and now in his senior year he wonders what to do.

Or a girl confides that she has always admired the sisters and sometimes thought of herself as one of them. Still she likes children and has much fun on dates. She sums up the situation with a sigh, "Now I'm more confused than ever!"

In all these situations where the individual describes conflicting desires for the married state and the religious life, it may help to take the vocation of marriage and work toward a solution. If you do not find an answer that way, try the religious state. In nine out of ten cases there will not be any necessity for the boy or girl to live in the single state in the world, so you are generally safe in using this dilemma.

Accordingly, you begin by inquiring into the person's social life. You invite him or her to tell you about dates, friends, romances. All the time you are alert for any evidence of the attitude of the one interviewed toward these experiences.

Some recruiters think this probing is particularly important in dealing with girls. They want to ask, "Have you ever noticed a sense of emptiness on your dates? Has it ever seemed that you were looking for so much more than you actually had?" When the answers have been "yes," these recruiters have said to the girl, "Maybe you are looking for a different kind of companionship . . . a different kind of love. It is a point to think over."

As the interview progresses, you have the boy or girl describe what is the ideal courtship, the best kind of engagement, and the perfect marriage. Then you ask, "Is that what you want?"

"I don't know," the youth will probably reply.

"There must be some way to settle this doubt," you explain. "You are considering either marriage or the religious life. You must choose one or the other. Would it, then, be prudent to choose marriage first?"

"No," the boy or girl will answer.

"Why?"

"Because there is no backing out, once you get married."

"Then," you ask, "would it be better to try the religious life first?"

This is the crucial point of the youth's thinking. Some will smile in immediate agreement and answer, "I suppose so." Others will want a little time to think the matter out.

One danger in using this dilemma is that it is so easy to slip into a disparaging attitude toward marriage. If this happens, the whole equation is destroyed! You are not asking the boy or girl to choose between two states, one good and the other bad. Both are good, and the choice is rather which should be tried first.

At this stage most recruiters explain the reason why the Church has such a long probation before a person becomes a priest or religious. It takes years to get ordained or professed, and this allows ample time for an individual to make up his or her mind.

Meanwhile, if the boy or girl is happy, the right vocation has been found. If he or she is not happy, it would seem that marriage is the right choice.

Such an argument, as is evident, cannot be conclusive. It makes no allowance for those cases where a boy or girl may be called to the lay apostolate or obliged to remain in the state of virginity in the world. Generally, though, in the preliminary stages of the interview you will have uncovered the reasons why a person should join some lay institute or remain single in the world. Not uncovering such reasons, it is safe to presume that the person's choice will be between the married and religious states. Thus far only is the approach valid.

NO FORCING OF A DECISION

"One thing a counselor should not do," Father Gerald Kelly, S.J., warns in an article entitled "Vocational Counseling," in the *Review for Religious,* "is to make the decision for his consultant. A divine vocation is a grace or, perhaps better, a series of graces culminating in the light to know the divine will. It is a grace given to the individual, not to his counselor; and no decision of the counselor is a safe substitute for it.

"The counselor's function," Father Kelly continues, "is to help the consultant clear up his own doubt. One way of doing this is to inquire into the reason for the doubt. It may be that the consultant is habitually indecisive, or habitually dependent on others for his decisions. If this is the case, he seems to lack the maturity necessary for embracing a permanent state of life and should first acquire this maturity by learning to make decisions for himself. Or it may be that the 'doubt' is rather a misunderstanding of the certainty required for a vocation. Some young men and women apparently think that an extraordinary degree of certainty is required for this decision. Through their ignorance they look for an illumination that has the force of a private revelation. Their entire difficulty may clear up if it is pointed out to them that the grace of vocation may well be indicated in a quiet judgment to this effect: 'As far as I can see, this or that state of life seems best for me.' "

However, in stressing these "mechanics" for clearing up doubts and reaching decisions, we do not want to overlook the function of prayer. Since a vocation is a grace or series of graces, it follows the law of distribution of graces. Hence, the one who is making the choice must be reminded to pray. You, the recruiter, must pray. Also all who are interested in the happy outcome must pray. God in His ordinary providence gives grace in answer to prayer for grace.

SUBSEQUENT INTERVIEWS

In "The Personal Interview as an Aid to Recruitment," published by the Marianist Vocation Service, emphasis is placed on the fact that you cannot expect to get everything accomplished in the first interview.

"Don't expect to break down the student in one interview," we are told. "Some will co-operate, but the vast majority will not feel at ease the first time. These tend to hold out much important information. Expect to get the 'run-around' the first couple of interviews. But analyze, think, and try to discover contradictions. Wait for future interviews. Sometimes five or six interviews will be required before you have the absolute confidence of the student."

Even if it should take five or six interviews for an individual to open up, the time has not been wasted. Meanwhile you have been building up an appreciation of the supernatural life. This requires time and much personal contact.

Any boy or girl who expects to give all to God should be going as frequently as possible to Mass and Holy Communion. But it never does simply to recommend daily Mass and Communion. You must give reasons and motives. You must elicit the youngster's generosity gradually by showing the many graces that flow from intimate contact with Christ in the Eucharist. You must teach him or her to particpate in the Mass . . . to live the Mass.

During this same time you encourage the youngster to select a regular confessor, and you also explain what he or she should expect from this spiritual guide. Many priests will gladly hear a person's confession regularly, but they will not give special direction unless asked. The youth, therefore, must be told how to request this special help, how to get advice on prayer, and how to make a daily examen.

Many of the problems that will arise at this time will spring from ignorance regarding certain aspects of the religious life. A girl, for example, may imagine that when she goes to the convent she will thereby divorce herself completely from her family. She rebels against this hardship and is a little ashamed to mention it in conference. Somehow it seems to her to be a weakness. If, therefore, in an interview you explain the relation of a sister with her family, the girl's face will light up. As you go on to tell the girl about visits she can have from parents and relatives, letters to and from them, and visits home during her professed life, the problem will be dissipated.

Again you may run into a boy who seems to be an excellent prospect. He is eager to do all that God wants. He has long been a daily communicant and delights in serving on the altar. His natural qualifications are evident, but something holds him back. As you talk, the subject of tuition comes up. A casual remark, like "No deserving boy is ever kept away for lack of money," opens the floodgates of his confidence.

Suddenly he blurts out, "That's it, Father! I can't go to the seminary because we can't afford it. Dad insists that everyone gets the same education, and there are five other children in the family."

Your explanation of the financial arrangements at the seminary thus opens up the chance for another vocation.

At the Sixth Annual Sodality Directors' Meeting in St. Louis, Missouri, Father James O'Neill, S.J., said that he checks on four qualities in every boy or girl he directs. They are:

1. Health;
2. Academic background;
3. Ability to get along with people;
4. Love for chastity.

"In handling these subjects who seem to be called to the religious life," Father O'Neill said, "I give them a six months' probation. During that time each one visits me every two weeks. I tell him or her about the intellectual and volitional nature of the religious life, but I do not stress the emotional. I also ask the individual to make a daily fifteen-minute visit to the Blessed Sacrament. During this time the boy or girl is not to say the beads, but try to achieve the realization of Christ in the Tabernacle, the lovely side of the human Christ, and to learn to chat with Christ 'cor ad cor loquitur.' "

Commenting on this same subject at the Vocation Institute, Father John P. Kennelly said, "It is absolutely necessary to have an individual come for spiritual direction from eight to twelve times. This will enable you to check and develop the supernatural motives, examine the background, the moral, physical, and mental abilities, and the person's willingness to attempt the life.

"You have to know the boy or girl," he insisted, "as well as you possibly can. In each subsequent visit you have to keep coming back to the question: 'Why do you want to be a priest . . . or a religious?' It seems to me that many of us who are spiritual directors do not emphasize enough the joys, the consolations, the thrills, the happiness, the great reward of loving and serving Christ. Too many times we look only at the negative side. We worry about giving up this and giving up that. If only we could look at how much we can please, how much happiness and joy we can give, the service of God would offer a greater incentive to youth."

ADDITIONAL POINTERS

Most recruiters recommend that you keep a file card on each person interviewed. But it is never wise to write during the interview. That always arouses the suspicions of the youth and he or she is curious as to what you have put down. It is better, therefore, to wait until the person has left the room, then jot down any important facts with your general impressions. These observations will be of invaluable help in future interviews.

All individuals, you will learn, are different. Some will come from excellent family backgrounds, and hardly any questions will be necessary. They tell you about their desires, and you merely lead them on to the final decision.

Others will come from a poor environment and you will

wonder how much the boy or girl has been influenced by parents or surroundings. Christ's words, "A bad tree does not bring forth good fruit," are a warning. If the parents are not practicing Catholics or are lacking in generosity toward God, it is important to check their son or daughter on these points.

Also if anyone has been influencing the youth's decision one way or the other, you should know it. You should likewise know if there has been any tension or difficulty at home. Usually these things will come out indirectly in remarks that are made during the interview. But if they do not, you should ask about them.

In counseling older prospects it is often well to remind them to be very prudent in settling their affairs. Since there is the possibility that the individual may return home, it is always better to take a "leave of absence" from a job, rather than to resign outright. However, it should be pointed out that a two or three weeks' vacation is never sufficient time to test one's vocation.

If the person has a car to dispose of, it is better to sell it than to leave it with a relative. The same goes for other chattels. The individual should be free of all these worries and concerns when it comes to finding out whether or not he or she has a genuine vocation to the religious state.

THE FOLLOW-UP

Since the purpose of the first and subsequent interviews has been to gather information that will help not only in forming judgments on the individual's vocation but also in counseling that person, it is often most helpful to visit the prospect's home. There you see the influences that molded the character, disposition, and temperament of the person you are directing. You also have a wonderful chance to enlighten the parents and dispel any prejudice they may have.

If in the course of the interview you mention how you would like to meet the individual's family or see the home, an invitation will generally be forthcoming. Sometimes the boy or girl will mention the matter to the parents, and even when they oppose the idea of a religious vocation, they are generally willing to see and talk to the priest or religious. They may feel honored at your coming, or they may be curious, or they may want to argue. In any case, you are invited.

The visit to the home should not only be social in nature, but also informative. If the parents have not opposed the son's or daughter's vocation, it is a good idea to bring along any pictures, slides, or films you may have on your seminary or religious institute.

The parents are most anxious to know where their son or daughter is going to be trained. They want to know what the life is like. . . . What is the order of the day? Will it be possible to receive mail? Can they send candy, cakes, and suchlike delicacies on his or her birthday? Can their son or daughter come home for the holidays? What kind of clothes will be needed? How much is this training program going to cost?

By working in explanations of all these subjects you will often win over the parents and find that they become enthusiastic supporters of the idea. When they have been opposed to the idea, such explanations often refute their objections.

It is also well to explain how such a vocation is a compliment to the parents. When God selects one of their own, it is proof that they have reared their family in a true Christian manner.

Then to avoid embarrassment later on, it is well on this first visit to explain that the parents' approval does not assure the son's or daughter's acceptance into the religious state. It is only one of many requirements and after everything is considered, you will let them know.

Only when you have gone through these preliminaries and assembled the facts are you in a position to make a judgment as to whether or not the individual should try out for the priesthood, brotherhood, or sisterhood.

CHAPTER VI

Judging Prospects

IN THE seventh chapter of the Book of Judges we are told that when Gedeon, son of Joas, was preparing to fight against the Madianites, he was able to muster only 32,000 Israelites. These men seemed hopelessly outnumbered by the 120,000 warriors of Madian.

Since the Lord wanted no halfhearted men in His service, He told Gedeon to proclaim: "Whosoever is fearful and timorous, let him return home."

This announcement eliminated 22,000 men, and as Gedeon considered the 10,000 soldiers who were left, the Lord said: "They are still too many. Bring them, therefore, to the waters, so that I may try them."

When the Israelites had come down to the waters, the Lord instructed Gedeon: "They that shall lap the water with their tongues, as dogs are wont to lap, thou shalt set apart by themselves. But they that shall drink bowing down their knees, shall be on the other side."

Now the number of the men who lapped water, taking it with their hands into their mouth, was 300. The rest, unmindful of the self-restraint they should have practiced, dropped down on their knees and drank directly.

Some might argue that these tests were quite arbitrary, but they were the way the Lord sifted out the weaker and more sensual men from the army of Israel. Though the requirements were so strict that only 300 remained out of 32,-000, still there were sufficient soldiers to defeat the mighty army of Madian. The cause of Israel did not suffer because of the high standards demanded of those who served it.

The same can be said of the Church today. Though the requirements for the priesthood, brotherhood, and sisterhood are very high, still there are sufficient youths with all the necessary endowments of nature and grace. We must search them out, but in doing so we must never lower the norms. Quality is more important than quantity.

CRITERIA OF A VOCATION

In Canon 538 of the Code of Canon Law we are told, "Any Catholic, who is not hindered by some legitimate impediment, may be admitted to religion, provided his motives are right and he is capable of discharging the obligations of the religious life."

In this directive we have the criteria of a religious vocation, namely, *the absence of any legitimate impediment, a right intention,* and *suitability.* These three things we must look for in every boy or girl who wishes to enter the service of God.

For judging those who aspire to the priesthood we have practically the same directives. The decision of the Papal Commission of 1912, approved and promulgated by St. Pius X, tells us to look for young men who have "a right intention and suitability in those gifts of grace and nature, uprightness of life, and sufficiency of learning, which offer a well-founded hope of their fulfilling well and worthily the office and obligations of the priesthood."

Accordingly, let us take each of these criteria, analyze it, and show how it must be applied to the youths we meet.

ABSENCE OF IMPEDIMENT

Our first responsibility is to eliminate all of those whom the Church considers unfit for admission to either the priesthood or the religious life. In particular cases, it is true, dispensations can be obtained from the prescriptions of Canon

Law. But it is obviously the mind of the Holy See that we refrain from encouraging such types.

Thus in Canons 984 and 987 we are told that the following classes of young men are debarred from the priesthood:

1. Those of illegitimate birth, unless they have been legitimated or have made solemn profession;
2. Those who are defective in body or who, on account of weakness, cannot safely, or on account of deformity, cannot becomingly, perform the functions of the altar;
3. Epileptics, the insane, and the possessed, who are now or who have been formerly in this condition;
4. Bigamists, who have validly and successively contracted two or more marriages;
5. The sons of non-Catholics, as long as their parents remain in their error;
6. A man who has a wife, as long as his wife lives;
7. Men bound to common military service by the civil law, before they are fully discharged;
8. Neophytes, that is, new converts, until the bishop thinks their faith is sufficiently tried.

Canon 542 lists for us the various types of individuals whom we cannot accept into the religious life. The directives bind for both sexes and are given without prejudice to the regulations laid down in the constitutions of the various institutes. There is also a distinction made between those impediments which affect the validity of a person's admission to the novitiate and those which affect only the liciety.

Thus we cannot validly accept:

1. Those who have belonged to a non-Catholic sect;
2. Those who have not reached the age required for the novitiate, that is, fifteen years of age;
3. Those who come into religion under the influence of force, grave fear, or fraud, and those accepted by a superior under the same influences;
4. Married persons as long as the marriage lasts;

5. Those who are, or have been, bound by religious profession;
6. Those liable to punishment for a grave crime of which they have been or may be accused;
7. Bishops, whether they reside in their diocese or are only titular; even those just nominated by the Roman Pontiff and not yet consecrated;
8. Clerics who by ordinance of the Holy See are bound by oath to devote themselves to the service of their dioceses or to the service of the missions, for as long as the obligation created by the oath lasts.

We cannot licitly accept:

1. Clerics in Holy Orders, if they fail to consult their bishop, or if the bishop opposes the step on the grounds that their departure would be gravely detrimental to the good of souls, and that this detriment could not be avoided unless they stayed;
2. Those burdened with debts which they cannot pay;
3. Those with some special responsibility or other temporal business to attend to, by reason of which the institute might become involved in lawsuits or troubles;
4. Children bound to help parents in really straitened circumstances, and parents whose services are needed for the maintenance and education of their children;
5. Those who in religion would be destined for the priesthood but are debarred from it by irregularity or some other canonical impediment;
6. Finally, Catholics of the Eastern rites may not be received into the novitiate of an institute of the Latin Church without written permission from the Sacred Congregation for the Eastern Church.

In his commentary on the "Canonical Impediments to the Religious Life," Father E. Bergh, S.J., points out, "Illegitimate birth is sometimes found among the additional impediments in various congregations.

"It may be doubted," he says, "whether a general law

with respect to this point is necessary or expedient. Where the constitutions do not contain a prohibition of this kind, superiors are often heard to say that they are sorry they took such people. On the other hand, there are instances — and they occur more and more now that marriages are so often performed before a civil magistrate alone — where candidates showing all the desirable qualities and with no likelihood that the danger of a more or less hereditary taint would develop, would be excluded, if their rule were enforced.

"It would seem preferable," he concluded, "to make it possible for each case to be judged on its own merits, and not to introduce general prohibitions into the particular law, unless the necessary faculties for dispensation are given with them."

RIGHT INTENTION

After we have eliminated those who are impeded from the service of God, we must again scrutinize the group for their motives. We must find out the reasons each one has for wanting to enter the priesthood or religious life. If there is not a right intention, there is no vocation.

The intention, moreover, must be a true, determined, and sustained wish. It must be a positive act of will, and not just a vague desire to do something for God. It is not enough for a boy or girl to say, "I think I should like to enter." He or she must have a precise and particularized wish to achieve perfection by fulfilling the conditions of a definite life in a definite group.

The intention I am trying to describe can be expressed thus: "I wish to become a priest in the Passionist Congregation" . . . or "I want to become a sister in the Third Order Franciscans."

The motives for this intention must be morally good. They should also be similar to those for which the particular group was founded. Thus a boy should not join the Christian Brothers to avoid caring for a dependent parent. He should rather seek admission into the community that he might sanctify himself by the practice of the vows of religion and by devoting himself to the instruction of boys.

While lecturing on this subject during the 1953 Institute of Spiritual Theology, Father Paul Philippe, O.P., made some very helpful observations. "It is not required of boys and girls, especially those who are quite young," he said, "that they have a perfect and explicit knowledge of the double purpose of the institute. It is enough for them to wish to dedicate their life to our Lord, even without knowing well what the works of the institute comprise, provided that they remain content when the works are explained to them."

The youngster's intention, moreover, must be free. We cannot accept one who has not yet made a personal decision, but is coming simply because somebody has said it was the thing to do. A spiritual guide may tell the youngster that the signs of a vocation are evident, but only the youngster can make the decision.

Oftentimes we meet youths who have difficulty in making up their minds. They consider mainly the sacrifice involved in the priesthood or religious life and consequently feel no attraction. "This is not a bad sign," Father Philippe explained, "for if they master their natural repugnance, they give proof of great generosity. If they do not overcome it, they invariably give up the desire.

"Another point to remember," he added, "is that, although the religious life is one of continuing sacrifice, it must bring with it a happiness in the depth of the heart. Therefore, one should never advise a youth, for example, to choose a form of the religious life which does not please him, in order that he might make a more generous sacrifice to God. On the contrary, it is perfectly normal for him to enter where he will find for his soul the greatest possibility of letting his own gifts expand supernaturally in the service of God and neighbor."

SUITABILITY FOR THE LIFE

The third criterion of a vocation is whether or not the person is suited for the priesthood or religious life. God in His wisdom does not call youths to a way of life for which they are not fitted and in which they could not persevere short of a perpetual miracle. Therefore, when a person is unsuited for the service of God, we know that such a one is not "called."

A sister, for example, once referred to me a young man who wanted to become a priest. As soon as I met him I noticed that his right arm was crippled from infantile paralysis. It was distressing to break the news to him that he could not become a priest, since he was incapable of performing the work of a priest. Sister should have recognized this herself and not encouraged him in the assumption that he had a vocation.

An even more embarrassing situation arose recently when an elderly benefactress thought to join the community she had so richly endowed. All along she had been encouraged in the hope that she could become a sister and then obtain a permanent dispensation from the rule. The bishop was forced to intervene and explain to her that she had no vocation, since she was unsuited for the regular observance.

Suitability as a criterion of vocation means that one should be *physically, mentally,* and *morally* fit for the service of God. If one is lacking in any one of these three aspects, there is no call to the priesthood, brotherhood, or sisterhood.

PHYSICAL FITNESS

There is no need to belabor the fact that to be a priest or religious one must be able physically to live the life. The question comes up, however, as to what to do with those of weak, but normal, health.

Most recruiters are of the opinion that they should be

directed to the less strict communities, where they are more likely to persevere.

An individual who has been weakened by a contagious disease, like tuberculosis or some inherited venereal malady, though, should not be accepted. It can happen that these individuals are cured, but with the weak ones there is always danger of a relapse. The community would then be responsible with consequent expense and treatment in a sanatorium.

Cripples, as a rule, are considered unfit for the religious life and therefore excluded by most communities. However, if they are not completely incapacitated, there are some lay brotherhoods and lay sisterhoods which will consider them.

In this regard it is interesting to note that the Congregation of the Little Sisters of Our Lady of Seven Dolors was founded for girls who are deaf and mute. Its mother house is at the Institute Sourdes-Muettes, 3725 Rue St. Denis, Montreal, Province of Quebec, Canada. Most of the work of the sisters is at the Deaf-Mute Institute, where they teach, cook, sew, nurse, and do whatever else their talents permit.

Another unusual group is the Congregation of Blind Sisters of St. Paul, whose mother house is at 88 Avenue Deufert-Rochereau, Paris, France. This group is not represented in the United States, but two other French communities, now planning foundations here, will also accept girls who are totally blind. They are the Sisters of the Lamb of God (not cloistered), 47 Rue du Vieux S' Marc, Brest, France; and the Sisters of Jesus Crucified (cloistered), Brou (Seine et Marne), France.

In the United States there are several communities which will consider accepting partially blind candidates. They are the Sisters of Social Service, 1120 Westchester Place, Los Angeles 19, California; Sisters of Our Lady of Mercy, 68 Legare Street, Charleston, South Carolina; Sisters of St. Francis, 22 E. Douglas Street, Rice Lake, Wisconsin; and

Sisters of St. Mary, 4242 N. Austin Blvd., Chicago, Illinois.

In doubtful cases it would be well to contact Father Jean Marie Bauchet, Cumberland Hill, Manville, Rhode Island. He is especially interested in helping blind candidates and is in contact with all communities which receive such handicapped girls.

Closely allied with this physical well-being is a person's age. Canon Law sets a minimum but not a maximum age for judging prospects. However, nearly all groups set their own maximum age limits, for they have found that individuals of more advanced years do not adjust properly and often become a burden to the community.

In recent years, especially since World War II, exceptions have been made for servicemen. Several dioceses and religious communities will now accept them as a matter of course.

Several schools have devoted their facilities to training these belated vocations. Most prominent among them are:

1. St. Philip Neri School, 126 Newbury Street, Boston 16, Massachusetts;

2. St. Mary's College, St. Mary, Kentucky;

3. Jordan Seminary, Menominee, Michigan;

4. Holy Family Seminary, 2500 Ashby Road, St. Louis, Missouri;

5. Benet Latin School, Benet Lake, Wisconsin.

St. Jerome College, Kitchener, Ontario, Canada, offers an accelerated Latin course, which enables a student to take four years of credits in one year. Many of the other Catholic colleges offer Latin and other courses necessary to prepare a student for entrance into a major seminary.

Those who are interested in a correspondence course can apply to:

1. Loyola University Home Study Division, 820 North Michigan Avenue, Chicago 11, Illinois;

2. St. Henry's Seminary, 5901 West Main Street, Belleville, Illinois.

There are also vocational clubs for these older prospects. The St. Patrick's Clerical Club, 980 Park Avenue, New York, New York, helps older men find the place where they will fit into the priesthood. The Little Flower Mission Circle, 389 East 150th Street, Bronx, New York, New York, endeavors to direct older women to the right sisterhood.

MENTAL FITNESS

In judging a person's mental fitness, we must first of all determine if the individual has sufficient intelligence to understand the ideals and obligations of the service of God. He or she must be capable of grasping the meaning of the vows and performing the works demanded.

For the priesthood a boy is not considered to have sufficient intelligence unless he is capable of mastering all the subjects in the seminary curriculum. Most seminary authorities agree that this calls for at least a 110 I.Q. (It must be remembered, however, that intelligence tests differ somewhat in difficulty. It is always well to have scores from more than one intelligence test.)

To place this intelligence quotient in its proper perspective, Dr. Arthur D. Fearon in his book, *How to Counsel Others,* gives us the following table:

		I.Q.	% of population in U. S.
Above Average	Genius	130–	1 } 6%
	Very Superior	120–130	5
Average	Superior	110–120	14
	Normal	90–110	60 } 88%
	Dull Normal	80–90	14
Below Average	Border Line	70–80	5
	Feeble Minded		
	Moron	40–70	} 6%
	Imbecile	20–40	1
	Idiot	–20	

Religious superiors of brothers and sisters prefer their subjects from about 95–120 I.Q. They grant that it is possible to employ the less intelligent subjects in the humbler services of the house, like the kitchen, laundry, or garden. But if the duller members of the community cannot achieve an appreciation of the spiritual life and understand the conferences and spiritual reading, problems will arise. For this reason some claim that it is a very poor risk to accept anybody under 90 I.Q.

Writing in the *Review for Religious,* Sister M. Digna, O.S.B., points out that we have long used the findings of medical science in judging prospects for the seminary or convent. Why should we not do the same in the field of psychometrics?

In her article entitled, "A Tentative Testing Program for Religious Life," Sister Digna recommends the California Test for Mental Maturity, since it has several significant features. "This test," she says, "is both diagnostic and analytical. Also the scores may be interpreted in terms of mental ages and intelligence quotients. It includes items dealing with language factors, non-language factors, memory, spatial relations, logical reasoning, numerical reasoning, and vocabulary."

Sister then goes on to explain how the findings of this and similar tests will eliminate those who are unable to grasp the meaning of the religious life. The intelligence scores can also be utilized in determining the educational and vocational placement of religious.

"If the score places the individuals below the low average," Sister Digna warns, "it is very doubtful whether they will be useful in religious life, unless the community is willing to assign them to very simple tasks. Then these questions arise: How well will they be able to understand the meaning and implications of religious life? How much benefit will they derive from their novitiate instruction? And will the community be willing to assume responsibility for possible custodial care?"

At the other end of the scale is the exceptional student. A prudent recruiter must check here just as carefully as with the dull student. Prejudice in favor of talent may sometimes blind one to the absence of good judgment in the brilliant boy or girl. Because many of these exceptional individuals cannot be trained, they soon succumb to indolence.

Speaking on this subject at the National Catholic Educational Association in 1952, Father Kyran O'Connor, C.P., insisted that before accepting these exceptional students, religious superiors should make sure that they have a real love of study. For if they do not have a love of learning along with their talents, there will be little hope of their persevering.

This brings us to a subject of increasing importance nowadays, namely, that of testing a person's attitude, disposition, and personality. The Armed Forces in their recruiting and placement programs regularly use a multitude of these tests, and many religious communities have been testing their practicality for determining fitness for the religious life.

In the spring of 1954 Brother Lester Raszkowski, S.M., completed a survey of 283 communities of priests, brothers, and sisters in the United States. He had inquired as to whether or not they had a testing program for prospective candidates, and learned that 100 communities used some kind of psychological test or screening device. Seventy-one groups had a formal testing program, and twenty-nine used only the I.Q. or achievement tests.

The general attitude toward these tests seems to be that they can and do supply some additional knowledge about the applicant. All realize that no psychological test can ever be devised for testing a divine vocation.

Pope Pius XI in his encyclical *Divini Illius Magistri* condemned those who "advance the claim — none the less wrong, blasphemous and dangerous for being devoid of any foundation — that they are able to test by ordinary, purely secular examination or experiment the supernatural factors that may enter into a child's education, such as a divine vocation to the priesthood or religious life, and in general the mysterious effects caused in the human soul by grace, which though it elevates the powers of nature, yet infinitely transcends them and can in no way be subject to physical laws, since the 'Spirit breathes where It will.' "

The whole purpose of these tests is rather to cut down the mortality rate of candidates by confirming or denying certain convictions regarding the natural fitness of an applicant in the screening process.

"No test can give you more than 20-20 vision," Father J. D. Corcoran, O.P., stated in an excellent address on psychological testing at the 1954 Vocation Institute. "Where one's personal observation of a candidate is adequate," he said, "tests are not needed. This explains how the Church has managed to get along for twenty centuries without these helps. But when certain factors of a personality or temperament are obscure, then tests can often magnify those components which must be seen before a judgment is made."

Discussing this matter one evening with Father Albert Plé, O.P., I mentioned how in the beginning some communities seized upon these tests as sort of universal panaceas for all problems of acceptance or rejection.

"That is a stupid, ill-formed, and harmful attitude," he said. "We who are trying to work seriously in the psychological field are the first to deplore it, for it can only compromise our efforts.

"We must never become infatuated with psychoanalysis and psychological tests, nor yet must we let ourselves be tricked into rejecting everything to do with psychology. If we must not ask psychology for what it cannot give us," he insisted, "so, too, we must not refuse to use those of its discoveries which are valid and scientifically established."

MENTAL BALANCE

This brings us to the subject of the candidate's mental balance, which is absolutely necessary for admission into religion. Without a sound and healthy balance of mind no one can observe the vows properly or lead the common life normally.

In his "Negative Criteria of Vocation," Father Reginald Omez, O.P., lists this lack of balance as one of the principal causes of trouble in religious communities. "By this vague term," he says, "I mean certain habits of mind resulting from family, national, racial, social, or religious traditions and producing incurably erroneous ideas, especially about religion and religious life.

"Some distorted ideas, coming either from heredity or from environment," he said, "are so deeply engraved in the mind that humanly speaking there is no hope of correcting them. For this reason some international congregations have stopped taking postulants from certain races or ancestry or converts from certain religions, experience having shown that it is still premature to introduce such people to religious life lived in common, as they are unable to adapt themselves to it."

When an individual loses mental balance, psychiatrists distinguish two conditions that result, the paranoiac and the schizoid.

The paranoiac individual is recognized by a tendency to take things for what they are not. He or she will be in conflict with companions, suspicious of superiors, or complaining about surroundings. Most recruiters can detect this type individual as soon as they begin an investigation of home background, attitude toward companions and teachers, and the like.

The schizoid individual is generally isolated from the common life and acts peculiarly. A recruiter can spot this type when his or her words and gestures are out of harmony with what one expects of a normal person. A typical schizoid, for example, asked me to accept him for the seminary because he was so adept at making animal noises. Half the interview consisted in my listening to him cackle like a chicken and bark like a dog.

Needless to add, both paranoiac and schizoid individuals are unsuited for either the priesthood or religious life. It is generally a mistake to accept them, even though their cases be very mild.

NERVOUS TYPES

A person's nervous state depends a great deal upon the tendency he or she has to react with feeling or emotion. The so-called "nervous" individuals we will have to judge are those in whom this affectivity is not tamed or curbed by the will. According to Father Philippe, O.P., there are three classes of these individuals:

1. The emotive;
2. The neurasthenic and psychasthenic;
3. The hysterical.

"Emotive people," Father Paul Philippe, O.P., explains, "are impressionable to a morbid degree for the slightest reasons. They are recognizable by the trembling of the eyelids when they are speaking, by the readiness with which they blush and shed tears when they are recounting some personal episode, and the like. They are sentimental people, prone to an exhibition of sensitive affection, though rarely to sensual acts. They look for the affection of particular friendship without being aware of its danger. Generally these persons are sound and can be educated and corrected, provided that their hyperemotion is not too strong.

"The second class of nervous people," he said, "are restless, anxious, and obsessional persons. They are continually analysing themselves and ruminating upon their obsessions. In this we distinguish two forms: the neurasthenic and the psychasthenic.

"The neurasthenic individuals preoccupy themselves to excess with their physical health, believe themselves to be gravely ill, demand a specialist and take medicine for every imaginable malady. On top of this they are generally irritable, diffident, and gloomy.

"The psychasthenic persons do not suffer physically but morally. They are tormented souls. Generally you will find that they are the obsessed victims of scruples, particularly in regard to chastity. Incapable of dominating their obsessions, they are dominated by them and suffer exceedingly."

When I asked if the neurasthenic and psychasthenic individuals should be admitted to the priesthood or religious life, Father Philippe replied: "If the trouble is not too far advanced, and, above all, if after curative treatment there [is] . . . hope of a cure, they can be admitted, provided that in all other respects they are really good subjects. Otherwise, it is more charitable to them to seem cruel and refuse to accept them into the seminary or religious institute.

"The third class of nervous individuals," he continued, "are the hysterical. The most distinctive characteristic of this group is that they draw attention to themselves. They seek to be admired and want sympathy. The important thing is that all should esteem and notice them. All means are good to compass this end: pretense at piety, sanctity, mystical graces, ecstasies, stigmata, and the like.

"Hystericals are the craftiest people in the world. They seem to possess a special sense of knowing exactly who will serve their fundamental intention. They cannot even account for this because they are acting under the impulse of the subconscious, which in their case is abnormal.

"Such a class of persons must never be admitted to the priesthood or religious life. They will be a scourge to their superiors and a calamity for the diocese or religious community. From the moment anyone tries to show up their game, they become vipers, and they will call upon the intervention of the bishop, even the Holy See."

MORAL FITNESS

Generally speaking, a boy or girl is morally fit for the religious life when he or she is exercising in a sufficiently notable degree the natural virtues, as well as the religious virtues, and has a serious desire of seeking perfection in the seminary or religious community.

The natural virtues, which we should look for in a prospect, are:

1. Sociability;
2. Sincerity;
3. A right conscience;
4. An honest character.

It almost goes without saying that anyone who is not able to live peacefully with others in the community or who is habitually insincere should be excluded from the seminary or religious institute.

In his work on the "Negative Criteria of Vocation," Father Reginald Omez, O.P., states, "Life in common demands pliability, adaptability, good manners, broadmindedness, ability to put up with other people, and a capacity for shutting one's eyes to things or forgetting them."

Likewise, any individual who seems to lack a right conscience should be excluded. Experience has proved that those who do not have the natural foundation for goodness will be unable to acquire the religious virtues.

Care should be taken, though, to determine if the individual is really incorrigible on these points. It may well happen that a boy or girl has never received a proper education in these respects. Then, if such a one shows docility and a desire to correct these natural defects, after a long probation in which he proves his worthiness, he may be admitted.

The religious virtues, which we should look for in one who is morally suitable, are:

1. Piety;

2. Docility;
3. Generosity;
4. Chastity;
5. Charity.

First on the list is piety, since the religious life is a life of sacrifice and prayer. This virtue, though, is not too easily detected in youths. Many who are blessed with it would rather be called anything but "pious." It is sometimes so deep within the soul that its very depth makes it almost imperceptible. On the contrary, those youths who make a show of their religion give you reason to suspect that their virtue is superficial.

The practice recommended by most recruiters is that there be a check on the individual's attitude toward prayer and the use of the Sacraments. If his or her prayer is at a minimum . . . if there is no daily rosary or other devotion . . . if Holy Communion and Confession are received only every three weeks or once a month, it is not likely that such a one has sufficient piety. It would then be a poor risk to accept such an individual for the priestly or religious state. As soon as the first fervor wears off, he or she will leave.

It might be well to add that allowances are always made for the age of the individual. We do not demand of a youngster in eighth grade what we would expect of a high school senior. The least that recruiters ask of grade school prospects is that they go to Holy Communion every Sunday and Confession about every two weeks. They also make an occasional visit to church or recite the rosary.

Of high school students most recruiters expect Holy Communion several times a week and regular weekly Confession. They also expect some daily devotion, like the rosary, and occasional spiritual reading. This is not asking too much, for all the youths who have successfully completed the program of formation in the Bosco and Good Counsel Clubs do these things as a matter of course.

The second religious virtue which we look for is docility.

Without it no boy or girl can be trained in the religious life. The overconfidence in self and excessive independence of mind that is so often inculcated in modern youths make it very difficult for them to bind themselves by the vow of obedience, unless they have cultivated this spiritual pliability.

Needless to say, one who lacks this virtue should be excluded. In the same class are those who have an intractable disposition, a choleric temperament, or dominative character. They will never make out in the course of training, so it is a mistake to accept them.

The problem, though, will arise when you are asked to judge those individuals of a critical frame of mind. Such persons will always be complaining and finding fault with others. If their weakness is due to an ingrained pride, they are incompatible with the religious life. But if they are willing to humiliate themselves and make an effort to correct their faults, they can be taken.

If living in religion meant no more than carrying out the theological virtues to a high state of perfection and keeping the vows of poverty, chastity, and obedience, there would not be all this worry and concern. But the religious life is lived in common and requires submission of mind as well as act. Thus one who does not fit into this type of life can be said to have no vocation, regardless of his or her other fine qualities.

In an excellent paper, "Qualities Required in Candidates for Admission to the Religious Life," read at the First National Congress of Religious, Father Giles Staab, O.F.M.Cap., said that the next virtue on our list, generosity, was the most important one to be looked for in anybody presenting himself for admission to the religious life.

"The religious life," he explained, "is a challenge. 'Let him accept it who can,' Christ said to the young man who finally failed the test of generosity: 'If thou wilt be perfect, go, sell what thou hast, and give to the poor, and thou shalt have treasure in heaven; and come, follow me.' The religious life is by its very profession a sacrifice, and it is a sacrifice that limits permanently man's three greatest drives — personal freedom, personal possessions, and the sexual urge. The religious life is no ordinary sacrifice completed in one act, no matter how heroic, but it is a sacrifice that will transmute every day of the future and touch every act of every day."

If a person cannot accept a regularity of life, with rising in the early morning, a tiresome and uncomfortable habit, dependence on others for permissions, it is not likely that such a one will make a good religious.

We should also be distrustful of persons who are prone to sensuality in eating and sleeping. Those who smoke or occasionally use liquor, though, should not be put immediately into the same category. Today most youths have the opportunity to smoke and the majority of them have at least tried cigarettes. They also have access to liquor in various forms and many of them are regularly offered such drinks at home and elsewhere. These individuals are merely the product of our times.

The prudent recruiter, though, will remind them that most of these stimulants must be given up in the seminary or convent. Accordingly, if the boys and girls are really generous, they will be expected to cut down on the use of these things and prove that they have no attachment or addiction to them. If they cannot give them up, then there is grave doubt as to their fitness for the religious life.

CHASTITY REQUIRED

When we consider a person's chastity as a test of a vocation, we must judge not only if he or she can live a continent life alone in religion, but also if he or she can remain chaste in the works of the ministry. Some individuals are able to overcome all personal temptations, but the moment they get with others they are in trouble. Accordingly, if there is a serious doubt that any individual may be in proximate danger of a fall when he or she is actively engaged in the works of the ministry, it is better not to accept such a one into an institute of the active life. However, before dismissing the person it would be well to investigate the possibility of such a one fitting into a cloistered group and being able to live a normal and virtuous life there.

The fact that a person is not bothered with temptations against purity, moreover, is not always a sign that he or she has the virtue of chastity. It is true that you will find many wonderful youths who have this virtue of chastity and they have passed through the dangers of the world without blemish. On the other hand, there are others who resemble them through lack of temptation, but who simply have not developed physically and emotionally.

If the case is merely one of retarded development, the recruiter should wait until the individual has passed through the emotional and physical crisis.

If, after competent medical examination, the lack of such temptation is judged to be the sign of a general infantilism, with no positive hope of later development, it would be best to exclude such an individual. Such a one would always be a dead weight, a religious without personality, suffering from a painful inferiority complex. Often, too, such a person is at the mercy of solitary habits, the more tenacious the more infantile they are, because the will is too weak to conquer the habits and will not face up to the matter of purity humbly and resolutely.

With regard to prospects who have sinned against purity, we should stick firmly to the general principle; namely, that before accepting an individual into the seminary or religious institute, we should have moral certitude that at the end of the training, he or she will be able to profess and observe the vow of chastity forever.

THE FINAL TEST

The final judgment should be passed on how the prospect will fit in with the others of the group and work with them.

There are two test questions: "Is he or she charitable?" and "Is he or she sociable?"

Charity in religion demands that a youth have a liking for people and a joyful willingness to help them. It is a good sign when a prospect is of an obliging nature, willing to help companions, and not afraid to do the chores.

On the other hand, boys or girls who hold themselves aloof and will not offer themselves for the service of others should be considered very doubtful vocations.

"We have too many 'free-lances' in communities today," Father Staab warned at the Congress of Religious. "There are some religious who do a magnificent job, who are capable of almost unbelievable zeal, but it must be in their own way. They will burn themselves out for any cause, provided it is not for their order. They arrange their own life and their own work, they feather their own little nest, and God help the superior who happens to stick his head in to see what is going on!

"These rugged individualists may be capable and spiritual in their own way," he said, "but they are not religious. When judging the social balance of an individual, watch for the 'lone-wolf.' Does the prospect mix in the sports and games of his age group? Or, if he has not developed properly along these lines, is he willing to adjust himself?

"Finally, find out if he is given to substitutions for normal interests. Never trust the lad who concentrates on piety, because he feels inadequate with his own social group. Unless he changes radically, he will eventually sell his religious community for any interest that will satisfy his ego."

CONCLUSION

"All the elements that contribute to a thing," Aristotle observed long ago, "are required to make it good. The defect of a single element, though, is sufficient to make it bad."

That principle can serve as a practical norm for every recruiter. In judging prospects we must select only those who have all the qualifications of nature and grace. The defect of any important element is sufficient to assure us that there is no priestly or religious vocation.

On the other hand, we must remember that even if all the elements are there, it is not therefore proof that a boy or girl is called by God. It may well happen that such a one has no intention of becoming a priest or religious.

If all the individuals who are endowed with the qualifications for the service of God had to enter religion, simply because they were well fitted for it, we would have to take in several million Catholics! Suitability is a necessary but not a sufficient condition. To enter religion a person has to have, in addition, the positive will to be a religious, which we treated under "right intention."

Of the three criteria or evidential signs of a vocation, theologians list the right intention as principal. The others, it is true, are necessary conditions. Each is infallible in its own negative aspect. Accordingly if a person lacks health, intelligence, or moral fitness, we can say that such a one is not called by God.

But the right intention, being a positive sign, must be proved. Its existence cannot be taken for granted. No matter how blessed a boy or girl may be, both naturally and supernaturally, we cannot say that such a one has a vocation, unless he or she wants it.

Finally, in making our judgment, we must remember that the good of the diocese or institute must always take precedence over the individual. We must never accept a person for an active community simply because he or she is a soul to be saved. If the best that can be said of a doubtful case is that he or she will do no harm, most recruiters will not accept such a person. He or she will always be an ineffectual individual, and the diocese or religious order is better off without that type.

Cardinal Verdier recommended three questions in these cases:

1. "What will this person be like when he or she is forty years of age?

2. "Will he or she be happy in the priesthood or religious community?

3. "Will he or she contribute to the good of the diocese or community?"

Only when all three questions are answered favorably is it prudent to accept a doubtful prospect. However, we should not go to the other extreme and demand that a youth be perfect in every point before acceptance. It is sufficient for such a one to have the right intention to tend to perfection. He or she does not have to be free of every fault, but only have the will to progress and willingness to be corrected during the course of training at the seminary or novitiate.

CHAPTER VII

Overcoming Parental Opposition

EVER since Mary and Joseph heard Jesus ask, "Did you not know that I must be about my Father's business?" parents have felt a catch in their throat and a twinge in their heart when they have heard a son or daughter express an interest in the service of God. Some heroic parents, despite the realization that they must be separated from their children, have smiled encouragement. But all too many have thought principally of themselves and bitterly opposed the call of Christ.

One tragic example of this parental opposition was the case of Elmer O'Connor. "You're too young to know your own mind!" his father had told him when he asked permission to become a Christian Brother.

A year later came graduation, then the draft. Uncle Sam asked no questions about parental likes or dislikes but simply took the boy into service. Within a few brief months he had finished his boot training . . . gone overseas . . . and been killed in battle.

Only when the chaplain sent home a picture of the Sacred Heart, found on his son's body, did the benighted father realize the mistake he had made. For on the back of that picture was scrawled in Elmer's boyish hand a simple plea for the life he had been denied.

"I beg You, dear Sacred Heart," he wrote, "to guide and protect me during my remaining days in service, and bring me back safely after this conflict that I may follow out my desire to enter the religious life, if it be Your holy will."

God wanted Elmer and took him . . . though the father
was still unwilling to give him up!

NUMBER OPPOSED

This true story can be matched by countless illustrations
of what other parents have done. Some few have favored
the religious vocations of their children; many others have
opposed them.

In his monumental study, *Environmental Factors Influencing Religious Vocations,* Father Thomas S. Bowdern,
S.J., tabulated the replies from 1561 young men and 2453
young women who gave themselves to the religious life. They
had successfully followed their vocations, but the inquiry
tried to ascertain the number who had endured some degree
of pressure or opposition at home once the vocation was
known. Fifty-nine per cent of the men and 72 per cent of
the women admitted such pressure or opposition. It ranged
all the way from simple ridicule to downright physical
violence.

Father Jude Senieur, O.F.M.Cap., writing in *Vocational
Notes,* commented that in the past two years well over a
hundred boys and girls have come to him with the sad news,
"My parents don't want me to be a priest or religious. What's
wrong, Father?"

My own observations have confirmed the judgments of
these two prominent vocational directors. Only about a third
of all the prospects I have interviewed during vocational
campaigns, school programs, and retreats have acknowledged
any help or encouragement from their parents. Fully two
thirds of all these young men and women have admitted a
measure of opposition from parents and relatives the moment
they spoke about going to a seminary or convent. Some actual
cases will illustrate what I mean. Only the names have been
changed.

Bill Meyers, for example, told me that when he first
brought up the subject of the seminary his parents only

laughed. Bill was serious and persisted in his desire. After he sent in his application, the seminary recruiter called at his home. The parents refused to speak to the priest. Later Bill was threatened by his father with expulsion from the home, and the mother sobbed that she had lost the love of her son. Even his brothers and sisters tried to talk him out of his resolution. Fortunately Bill persevered in his determination and finally left for the seminary.

I remember, too, a painful evening with the Bisignanos. Their daughter, Rita, wanted to go to the convent, and I had agreed to intercede for her. The father eventually gave in to our arguments and pleas, but the mother remained adamant. Rita left for the convent amid maternal sobs and screams. Later the mother went on a hunger strike, and the father, regretting his permission, demanded the daughter's return.

Another case was that of Mike Petroski. He was the family's pride and joy, and his father frequently spoke of taking Mike into his business. But the boy expressed a preference for the diocesan priesthood. Long arguments ensued, and when Mike finally left for the seminary, his father refused to say good-bye. On subsequent home visits the dad wouldn't even speak to the boy.

Opposition to Jeannine Landreau's vocation was just as strong but much more subtle. On graduation her father bought her a convertible as an inducement to drop her ideas about the convent. Mother insisted on her dating practically every evening. When she finally managed to get to the convent, her parents continued their subtle opposition. Each visiting Sunday they came out in Jeannine's convertible and brought along a suitcase full of her nicest clothes. "Wouldn't she come back with them?"

Many of these examples from real life would be hard to believe were it not that they are so common. The saddest part of the whole business is that so many of these families — like the O'Connors, Meyers, Bisignanos, Petroskis, and

Landreaus — are all considered to be "such good Catholics."

Surely the Holy Father, Pope Pius XI, was thinking of these families when he wrote in his encyclical *Ad Catholici Sacerdotii:* "It must be confessed with sadness that only too often parents seem to be unable to resign themselves to the priestly or religious vocations of their children. Such parents have no scruple in opposing the divine call with objections of all kinds. They even have recourse to means which can imperil not only the vocation to a more perfect state, but also the very conscience and the eternal salvation of those souls they ought to hold so dear. This happens all too often in the case even of parents who glory in being sincerely Christian and Catholic, especially in the higher and more cultured classes."

OBJECTIONS REFUTED

In the Book of Ecclesiastes Solomon remarks: "There is nothing new under the sun, neither is any man able to say: Behold this is new." How truly this applies to the complaints of parents! After combing through over five thousand written objections of mothers and fathers to religious vocations, I have found that there is nothing that hasn't already been heard and refuted many times over.

Parental opposition always seems to fall into one of five categories:

1. The son or daughter is too young or too immature for the seminary or convent.

2. There has been undue influence brought to bear upon the youngster.

3. The nature of the religious life precludes the possibility of their child's having a vocation.

4. The lesson of experience proves that their son or daughter should not attempt the religious life.

5. The child's obligation to the parent rules out the idea of such a vocation.

Let us take each of these objections, show their variations, analyze them, and give the refutations.

"TOO YOUNG TO KNOW"

The first and most obvious objection of parents is that their son or daughter is "too young to know." This applies to all eighth grade graduates and even to many high school students.

The first part of this argument is quite hard to refute, since it is a half-truth. Certainly boys and girls at fourteen or fifteen years of age do not know what the priesthood, brotherhood, or sisterhood really entails. But they can know at that age whether or not they want to find out about such a life for God.

Even at eighteen or nineteen a young man or woman knows little about the nature of the religious life. But the same can be said of the married state. What do youths know about marriage until they get into it? All these lovers know is that they want each other and are willing to make any sacrifices necessary. The same spirit motivates those who want God.

The God-Man was going about His Father's business when He was twelve years of age. Many parents who are blocking vocations today were themselves married in their late teens.

Movie stars and TV and radio personalities are able to have romances at seventeen and eighteen while all the country applauds. Teen-age sport idols are held up to the admiration and imitation of youths. But let someone of the same age as these headliners mention interest in the cloister or missions, and there is a chill silence. An eighteen-year-old boy is old enough to die for his country, but he is not old enough to go to a seminary. An eighteen-year-old girl can take on the responsibility of a family, but she cannot put on a postulant's garb.

The position of such parents is even more illogical when we point out that a boy or girl entering religion does not thereby take an irrevocable step. He or she merely tries to find out more about the priesthood or religious life. The seminary or juniorate insists on a probationary period and, by presenting both sides of the problem, helps aspirants to make a more intelligent decision.

When a youth is in doubt as to whether God calls to marriage or the religious state, it is never prudent to choose marriage first . . . with the intention of attempting the religious state if one does not find happiness in marriage. Rather one should investigate the religious life, and if one finds happiness there, then one has found the proper state. If one does not find happiness in a seminary or convent, then marriage must be the vocation.

Some parents have admitted that their sons or daughters are capable of making a choice early in life, but they merely want their youngsters "to take a little more time" . . . "finish high school or college first" . . . "wait a year."

Father Van Antwerp answers such parents with their own type argument: "Suppose a rich uncle left your child $5,000. Would you say that the money should be left outside for a few days; then, if nothing happened to it, it could be taken up? Certainly not! But you want your child to act just as foolishly in regard to the gift of God!"

In the Seraphic Society's *Vocation Aids* Father Francis Xavier Maynard, O.F.M., develops an argument from psychology. He points out that the best time for a youngster to plan for the future is just this period in question, "the time between the ending of puberty and the beginning of adolescence. Here a child is best able to decide what he or she wants to be and do. Later on there is no such time of calm decision, for other forces come to bear upon the child and he or she begins to vacillate."

The best refutation, though, seems to be a combination of both arguments. You start by showing that it will not be any easier for a parent to part with a child after "a little while" . . . "after high school" . . . or "a year from now." In

fact it will be just that much harder, for the parent will have
come to depend that much more on the son's or daughter's
companionship. Meanwhile, God will have been denied that
much service.

During this delay many things can happen. God's call is a
delicate thing. It is not demanding. It forces no one. It can
very easily be drowned by the noise of the world or the
appeal of other interests. In the end one of two things will
happen: either the son or daughter will still be eager to go
and the pain of parting will be emphasized by the delay, or
God's invitation will have been forgotten and the parent
must answer in Judgment for keeping the child from God's
service.

"SEE THE WORLD FIRST"

Many mothers and fathers will nod in perfect agreement
with these arguments and then come right back with this
objection, "Our children know almost nothing about life
in the world. Until they have seen the world, we'll not give
them permission to leave home."

In analyzing this objection we have to determine just
exactly what the parents mean by "seeing the world." Surely
they are not thinking of a tour with the National Geographic
Society. Neither can we accuse them of wanting their sons
or daughters to see the seamy side of life or get a taste of sin.
The only thing they can possibly mean is that they want their
youngsters to have a chance for the innocent joys and pleasures of life.

Unfortunately, though, parents rarely see the dangers in
such a plan. Father Daniel A. Lord, S.J., illustrated the error
with an incident from real life. "A beautiful girl," he said,
"came to me some ten years ago, eager to enter God's service.
I have never met a lovelier soul. She was innocent, wholesome, generous. It was a clear vocation, and I prayed God
to give her the strength to accept it. But her mother wanted
her to see a bit of the world first and refused to permit her

to enter for at least three years. So the daughter obeyed and was rushed off to a whirl that was a stunning surprise to the child. In the end the girl ran away with a man who was a rake if there ever was one. After their first child was born, the young husband left her for a new love. The poor girl came back to her mother with her baby and her ruined life. I have often wondered what the mother thought as she held her daughter in her arms."

To refute this type of argument, it is best to ask the parents to name the particular pleasures of life that they consider so important. Which ones contribute so much to a person's happiness? Which ones are so necessary to their child's well-being?

Since good and wholesome pleasures are also found in religion, it is but a step to show how seminarians and postulants have as much fun — and even more — than their companions at home. It is safe to say that they have more laughter, more gaiety, more games, more genuine enjoyment than anyone else their age. Too few of the laity know much about what goes on in religious houses. If they did know, they would feel foolish indeed when they argued for the "world."

One mother commented to me after her first visit with her seminarian son, "I can't tell you how surprised I am. I never knew boys could have so much fun and real enjoyment. When my son left home I was quite concerned about whether or not he would like the life. After seeing him this afternoon I can never again doubt but that he is in the right place. My only regret is that I didn't know this beforehand. It would have saved me a lot of worry."

When you run across cases of parents who are afraid that their children will not know the facts of life before they take the vow of chastity, you have a much simpler situation. All you need to do is point out how in the seminary or convent their youngsters will get the whole truth about human love and sex — but from God's viewpoint. The only thing they don't get is a sordid or prejudiced approach. All seminarians or novices are better informed before their vows than most couples on the verge of matrimony. A cursory glance at their courses of instruction will quickly confirm these arguments.

Parents need never fear that their children are going to be accepted in the priesthood or religious life in ignorance of what they are giving up. They will be innocent, it is true, but it will be an informed innocence that makes their decision not only an intelligent one but a very meritorious one.

As for the complaint that "older candidates are better, more balanced," we can only point out that this is a begging of the question. Seminaries and religious institutes are much more concerned about the balance and maturity of their subjects than any parents.

During the probationary periods for the priesthood, brotherhood, or sisterhood, all candidates are introduced gradually into the ways of the spiritual life and the rules under which they will live. During this period they are permitted either to visit their homes or to have their parents come to see them. If there is any doubt about the maturity or balance of the candidates, the superiors always advise a year or more back home. This gives them a chance to prove themselves.

But when there is evidence of a sincere determination and all the qualifications for the religious life, the sooner the choice is made, the better it is.

"TOO MUCH PRESSURE"

Because human nature does not like to be "talked into" anything, many parents feel they are on solid ground when they object to their children's being talked into the priesthood or religious life.

"This isn't my daughter's idea," a mother will explain. "It is just that Sister has talked her into it."

"My son is too impressionable," a father will say. "The priests have pressured him into this decision."

"This is just a youthful enthusiasm," others will add. "What can you expect after an emotional appeal of a retreat . . . a mission . . . or even a day of recollection?"

In the eyes of many parents any type of vocational promotion is simply a clever conspiracy, like the advertising tactics of unscrupulous businessmen, to trick their sons and daughters into the service of God. One drums up interest in the religious life the same way one drums up an ice-cream trade. It is not the influence of grace that gets candidates but the glib tongue of some recruiter. God doesn't sweep boys and girls off their feet, but the excitement of a vocational rally does. In fact God has nothing to do with such things. They are all a big hoax put on by priests and religious who want more recruits for their line of work.

The illogic of these arguments has always been so evident to us that I am afraid that many priests and religious have been inclined to shrug them off without adequate explanation. We must not minimize this form of opposition or underestimate the degree of parental hostility it arouses.

Whenever there is a suspicion of pressure on the child, the parents are immediately on the defensive. The home, where the vocation is expected to flower, is turned against us.

To overcome this opposition we will have to convert the parents. Once they understand a religious vocation they will be more inclined themselves "to talk their children into the idea." With the right approach they can become the best possible recruiters for Christ.

Fortunata Caliri, writing on this subject for the *Catholic World,* stated, "If parents could be taught the true meaning of vocation, if they could be made to realize the importance of including the religious life among the various things in which they try to interest their children, then religious vocations will come from the home where they belong, and all this stupid fear and unhappiness resulting from false notions will vanish."

It seems to me that most of these parents, who object

that pressure has been brought to bear on their son or daughter, have taken a little too literally what they have heard in sermons or read in vocational literature. The priest tells them in Church that "a vocation is a call from God." They pick up a Catholic magazine and see an advertisement for some seminary or convent with a finger pointing out at them and a caption entitled, "Is God Calling You?"

Then, when a son or daughter of theirs claims a vocation, these literal-minded parents immediately want to know what priest or religious has been after their child. They know their youngster has not received any "call" from God. Certainly there hasn't been any private revelation, nor public one either. No angel has spoken to them. In fact there has been nothing out of the ordinary.

If the son or daughter persists in the idea that he or she has been "called," that only proves that some priest, brother, or sister has been trying to act the part of God Almighty. Then Mother or Dad gets excited and wants to come right down to the rectory or convent and tell us a thing or two.

In order to correct these mistaken notions — and the consequent opposition — we must point out what we mean by a "call from God." It is really nothing extraordinary. The "call to the religious life" is very much like the "call to marriage."

Parents know about their own vocation of marriage and how it demands certain qualifications. They also know that God has given them special graces for their state of life. From here you go on to show that there are similar qualifications for the religious life and certain graces necessary for that state. When one has these qualifications and graces, one has a "call from God." There are no miracles nor revelations expected.

Once mothers and fathers have grasped these ideas, the opposition will crumble. They will understand, moreover, that when God "calls" their son or daughter, as He does through His representatives, He is not giving them an insult or an injury but rather a delicate compliment and a new honor.

Finally, we point out the fact that only a small percentage of those who enter seminaries or preparatory school ever end up as priests or religious. Certainly this is not the result of "high-pressuring." Although the Church needs thousands of priests and religious, she never lets that need influence her choice.

If the candidates prove their qualifications, they are accepted. If any of the qualifications are lacking, candidates are sent home, regardless of who they are or who their parents may be.

It is true that seminarians and novices are given every opportunity to prove themselves and reach their desired goal, but nothing is rammed down their throats. In fact, before a boy is ordained to the priesthood or a girl is permitted to take her religious vows, both must swear with their hand on the Holy Bible that they are taking this step freely and with full knowledge of what they are doing. In no other state of life does the Church require such rigid precautions to insure absolute liberty and freedom of choice.

''MY CHILD WON'T BE HAPPY''

In the opposition arising from the nature of the priestly and religious life some parents find all kinds of matter for argument. The first and most obvious complaint is that the priesthood, brotherhood, and sisterhood are unnatural forms of existence. Accordingly, no son or daughter of theirs could possibly find happiness in such a life.

We priests and religious can hardly be expected to appreciate this point of view. We have already experienced some of the "hundredfold" promised by God in this life, and we anticipate the joy and happiness that will be ours in eternity. We also know that our parents will share in our rewards and honors in paradise.

But if we are to analyze this form of opposition we must

put aside the "paradise viewpoint" and try to look at the matter as these objecting parents do.

From the moment their child came into the world these parents have worked, sacrificed and suffered to give their youngster the best they could. They have spent their lives trying to insure the happiness of their boy or girl. Accordingly, now when they obstinately refuse permission to their child to enter the service of God, they do so because they cannot see how it will be conducive to the happiness of their child.

These parents have either let a single unpleasant experience with a priest or religious blind them to the true nature of life with Christ, or they have simply accepted the pagan notion that the vows of poverty, chastity, and obedience are instruments of frustration. Since they cannot understand such a life, they will not accept it as the vocation in which their child can find happiness.

This state of mind is refuted by an appeal that is partly emotional and partly intellectual. You approach the parent with great kindness and sympathy. These virtues will generally wear down even the most obstinate objectors. Your intention is not to condemn their mistaken judgments but simply to point out their best interests.

Your arguments will all be in terms of the parents' interests. They want the happiness and security of their children. They are also interested in the honor that will accrue to them from the success of their children. You will show them, therefore, how a religious vocation guarantees success and happiness for their child and great honor and reward for themselves.

A good example is the case of Father O'Callaghan, S.J., heroic chaplain of the aircraft carrier *Franklin*. When he went to the White House to receive the Congressional Medal of Honor, his mother went along with him and shared in all the glory of the nation's acclaim. This was her boy, and her training had helped to form the character that measured up so magnificently in time of trial.

Then you can show how more than in the glory of her son's physical strength, this mother shares also in the merit of the Sacraments administered, the words of comfort uttered in that trying hour, and the eternal reward for every Mass of his, sermons delivered, confessions heard, and all his other works for the love of God and men.

You can also point out that another source of deep happiness for parents is that they share with their son or daughter in religion the most joyous moments of their life — their reception of the habit, profession, ordination, First Mass, and the like.

James Costin, writing in the *South Bend Tribune,* summed up a parent's attitude very well after his own daughter had received the religious habit: ". . . she comes back with the ten others in her little band. Proud as can be, all of them. Wearing the habit proudly, but with such humility, too. There she is, that little one, right over there. That's your own, no kidding. You wonder more than ever, at such a momentous time in the life of your first born, how something like this could happen to a guy like you. Yes, sir, that little one right over there, wearing for the first time the fluted cap and the black robes of her new way of life, is your own. Doesn't she look — well, just like she's always wanted to look since she was old enough to have made up her mind about anything? So peaceful, so happy, so contented. You wonder, and you wonder again, how something like this could happen to a guy like you."

Once the parents begin to feel that we are as interested in their child as they are, they will begin to listen to our reasoning. When they finally realize that we have an open mind, including a high regard for their own vocation in marriage, they will begin to open their own minds and become more generous in their attitude toward us.

"BUT THE LIFE IS SO HARD"

Sacrifice is always difficult and irksome to human nature, so by taking this theme other parents think they have an irrefutable argument. Nobody likes to rise early in the morning, work long hours, have a monotonous grind day after day, never see new faces, eat coarse food, and live in plain surroundings.

Deep in their own hearts these parents know that the picture is a little exaggerated, but the objection is sound. The service of God is something hard, unexciting, and sacrificial. It is not a life for one you love!

In taking this argument apart, you naturally correct the exaggerations. Priests and religious generally live in plain quarters, but they have every necessity of life and most modern conveniences. Most of them have more than the average lay person. The food, too, may be plain, but it is wholesome, and there is a wide variety. By and large they eat as well as anybody else.

Early rising isn't such a hardship if you retire early. Religious rules, moreover, guarantee members between eight and nine hours' sleep a day if they want that much.

As for the work, it may be arduous, but it is never unpleasant. The only things that are really hard or monotonous are the things one doesn't like to do. If you enjoy what you are doing, you certainly don't complain.

The hours may be long, but what successful businessman hasn't worked overtime? What devoted mother can say she has time on her hands? Worth-while things always take time, but no one notices that when one is happy in the work.

The real sacrifice and hardship of the religious life is never brought up by objecting parents. They see only the externals and little realize that the most difficult thing about the lives of priests or religious is that they never see face to face the One to whom they have given their heart.

Religious live under the same roof with Jesus, receive

Him each morning in Holy Communion, and visit Him many times each day. But all His beauty and charm are concealed under a thin wafer of bread. It is not until the eyes of their souls are opened in death that they see Him as He is. This living in faith is what is hard!

At this point some recruiters have thought it a good idea to turn the argument against the parents. In marriage can they guarantee that their son or daughter will find an easy, but wonderfully varied and exciting, life? Can they promise that there will be no unhappiness, disappointment, or disillusionment? What is the percentage of successful and happy marriages in their family?

Christ, on the other hand, promised to everyone who would follow Him eternal life and a hundredfold of happiness in this present life. He promised them their salvation and a hundred times as much happiness on earth as they were giving up. Can parents promise that they will not only save their children's souls but that they will make them a hundred times happier than they are now?

As this objection is reduced to an absurdity, mothers will sometimes make a compromise. "If a son of mine wanted to be a priest, I wouldn't mind. They have so much more liberty and have an easier life. But there is no denying that a sister cannot get out and visit her friends much. People don't respect them either, as they do a priest."

"This objection is true in part," Father Daniel A. Lord, S.J., says in his excellent pamphlet, *Shall My Daughter Be a Nun?* "It is exactly like saying that the life of a good woman is usually harder than the life of a good man. He has the excitements of life; she has the commonplaces. He has variety; she has monotony.

"When fathers and mothers look at their children, which can honestly say that the children have cost them more? Isn't it the mothers who suffered for them, deprived themselves of so much for them? Which has the larger measure of freedom and the larger outlook on life, a man or his wife?

When a man and a woman start together in the business world, no one has any doubts about which has more opportunities and the smoother road ahead. It's the man every time.

"But does that mean that the man is doing better work or pleasing God better or winning a greater reward? No one is silly enough to think that.

"So the priest is the man and the nun is the woman. But remember this too — greater privileges bring greater responsibilities, for which the priest will have to answer some day. Sometimes I shudder when I think of the difference between what I actually do as a priest and what I ought to do. It probably would be a great deal better for me if I were a woman serving as Sister Cook in some little orphanage. And when I'm honored by people, I stand balanced between two precipices; shall I take the honor and admit that I'm a pretty clever and competent fellow after all, or shall I admit that I don't deserve a tenth of the honor that is being given me? I have freedom to move about, but sometimes that means moving about in the midst of temptation when I should be much safer if my duty did not take me out on the firing line. I have freedom to move, but my movement gives temptation freedom to reach me. I have not the warm, protecting arms of a cloister around me — and sometimes, God knows, I wish I had!"

OTHER OBJECTIONS

These arguments from the nature of the religious life can be extended almost indefinitely. The moment you answer one, another can come to mind. I remember arguing with one parent who claimed that his gifted son would only waste his talents in the priesthood.

Patiently I explained that just the exact opposite was the case. In the priesthood, under the competent personal guidance of the best teachers, his talents would be developed. In the seminary he would get a superb education — one his father couldn't hope to give him in the world. Then the great variety of activities in the Church would be a constant challenge to his son throughout life.

No sooner had I paused for breath than the same parent started off on another objection. "Really, Father," he said, "my boy is not good enough for such a noble vocation."

Other times I have heard parents say that their sons couldn't be meant for the priesthood because they loved sports too much. Their daughters, too, were not qualified for the convent. They loved parties too much . . . or dancing . . . or nice clothes. Sometimes the argument is from personality; again it is from the temperament of the child.

I asked Father Leon Grantz, C.P., what he thought of the parental opposition to a vocation on the ground that it stifled personality and individuality.

"If there is anything more prejudiced than that," he exclaimed, "I would like to hear it! I teach in the seminary, and I've never seen a single priest or student with a smothered personality. Everybody has different interests, concerns, hobbies. At recreation you can hear anything from an argument on which team will win the National League pennant to what's wrong with Plato. You can't listen to them for five minutes without realizing that they have never succumbed to pressure, propaganda, nor publicity. It is people outside that are repressed, not us!"

Certainly if the laity knew more about life in rectories, monasteries, and convents they wouldn't dare bring up some of the foolish objections they do. The evidence is much to the contrary. Religious men and women successfully operate colleges, high schools, grade schools, parishes, hospitals, social service agencies, and missions. Priests, brothers, and sisters are recognized leaders in every important phase of life.

No club or business organization can claim a better balance of talents and abilities than the average religious community. It is only ignorance that makes a lay person assume that in religious life the individual is subordinated.

It has been ignorance, too, that has prompted parents to tell me that the religious life frustrates all normal human desires for children. "One cannot give up fatherhood or motherhood," they have said, "without consequent loneliness and heartache."

In the very same breath with which these parents objected they called me "Father." I didn't laugh, but I knew they had forgotten that we are spiritually parents to all God's children. Through Baptism we give every Catholic youngster its spiritual life. As the child grows we instruct and care for it. This sublimated and spiritualized paternity more than makes up for what we lack physically.

They have also forgotten that many sisters are called "Mother" for the same reasons. These women often devote more time to the care and rearing of children than the physical parents. Can any girl be blamed then if she prefers a spiritual motherhood to that which is physical?

LESSON OF EXPERIENCE

Many parents that are much too wise to be taken in by some specious argument from the nature of the religious life will turn right around and try to argue from their own experience. They have had a relative or friend who entered the seminary or convent, and that person never persevered. Someone of their family tried the life and came back. If such individuals couldn't make it, certainly it would be foolish for their son or daughter to try it.

Behind these objections there seems to lurk the age-old assumption that parents-are-always-right. It is the judgment of the parents pitted against that of the priests and religious. Who are right? The parents claim that they are, and immediately we priests and religious are faced with another form of parental opposition.

In meeting their objections we simply make a plea for fairness. Regardless of what others have done, if the child has the qualifications and has expressed a desire for God's service, he or she is entitled to a right-of-trial. That is all we ask. Let the youths prove themselves.

We can point out, moreover, that the principal function of a minor seminary or juniorate is to test candidates for the priesthood or religious life. Only those that prove themselves worthy can continue. Actually a small percentage of those who start out in the religious life ever take final vows or get ordained.

Some nationalities, like the Irish, have such an esteem for the priesthood and sisterhood that they fear the idea of having a "spoiled priest" or a "spoiled nun" in the family. Others just come out categorically with the statement, "All ex-seminarians and ex-novices are blighted individuals." For these reasons the parents feel quite justified in protecting their sons and daughters against making any such mistake.

Basically this opposition seems to come from ignorance. It is as if the parents suspect that their child is spoiled if he or she tries out the religious life and then comes back. They forget that this only proves that their child is better than all the others who cannot think of trying such a life. As a rebuttal you can paraphrase the old adage, "It is better to have tried and lost, than not to have tried at all!"

There is scarcely any large parish that does not count many successful lawyers, doctors, and businessmen who have spent some time in a seminary or juniorate. Hardly any group of Catholic women can be found that doesn't have one or more mothers who spent a while in a convent school.

Today there are over a half-million ex-seminarians and ex-postulants in the United States. Most of them are outstanding Catholic lay leaders, wonderful fathers and mothers. They look back with pride and gratitude on the days they were privileged to spend in a seminary or convent. It was the way God prepared them for their vocation. Also I am sure, from talking with so many of them, that if they had the chance they would do it over again!

Another argument that parents sometimes give you is that

they have run into priests and sisters who are not happy in their vocation. They want to keep their children from such a tragic choice.

With this fact of experience we can only agree sadly. But without being too critical we can immediately point out that the individuals these parents have met are not generous souls. Certainly they have not given themselves completely to God.

For there is no such thing as an unhappy priest or religious who is really in love with Christ. Simply challenge these parents to ask any of the thousands of priests and religious who are giving God a wholehearted service what they think of the matter. Their eyes will reflect their answer even more quickly than their lips.

As I write these reflections, memories crowd in upon me. I remember an old priest in our Passionist Monastery, who once commented from a bed of pain, "I have known so much happiness in my life that I sometimes fear that God has been giving me my heaven here on earth!"

Another time I had just anointed an old sister. She had lived over sixty-seven years in religion and was now going to meet her God with a confident soul and full hands. Curiously I asked, "If you had it to do over again, Sister, would you spend so much time in a convent? There is so much good to be done outside."

Her eyes twinkled as she looked up at me and said, "Go chase yourself!"

"I'm serious, Sister," I argued. "I meet many parents that speak this way. What should I tell them?"

"Pretty soon," Sister continued, "I am going to see Jesus. I have spent a long time working for Him. If He has forgotten anything, I'm sure going to remind Him. But He can't forget, and He won't forget. And you know, Father, I just can't wait to see what He has prepared for me. I just can't wait. . . ."

As Sister's voice trailed off through weakness, I got up

and tiptoed out of the room. At that moment I think I came closest to understanding what a vocation really is and heard the best refutation of those who object because they know of failures.

OBLIGATION TO PARENTS

The last and most difficult form of parental opposition comes from those parents who feel that their children owe them something. It is as though their children had contracted debts and must now discharge them. Rarely will this objection be put into words, but you can sense that it is the thought behind the things they say.

For instance, you will hear this remark, "Leaving home is no way to show gratitude to us for what we have done."

Or: "We parents have an investment in our children. It is only fair that we get some return on it."

In public this type of parent may even become quite enthusiastic about some family that has three girls in the convent and a boy in the seminary. But privately they will remark that such youngsters must be a "little queer" and it is certainly "very selfish of them to leave their parents that way!"

To analyze and refute this type of opposition we have to lay all the cards on the table. Just exactly what do the parents expect of their children in the way of repayment? Is it that they want reverence, respect, gratitude, obedience, and love? If so, we agree with the parents most heartily and insist that their children thus repay them.

But if the parents mean they want something back in a financial form, then we must remind them that their children do not owe them anything in dollars and cents. Only when parents have suffered misfortune or are unable to take care of themselves does filial love obligate their children to see to their support.

Simply because parents want to pay off a new house or purchase a new car is no reason to keep the children home.

Neither can they for these reasons obligate any of their children to take a job and turn over the pay check to them. Nor can they insist that their oldest son or daughter assume the obligation of educating younger brothers and sisters. The older ones may do this out of charity, but it is not a matter of strict obligation. Parents may not alienate their responsibilities simply because they have grown sons or daughters.

All that obedience demands is that the children conform to the reasonable wishes of their parents in regard to their training and domestic order. It does not include the whims of their parents or the ideas Mother and Dad may have on their religious vocations.

Obedience is due first to God, then to parents. Accordingly, when there is a conflict, children must first follow the divine will.

When parents rashly contradict the divine invitation and refuse permission for their children to enter the service of God, the children can go without parental approval. There is no question of disobedience, for when the parents go against the superior will of God, they cannot demand submission from their children.

However, since there can be legal repercussions if these benighted parents appeal to the civil authorities to force the return of their son or daughter, most seminaries and religious institutes will not accept a candidate until he or she is of legal age if the parents should withhold consent.

Writing in the *Ecclesiastical Review,* Father Winfrid Herbst, S.D.S., has this to say about such parental opposition: "In this matter the parental will is not a manifestation of the will of God, so permission of the parents is not strictly necessary. If the son or daughter is of the required age, say at least fourteen or fifteen years old, he or she is quite justified, after consultation with others who are able prudently to advise, in disregarding the parental wishes when they are opposed to the manifest call of God."

When dealing with these parents we should point out to

them that they are on very shaky ground when they start talking about "obligation" and hinting that their children are "sinning against obedience." If there is any sin, it is on the part of the parents!

St. Alphonsus Liguori in his *Homo Apostolicus* says, "Parents, who without a just and certain cause prevent their children from entering the religious state, cannot be excused from *mortal* sin; and not only parents, but any one who prevents another from following a religious vocation sins *mortally*."

This is a very hard doctrine but one that sometimes needs to be emphasized with modern parents. Opposition is noticed especially in the case of daughters going to the convent, so it might be well at these times to remind them that the Fathers of the Council of Trent in their Twenty-Fifth Session anathematized "those who shall in any way and without a just cause impede the holy wish of virgins or other women to take the veil or pronounce vows."

SEPARATION FROM LOVED ONES

Most parents, as soon as they realize that they are theologically in error and that there is danger of sin if they continue in such convictions, will veer off into arguments that the child is obligated to love them. That is all they want.

"When our children leave for religion," they claim, "we have lost them. Barriers are immediately thrown up between them and their family."

Others take a more pleading tone. "You can't blame us for loving our children and not wanting to see our home broken up. Surely God understands."

Since this is a very emotional argument, you should appeal to some touching examples and prove that "the one you give to God is the one you keep for yourself."

Father Daniel A. Lord, S.J., for example, tells of a deathbed he once attended. "This splendid mother had been blessed with four daughters and two remarkably successful sons. Three of the daughters had married; her favorite became a nun; the sons, of course, had established their own families. It was the last day of the mother's life, and she seemed to realize that the end was near. Her six children were around her bed, praying with her, listening to her last requests, making the end as quiet and peaceful as possible. Night came and no one moved. Then the mother looked around at her children and smiled slightly.

" 'It is getting late,' she said, 'and I'm tired. Children, run along now to your families. They will be waiting dinner for you, and they need you.'

"They rose and stood beside her bed, torn between their desire to stay and their duty to their families. Then the mother turned to the daughter who was a nun and said, 'Helen, you stay with me.' "

That, Father Lord points out, is the perfect example of what a child in religion means to a parent. This mother, as she came to die, knew that between herself and her other children had come other loves. Only the daughter who was a nun had never brought in any human obligation that might now stand between them.

A similar account was published a few years ago in the *Mission Helpers Review* under the title of "The Daughter I Gave to God." It told of how a mother lost her youngest child and turned in her grief to the one she had in religion.

"Miriam met me," this mother wrote, "with a look of such peace and happiness as I have never seen on the face of any of my other children. We talked for a long time. Under her deep understanding and true sympathy I found myself laying bare my soul's worries, my grief, my cares, my problems, probably all enlarged in view of Ann's sudden death.

"Gradually each trouble disappeared as the nun beside me unfolded the beauty, sweetness, and peace in the age-old mystery of God's loving providence. It was the first time I had ever come spiritually close to any of my children. Later, as I knelt in the chapel, I knew that however blind I was to the fact, Miriam was really God's gift to me. All the anguish, bitterness and resentment I had felt at her entrance into religion vanished like smoke in a high wind.

"Since then the passing years have only served to increase the bond of companionship. If happiness comes in an unusual way, then Miriam must share it. If there is a puzzle to be solved, Miriam always finds a way out. If sorrows and cares appear, it is always Miriam easing the pain. . . . That is why she, now that all my children have gone from the old home, seems nearer than the rest. That is why I agree that 'the child you give to God is the child you keep.' "

HOW TO SOLVE THE PROBLEM

So far I have analyzed and refuted forty-two different objections from parents, but even that number is far from being a comprehensive listing of the arguments you will meet. In this I have not attempted to show all the objections there are but only to show the different categories into which typical parental arguments fall and the best ways of refuting them.

Now we come to the final investigation of the different approaches to a solution of parental opposition. Here again I have had the help of countless recruiters, research specialists, and interested parents. From our discussions and studies it has seemed to us that there are five ways of dealing with the subject, determined by its five different aspects:

1. There is the emotional appeal when the problem is predominantly emotional.
2. There is a genetic problem that must be handled by a careful treatment of national characteristics and hereditary traits.
3. There is the consideration of the environmental factors influencing both parent and child.

4. There is the dispelling of ignorance and reasoning to a conclusion, when the problem arises from ignorance or prejudice.

5. Finally, there is the spiritual approach, when the problem springs from the religious background or spiritual attitudes of the parents.

THE EMOTIONAL APPEAL

This approach has already been alluded to in the treatment of several objections that were founded in parental feelings. It makes itself felt to greater or less degree in all arguments the parents put up. You can tell it is there when Mother and Dad become misty-eyed or wipe away a furtive tear.

Many recruiters find it helpful at this point to inject a few emotion-toned words themselves and play upon the sentiments of admiration or sympathy.

I remember attending a Sodality program for students and parents at which a very talented vocalist sang, "I'm the Daddy of a Nun." Later they announced the names of all the proud fathers and mothers in the audience who had a son or daughter in religion. In the congratulations that followed most of the fortunate parents were bursting with pride and joy, and many of the others wished they had a son or daughter in the service of God.

Father Simeon Heine, S.A., told me that he often uses this emotional appeal in recounting the story of how his holy founder, St. Francis of Assisi, not only defied parents and left home but also helped St. Clare do the same.

"I tell these mothers and fathers about the way Francis helped Clare to elope into the cloister. I paint the whole scene of how she escaped through a hole in the wall, fled through the woods, and was received into the convent at midnight by the light of torches.

"Then I go on to show how the world acclaims any girl

a heroine who lives up to her convictions and is willing to endure any trial for her love. Juliet, for instance, was willing to undergo any sacrifice to prove her love for Romeo. The world has sympathy for Juliet, and it applauds the Friar's help to that girl in her hour of need. Isn't it inconsistent then to condemn the help Francis gave Clare in a similar trial . . . or to criticize the modern religious who tries to help a boy or girl run off with God."

THE GENETIC APPEAL

In taking up the genetic appeal I recall a remark made by one of my old professors. "It always takes a Dutchman to understand a Dutchman." Certainly that adage applies to this form of parental opposition.

No one denies that a Dutch parent will take a much different stand on this matter from that of an Italian. A Polish mother will argue differently from a French one; and an English father is altogether different from an Irish one. A recruiter, therefore, must recognize these differences and evaluate all the national characteristics and hereditary traits.

This is partly the reason for the success of the Friends of Our Lady. This organization was started among parents of religious in Pittsburgh, Pennsylvania, by Father Jude Senieur, O.F.M.Cap., in 1948. He had come to the realization that the best persons to answer parental objections were parents of the same racial and social background.

Since these people had already let their child go to a seminary or convent, they knew how to argue others into giving a like permission. Certainly they could talk to their friends and neighbors more convincingly than anybody else. The Italians among them knew the best way to appeal to the Italians; the Germans knew how to approach Germans; and the Irish knew how to handle the Irish. It started with five individuals and now numbers many units, not only in Pennsylvania but throughout the country.

ENVIRONMENTAL   FACTORS

Poverty or lack of money is another reason why parents will sometimes seek to oppose the vocation of a son or daughter. When pinned down on this point, one father said a little bitterly, "Even the Apostles wouldn't have followed Christ if He had charged them $500 a year!"

You can explain all you want that tuition is unimportant and that allowances will be made for those boys and girls who cannot afford the full payment. But the parents will still hold them back, for they are a little hurt and a little ashamed.

When the Catholic University Clerical Conference took up the study of priestly and religious vocations in 1945, this environmental problem was given particular attention. Many aspirants for the seminary or convent had been blocked because their parents had not had enough money.

To combat such financial embarrassment they recommended the establishment in each parish of a Regina Cleri Society. Such a group is quite simple in its organization and, as already mentioned, is based on the idea that candidates for the service of God are truly sons and daughters of the parish. As such they are entitled to the full support of the parish, both spiritually and financially.

The society attempts to solve the problem of supporting vocations not by charity but by co-operation. The parish is divided into a suitable number of areas, with two persons, called promoters, assigned to each area. There is a president, a secretary, and a treasurer for the group, and they arrange that the promoters call upon every Catholic family in their area once a month. These promoters explain the purpose of the Regina Cleri Society and ask the parishioners for their co-operation.

Everyone who promises either to say a prayer daily for vocations or make a donation for the support of candidates for the priesthood and religious life becomes a member of the group. A membership card containing a picture of our Lady and a prayer for vocations is given to everyone who co-operates. The promoters also distribute literature concerning vocations and try to clear up mistaken notions that some of the people have about the requirements of the priestly and religious state.

All money collected by the promoters is turned in at monthly meetings to the treasurer, who then deposits it in the bank under the society's name. All tuition bills for the parish's religious candidates are sent directly to the treasurer of the Regina Cleri Society, who pays them by check. When necessary, the Society also takes care of the dowry for any girl entering a cloistered community.

Where such a group is active, many of the environmental problems are eliminated. If the young man or woman is worthy, capable, and approved by the pastor, there is no material obstacle to hinder such a one from going to the service of God.

DISPELLING IGNORANCE

When a parent's opposition springs from ignorance, the obvious solution is to instruct such a one. This can be done by sermons, distributing informative literature, and personal instructions.

This whole question was considered at great length by some 162 Vocational Club moderators at the 1953 meeting of the Midwest Vocation Association. Their recommendations were to have more parent-religious meetings and discussions. Many of the communities represented planned open-house programs for the following March, and where the program was followed, they reported that many parental misconceptions were dissipated.

One pastor, intent upon dispelling the ignorance he found in his parish, chartered two buses and took over fifty parents on a pilgrimage of nine seminaries and novitiates. On the way they all prayed for an increase of vocations. At each place they visited the chapel, toured the buildings and grounds, saw the students, and partook of light refreshments. "Parental reactions," Father said, "were most interesting. Many of them remarked: 'These youngsters certainly are a lot happier than I thought' . . . 'It is so clean here' . . . 'You'd never dream this is the way they live.' All of them came away convinced that the religious life offers more than it demands."

An even more successful program is that carried on by Monsignor Martin Muzik of St. Eulalia parish, Maywood, Illinois. Every two years he holds a Vocation Forum. As part of the affair each child in the school is dressed as a priest, brother, or sister, and each participates in a pageant at the end.

The Forum lasts three days. On Sunday morning at all the Masses there is a sermon on vocations to the religious life. That evening there is a panel discussion on "What to Look For in a Religious." Next evening there is a talk and discussion on the "Making of a Religious." Sometimes a film is shown. The last night all the children are called up to the stage to explain the life and work of the community they represent. There is special recognition given to all parents who have a religious in their family, and awards are given to the winners in a vocation essay contest.

This program has produced results, for each year Monsignor Muzik has sent several boys to study for the priesthood or brotherhood and several girls to prepare for the sisterhood. "Parental opposition," he says, "is rarely evident. Most of my people now glory in the privilege of having one of their own flesh and blood called to the religious life."

THE SPIRITUAL SOLUTION

In a way the spiritual aspect of the problem underlies all our other considerations of parental opposition.

Sometimes it may be a misguided parent who, though a

daily communicant, refuses to recognize the voice of God in the child's vocation. I was once invited by such a father to give a talk to other parents of his group on what they could do to promote vocations in their own families. Meanwhile this man was using every trick he could think of to thwart his own daughter's going to the convent!

At other times the vocation of a son or daughter will be a reflection on the spiritual generosity of the parents. This is especially true when the mother or father is not very faithful in the practice of religion. The condition is only aggravated in many mixed marriages or where there is a bad marriage. When their child wants to go to religion it is like a reproach to the parents.

Father Edward F. Garesché, S.J., brought out this point in a thought-provoking article he read at a Vocational Conference of the Missionary Union of the Clergy. "Homes full of faith and fervor," he said, "where both parents are good Catholics . . . and where religious influences are strong and deep, are nurseries of vocations. Those of weak or bad Catholics . . . materialistic and selfish homes . . . give no children to God."

The same idea was developed in an article by Father Joseph H. Eckert, S.V.D., entitled "Vocations and the Catholic Family." "If priestly and religious vocations," he wrote, "are to be more plentiful in the future, it will be necessary to weed out the spirit of secularism and all that it implies and restore the Catholic family to its pristine lustre and significance. It must be divested of its streamlined modern character of worldliness and love for pleasure and reclothed in the old-fashioned robe of strict discipline, deep faith, and a spirit of sacrifice. Catholicism must be visible not only on Sundays but throughout the week and permeate every phase of home life. Only then will we solve our problems and have in the home a gilt-edged guarantee of more vocations."

The best spiritual solution, though, was the one expressed

by Pope Pius XI in his great encyclical *Ad Catholici Sacerdotii*. It makes a fitting conclusion to this study of parental opposition.

"The first and most natural place," the Holy Father wrote, "where the flowers of the sanctuary should almost spontaneously grow and bloom, remains always the truly and deeply Christian family. Most of the saintly bishops and priests, whose 'praise the Church declares,' owe the beginning of their vocation and their holiness to the example and teaching of a father strong in faith and manly virtues, of a pure and devoted mother, and of a family in which the love of God and neighbor, joined with simplicity of life, has reigned supreme. To this ordinary rule of divine providence exceptions are rare and only serve to prove the rule.

"In an ideal home the parents, like Tobias and Sara, beg of God a numerous posterity 'in which Thy name may be blessed forever,' and receive it as a gift from heaven and a precious trust. They strive to instill into their children from their early years a holy fear of God, and true Christian piety. They foster a tender devotion to Jesus, the Blessed Sacrament, and the Immaculate Virgin. They teach respect and veneration for holy places and persons. In such a home the children see in their parents a model of an upright, industrious, and pious life. They see their parents holily loving each other in our Lord, see them approach the Holy Sacraments frequently and not only obey the laws of the Church concerning abstinence and fasting, but also observe the spirit of voluntary Christian mortification. They see them pray at home, gathering around them all the family, that common prayer may rise more acceptably to heaven. Finally, they find them compassionate toward the distress of others and see them divide with the poor the much or the little they possess.

"In such a home it is hardly possible, that while all seek to copy their parents' example, none of the children should listen to and accept the invitation of the divine Master:

'Come, follow Me, and I will make you fishers of men.'

"Blessed are those Christian parents who are able to accept without fear the vocations of their children, and see in them a signal honor for their family and a mark of the special love and providence of God. Still more blessed, if, as was oftener the case in the ages of greater faith, they make such vocations the object of their earnest prayer!"

CHAPTER VIII

Recruiting Programs

THERE is a beautiful old legend that tells how, when Christ ascended to His Father, the angels gathered around Him and asked about what He had found upon earth.

"I found My Father's children divided one against the other," He said. "I found their minds darkened by error, their hearts heavy with failure, and their lives made wretched by sin. But I established a Church and gave My followers sacraments and precepts, with a creed and a cult, to remedy the situation."

"Whom did You place in charge of this program?" the angels asked. "Did You create other seraphim and cherubim to save the world?"

"No," Jesus replied. "I picked twelve men, whom I made priests. Another group of men and women I made religious. These followers of Mine will make known the Church, save souls, and change the world."

The angels almost in pity protested: "But these poor priests and religious are so weak and unknown. Suppose they fail?"

The answer of Christ, as this legend goes, is the thought I would leave with you. "They cannot fail," He said, "for I have made no other plans."

The moral is obvious. There is a divine purpose in what we do for vocations. Christ's program for the Church and for the world depends for its fulfillment upon us. May we never fail Him!

As a help toward a better understanding of what can be done *for more vocations,* I have included in the following survey all the different vocational endeavors in this country. By grouping the works of the principal dioceses, religious communities, and youth organizations under one outline, I hope the whole vocational program can be more easily comprehended.

Moreover, this summary of projects and programs, already alluded to in preceding chapters, may serve as a norm for those experienced in the work and a guide for those who are starting.

THE DIOCESAN PROGRAM

The diocesan program begins with the bishop either appointing a vocational director and committee, or delegating this responsibility to one of his priests. When he chooses to delegate another, generally it is the superintendent of schools or the director of the Propagation of the Faith.

The most successful programs have generally started with the selection of a "Vocations Committee," made up of representatives of the various religious communities in the diocese. The diocesan director of vocations has then served as chairman of this group.

After the establishment of this organization it has been the practice in most dioceses to seek affiliation with the *Pontifical Work for Priestly Vocations.*

"The primary purpose of this *Work,*" as Pope Pius XII pointed out in his *Motu Proprio* on the subject, "is to intensify among the faithful, by every means, but particularly through the lay groups presently existing in the diocese, the desire of promoting, safeguarding, and assisting ecclesiastical vocations. The second purpose is to disseminate the right knowledge of the dignity and necessity of the Catholic priesthood. The third purpose is to unite the faithful of the whole world in a communion of prayers and pious exercises."

The promotion of this work is under the direction of His

Eminence, Joseph Cardinal Pizzardo, Prefect of the Sacred Congregation of Seminaries and Universities. His inspired leadership has been responsible in great part for the awakening of interest in vocational promotion, and it is his desire that branches of the *Pontifical Work* be established throughout the world.

The diocesan units, in turn, affiliate local societies and local branches of national societies. They also affiliate religious communities, groups of children, the sick, and other interested individuals. Thus through the *Pontifical Work* all have unified aims and ideals.

The special days of prayer for vocations, recommended by this *Work,* are the Ember Days, the Solemnity of the Blessed Virgin Mary, the Solemnity of St. Joseph, and the feast of SS. Peter and Paul.

Interest in this subject of vocations has been all the more intensified when the bishop has stressed its importance at the clergy retreat or selected it as the subject for discussion at one of the clergy conferences.

In many places the people are kept aware of the matter by talks from the bishop at time of Confirmation or ordinations in their parish church. Archbishop Mitty of San Francisco, for example, has found it very effective to speak on vocations during his Confirmation tours. At the other end of the country Archbishop Hurley of St. Augustine, has arranged for ordinations in different parishes of his diocese, so that people in practically every large area can see the ceremony.

Equally important is the regular course of instructions for the laity. This is generally worked into the diocesan sermon outlines, as is the case in the Archdiocese of Chicago. There the outlines for the month of March give sermon material on:

1. The Signs of a Vocation;
2. How to Overcome Difficulties;
3. The Apostolate That Lies Open;
4. An Appeal for Generosity.

The advantage of these four instructions or sermons is that parents begin to talk about the priesthood and religious life. They then learn more about the importance and dignity of the service of God. They also come to realize that they should not stand in the way of their sons or daughters and that they may even sin if they prevent their children from following their vocation.

Finally, since prayer is such an integral part of all the Church's vocational work, each diocese generally publishes a special vocational prayer. In this the bishops are simply following the example of Christ who exhorted the apostles to "pray to the Lord of the harvest that he send laborers into his vineyard."

Moreover, in the Archdiocese of Kansas City Archbishop Hunkeler encouraged his pastors to say the Votive Mass of Christ the Eternal Priest on the first Thursday of each month and to have their parochial school children attend.

In Pittsburgh Bishop Dearden encouraged a holy hour for vocations at the Cathedral. This was made a big affair, and youths from all over the city were invited to attend.

In Springfield, Massachusetts, Bishop O'Leary started an annual novena for vocations, from Ascension Thursday to Pentecost Sunday. This is the most nearly ideal time for vocational promotion, and this practice is one that could well be adopted universally.

THE DIOCESAN VOCATIONAL DIRECTOR

Since all vocational programs depend upon their directors, the success of any diocesan campaign is in proportion to the effort the director puts into it.

One of the first moves of a diocesan director is always to arrange a meeting with all grade and high school teachers in the diocese. If he does not have the co-operation of the teachers, he will accomplish nothing. At this meeting he outlines his program and asks the assembled teachers to contribute their ideas.

In some dioceses, like Trenton, weekly conferences or days of recollection are arranged in different parts of the diocese. Pastors and teachers are encouraged to send any likely prospects to these affairs.

The director, too, arranges with the seminary authorities for an open-house celebration to which he brings all the boys of the diocese who are interested in the secular priesthood. Often, though, he can find help from Serra Club members in working out the details of such a program.

In the Archdiocese of Chicago on the second and third Sundays of March the various communities of sisters select one of their convents and invite all interested girls to visit them. These open-house programs are held from 2:00 p.m. until 5:00 p.m.

The girls are taken through the convent, given an explanation of the life and work of the sisters, and then after a visit to chapel, they are treated to refreshments. Each group spends about an hour at the convent, and when interest mounts, individuals are invited back for a longer visit and more thorough explanation. If a girl is interested in showing her parents through the convent, a day is arranged when this can be done.

The principal duty of the vocational director, however, is to arrange talks in all the schools of the diocese and follow up on the response. If he cannot do this personally, he should select other priests in the various areas of the diocese and have them in their respective areas give talks in all Catholic classrooms from the seventh to the twelfth grades inclusive.

After these talks on vocations, cards are passed out. On them the students are to designate whether they are "Interested in" . . . "Not interested in" . . . or "Merely curious" about the priesthood, brotherhood, or sisterhood.

All of those who check off "Interested" are called in for a personal conference. Afterward all necessary data on family and scholastic background are added to the card from the school file.

Where possible, vocational directors often establish a vocational club in those schools where there are many students interested in the priesthood or religious life. If they cannot handle the club personally, they help the local moderator by getting speakers for meetings, arranging for vocational films, and the like.

In some places, like Los Angeles, the diocesan director has a speakers' bureau and assigns priests or laymen for talks that are requested. In other places it is arranged that teachers exchange schools and address the student assemblies on the subject of vocations.

As a help in their work many directors publish a folder on all the communities in the diocese and send supplies of this advertisement to pastors for distribution in the parishes.

To keep the subject before the laity many directors send regular articles to the diocesan paper. Sometimes these are in the form of news stories; at other times they are simply explanations of some local community. Since most religious groups are eager to co-operate in this matter, the work burdens no one.

Once a year there is generally a vocational rally or exhibit. All the youths of the diocese are invited, along with their parents and friends. One or more talks are given on the need for vocations and the qualifications demanded of one who would follow Christ. Then the boys and girls visit the booths and pick up sample literature.

In a few places, like in the diocese of Boise, the director has been able to organize the seminarians and coach them to do a little promotional work during the summer vacations. This is beneficial, not only in that youths work most effectively with other youths but also in this that by selling the idea to others, they thereby strengthen their own convictions.

PROGRAM FOR RELIGIOUS COMMUNITIES

In setting up their own vocational program, all the reli-

gious communities which have been successful in promoting
vocations have set aside one or more individuals for full-
time vocational work. The effectiveness of this program is
proved by the fact that ten years ago, in 1945, there were only
thirty-four full-time recruiters for all the religious communities of the country. Today there are 319 priests, brothers,
and sisters giving their full time to this work.

In a community the official recruiter sets up the various
projects and co-ordinates the efforts of the different religious.
For help in this work there is generally a moderator appointed for each local house or school.

Where the diocese has a regular promotional plan, it is
the responsibility of the religious recruiter to study the plan
and follow its prescriptions exactly.

In the Archdiocese of Chicago, for example, there is a
voluntary association of forty-one religious communities of
priests and brothers, who recruit in all the schools of the
area.

The gist of the plan is that by agreement only three
recruiters, instead of ten or twelve, as formerly, will ask each
pastor for permission to give a vocation talk in his school
in any one year. In early 1951 a committee, chosen from
among the members of the group, divided the Chicago elementary schools into equal lists, taking into consideration
the size of the schools, their location, and the like. These
lists were then given to the vocation directors who wished
to give school talks. In each subsequent year the lists have
been rotated and assigned to different recruiters.

Each recruiter must himself seek the permission of the
pastors on his list and, if this permission is obtained, must
arrange with the school principal to give the talk at a convenient time. The vocation directors usually speak to the
seventh and eighth grades, and sometimes even to the fifth
and sixth grades. This plan, without overcrowding the school
schedule, offers the pupils a well-rounded view of the work

of the Church at home and abroad, as exemplified in the many activities of the various communities.

To implement and regulate this plan the Chicago group drew up a set of rules that all religious recruiters should follow. The essential points are that they pledge themselves to work for the cause of vocations in general without over-stressing the needs of their community. They also treat all aspects of the priesthood, brotherhood, and sisterhood and try to reach every school on their list. Then besides talking to both boys and girls, they make themselves available for adult groups, like the Altar Society and Holy Name Men.

The value of this co-operation of the religious recruiters with the diocesan authorities can be seen in the results from the Chicago schools. In the summer and fall of 1953, in addition to the 251 high school freshmen and the 21 students above the first year, who enrolled in the diocesan seminary, 151 candidates from the first year and 97 from above the first year enrolled with other religious groups. The brothers received 87 boys. Furthermore, of the 248 youths who entered religious seminaries or novitiates, 221 went to communities serving the archdiocese. Twenty-seven joined groups outside the diocese.

When giving such talks in the school the religious recruiter generally passes out "vocation-interest" cards. The boy or girl checks off his or her degree of interest, age, grade, name, and other general data. Those who claim they want to know more about the priesthood or religious life are interviewed personally. If the speaker is not able to do so, some other priest or religious is asked to take over. It is the follow-up work that produces results.

When it is impossible to have these personal interviews, then the recruiter takes the names of all interested youths and later sends them literature through the mail.

For these interested prospects many directors put out a monthly folder or form letter. It is printed in a very informal style and keeps contact with the youths. It also eliminates a great bulk of personal correspondence.

Finally, the director makes it a point to visit the home of each prospect who makes formal application to the seminary or religious institute. This serves as a further check on his or her background and often dissipates a great deal of parental opposition.

I remember one Mother Superior who pleaded most insistently that I help them get vocations. "But what are you doing about the matter?" I asked.

"We are praying very hard for vocations. We just completed one novena and are starting another!" she replied.

Prayer, I agreed, was quite important, but my question was, "What are you *doing* in a promotional line?"

Come to find out, that Superior had no one assigned to the task of vocational promotion and did no advertising. It was no wonder that they had practically no vocations. However, Sister made up for lost time by immediately appointing two full-time recruiters and sparing no expense on vocational literature and advertising. The following year they took in forty-two postulants!

THE PARISH PROGRAM

The success or failure of the parish program depends directly upon the parish priest.

Canon 1353 of Church Law states: "All priests, especially pastors, shall see that boys who show signs of an ecclesiastical vocation, are carefully preserved from the contamination of the world. They shall train such youths in piety, give them elementary instruction in the study of letters, and foster in them the seed of the divine vocation."

All parish programs are but the implementing of this directive of the Holy See, and the emphasis on "boys" does not imply that the priest must restrict his attention to those who will become priests. The Code is merely legislating for the more important matter, and takes it for granted that they will also foster vocations to the brotherhood and sisterhood.

Most pastors find occasion for a vocational talk in the course of their catechetical instructions, especially when they treat the subject of Holy Orders. They also use the occasion of a reception, profession, or ordination of someone in the parish as an opportunity for a sermon on the subject. Some even use the Sundays before Ember Days as regular times to remind their people to pray and to do penance that God may bless the Church with more vocations.

The parish priest also has a wonderful opportunity to promote vocations when he is teaching catechism to the school children. Some explain during the instructions on Baptism how youngsters should carry their faith to others. This is an appeal for the missionary life. While treating of the Eucharist they point out what a privilege it is to bring God down upon the altar. This offers occasion for comment on the power of the priesthood. Thus something will come up almost every week for comment or observation. One need only look for an occasion to talk vocations and it can be found.

In the confessional this instruction and guidance can be given even more effectively. When a pure and generous soul concludes his or her confession, the priest need only ask, "When was the last time you thought of being a priest . . . or brother . . . or sister?"

If the youth is sufficiently virtuous to attract your attention, chances are he or she has thought of the service of God. The answer will probably be, "Back in grade school" . . . or "In high school" . . . or "I'm still thinking about it."

The confessor should then ask why the individual gave up the idea . . . or why he or she is not doing something about it.

Girls especially are often very much interested in the possibility of becoming a sister, but they dare not mention the matter to one of their teachers. They are afraid that the sister will immediately urge them to take the step for which they are not yet prepared. The confessor, on the other hand, seems more disinterested. Accordingly, if he gives them an opening, they are eager to ask advice.

When, however, the priest meets a penitent who is not interested in finding out more about the service of God, he gets a simple answer, "No." That ends the matter. Any further questioning only embarrasses the youth. The important thing, though, is to give the penitent a chance to ask for advice and to show that one is willing to help.

Some parish priests pay particular attention to altar-boy groups. Father Joseph F. Kundinger of Scofield, Wisconsin, has averaged one boy a year from the parishes in which he has worked with altar-boy groups. He occasionally has them work around the church and the rectory, and once a year he takes the group for a visit to the diocesan seminary.

Father Richard Gabel of St. Joseph's parish, Tiffin, Ohio, holds an annual triduum for vocations. Since his program started five years ago, he has recruited eight seminarians and twelve girls for the convent. Each morning of the triduum, Mass is said for more vocations, and in the evening there is a sermon on some aspect of the priesthood or religious life, followed by Benediction.

Some pastors have invited prudent and influential laymen and laywomen to help them in recruiting vocations. These priests instruct their "scouts" on what to look for in candidates for the priesthood and religious life. They then send them out to round up likely prospects. All youngsters who seem qualified are interviewed by the pastor if they show any interest in the priesthood, brotherhood, or sisterhood.

Finally, some priests have arranged for a daily Mass for vocations, at least during Lent. All the parochial children are urged to attend this Mass and recite special prayers for vocations.

THE SCHOOL PROGRAM

The first effort here is always directed toward deepening the spiritual life of the students through prayer and more frequent reception of the Sacraments. Then comes a cultivation of a spirit of sacrifice and generosity.

In each diocese the bishop generally selects a special prayer for vocations. This should be displayed in each room at school and recited every morning before classes.

Emphasis should be placed on ejaculatory prayer, for many students have the idea that to pray means to say the rosary . . . or the stations. Not having time for these things they give up altogether.

Some teachers are content to have the youngsters add to their morning and night prayers the indulgenced petition, "Dear Jesus, please help me to become a priest (brother or sister), if it is Your holy will."

The plan used in the schools of the Archdiocese of Chicago recommends a novena for vocations, beginning on March 16 and ending on the vigil of the Annunciation. It also arranges for a day of recollection for the senior students to be held on a date selected by the pastor.

More frequent reception of the sacraments of Holy Communion and Penance cannot be stressed too much. In most school programs the teachers urge their students to receive these sacraments at least once a week. During times of retreat, Lent, and the vocational campaign, they are encouraged to receive Holy Communion daily and to go to confession weekly.

In the cultivation of a spirit of sacrifice and generosity, most zealous teachers give several short exhortations to the practice of these virtues, emphasizing the points recommended in the religion course.

Since the second purpose of the school program is to impart adequate instruction, time is always set aside for study of the service of God, with occasional plays and dramas, movies, debates, and the like.

The fundamental matter is covered in religion class during vocation week or month by having at least one period devoted to each of the following subjects:

1. Signs of a Vocation, i.e., Health, Intelligence, Moral Fitness, and Right Intention;
2. How to Overcome Difficulties, i.e., Parental Opposition, Poverty, and the Like;
3. The Apostolate That Lies Open, i.e., Parish Work, Mission Work, Teaching, Nursing, and the Like;
4. An Appeal for Generosity in Following the Promptings of Grace.

The supplementary reading generally includes those books and pamphlets which will supply the youngster with all that is needed for a well-balanced view of the service of God. General works, like the pamphlets *Follow Me* and *Follow Him* from the Grail Press, St. Meinrad, Indiana, are the type to promote. Books, like *Opportunities in Catholic Religious Vocations,* from the Vocational Guidance Manuals, New York 19, New York, are also very helpful.

The visual aids range from slide sets on various religious communities to sound and technicolor films on the training of a boy or girl. An inquiry through the office of the Chancery, School Board, or Propagation of the Faith will generally be answered with information concerning available materials.

Where the school program is most successful, it is always the result of confidence well placed. When the principal or superior appoints an individual vocational counselor, he or she should be given time from class to call in the various youngsters for conference and be given a certain amount of discretionary power in accepting or rejecting candidates.

In these same successful schools you will find that the principal has one of the teachers, or the local vocational moderator, publish a monthly vocational bulletin and see to it that the bulletin board is decorated regularly with appropriate posters.

It also helps when the retreat master, at the time of the annual spiritual exercises, gives a special talk on vocations. Many priests, though, do not do this unless reminded by the superior or one of the teachers.

Some schools have created a vocational atmosphere by having debates, quizzes, plays, and contests on various aspects of the priesthood and religious life. All of these things are good in that they keep the youngsters thinking and talking about the subject.

As the vocational program draws to a close, the most important project is a paper on the subject: "Why I would (or would not) want to become a priest (brother or sister)." This generally elicits a great deal of genuine response and is the best indication of how much interest the various instructions and projects have aroused.

It is also very helpful to build up a vocational reading library and encourage the students to use it. There are many stories of what goes on in seminaries and convents that make excellent reading for youths.

Lastly, there is the vocational club that meets on school time. Speaking at the Vocational Institute in New Orleans, Msgr. Edward A. Freking said that he visited one community whose teaching sisters were dying out. Because there were more deaths each year than professions, he asked, "What are you doing?"

The Reverend Mother replied that they didn't know what to do. "Then I will tell you," Msgr. Freking said. "Form vocation clubs in each of your schools and get the most intelligent, broad-minded, and likable nuns you have to direct them."

Happily the sisters followed Msgr. Freking's advice, and a year later they were averaging four vocations from each of their clubs. Another thing that surprised the sisters was that three fourths of the girls, whom they never suspected of having interest in the sisterhood, joined the clubs.

A FINAL THOUGHT

Bishop Landrieux of Dijon, France, once said: "There are vocations which manifest themselves; they must be fostered. There are vocations which are not conscious of themselves; they must be awakened. There are vocations which do not dare manifest themselves; they must be found and encouraged. There are vocations which are in fear of being lost; they must be reassured. There are vocations which meet with opposition; they must be strengthened. There are vocations which are paralyzed by poverty; they must be helped financially."

All of this is but another way of saying that a successful recruiter must get out and get busy. No matter what program is emphasized or what techniques are used, the recruiting will be successful only insofar as the recruiter prays, works, and sacrifices.

This calls for high motivation and the words of St. Vincent de Paul are worth pondering. "No matter how we seek," he says, "we shall always discover ourselves unable to contribute to anything greater than the making of good priests" . . . and we might add "good brothers and sisters."

Surely at death it will be a great consolation to look back on the vocations we have gained. The same pride and joy that an earthly parent has at the thought of sons and daughters left behind to carry on the family name will bless us. For we will leave our own spiritual progeny behind to carry on the work of Christ and His Church. We will not have failed Him!

"This is the sunlight in the final shadows," as Father Edward Murphy, S.S.J., expressed so beautifully. "This is the star in the deepening night. This is the talent that was not buried in the ground but duly increased. This is a pledge of that smile of God: 'Well done, thou good and faithful recruiter!'"

Bibliography

NOTE: This bibliography is not intended to be comprehensive of the subject. It is rather a convenient listing of those authors who are most quoted in this book and whose published works are available for reference.

DOCUMENTS AND SOURCES

Acta et Documenta, Congressus Generalis de Statibus Perfectionis, Pia Societa San Paolo, Rome, 1950

Acta Sanctae Sedis, 41 vols., Rome, 1865–1908; *Acta Apostolicae Sedis,* Commentarium Officiale, Rome, 1909 —

Alphonsus Liguori, St., *Ascetical Works: On the Choice of a State of Life,* 5th ed., Vol. II, Tours, 1881

American Ecclesiastical Review, The, Vols. I–CIX, Philadelphia, 1889–1943; *The Ecclesiastical Review,* Vol. CX, Baltimore, 1944 —

Bargilliat, M., *Romanorum Pontificum Monita et Decreta de Institutione Clericorum,* Berche & Tralin, Paris, 1908

Bouscaren, T. L., *The Canon Law Digest,* 3 vols. and Supplement, Bruce, Milwaukee, 1934–1953

Canonical Legislation Concerning Religious, authorized English translation, Newman, Westminster, Md., 1950

De Smedt, L. J., moderator of the Missionaries of the Congregation of the Immaculate Heart of Mary, who assembled the *Directorium Seminariorum* (in Sinis), Scheut-Pekini, 1949

Gasparri, P. Card., *Schema Codicis Juris Canonici,* ed. cum notis, Rome, 1912

Pius XI, *Ad Catholici Sacerdotii,* English translation, St. Anthony Guild Press, 1940

Pius XII, *Menti Nostrae,* N.C.W.C. translation, Washington, D. C., 1950

Thomas Aquinas, St., *Summa Theologica,* 6 vols., Taurinorum Augustae: Marietti, 1938; *Commentaria in Omnes St. Pauli Apostoli Epistolas,* 2 vols., Taurinorum Augustae: Marietti, 1917

BOOKS

Blowick, J., *Priestly Vocation,* Gill & Son, Dublin, 1932

Brady, Dominic, O.P., *An Analytical Study of Counseling Theory and Practice with Recommendations for the Philosophy of Counseling,* Catholic University Press, Washington, D. C., 1952

Carr, Aidan, O.F.M.Conv., *Vocation to the Priesthood: Its Canonical Concept,* Catholic University Press, Washington, D. C., 1950

Cotel, Peter, S.J., *A Catechism of the Vows,* Newman, Westminster, Md., 1942

Curran, C. A., *Counseling in Catholic Life and Education,* Macmillan, New York, 1952

Duffey, F. D., C.S.C., *Testing the Spirit*, Herder, St. Louis, 1948

Farrell, Edward, O.P., *Theology of Religious Vocation*, Herder, St. Louis, 1951

Gallagher, T. R., *The Examination of the Qualities of the Ordinand*, Catholic University Press, Washington, D. C., 1944

Gasparri, P., *Tractatus Canonicus de Sacra Ordinatione*, 2 vols., Paris, 1896

Gay, Msgr. Charles, *The Religious Life and the Vows*, Newman, Westminster, Md., 1942

Geremia di S. Paolo della Croce, *La Scelta della Vocazione*, Milan, 1946

Gibbons, J. Cardinal, *The Ambassador of Christ*, Murphy, Baltimore, Md., 1896

Guibert, Jean, S.S., *La Culture des Vocations*, Paris, 1907

Irenaeus, P., C.P., *Institutiones Juvenum Candidatorum ad Sacram Ordinationem*, Scala Sancta, Rome, 1937

Kane, George L., editor of *Why I Became a Priest* (1952); *Why I Entered the Convent* (1953); and *Why I Became a Brother* (1954), Newman, Westminster, Md.

Ladislaus a Maria Immaculata, C.P., *De Vocatione Religiosa*, Rome, 1950

Lahitton, J., *La Vocation Sacerdotale*, nouvelle ed., Paris, 1913

Lambert, J. M., *Le Recrutement et La Formation des Vocations Ecclesiastiques*, Oeuvre des Pretres-educateurs, Paris, 1942

Lord, Daniel, S.J., *Some Notes for the Guidance of Youth*, Queen's Work, St. Louis, 1945

Loret, *La Vocation, Principe et Pratique*, Editions Saint Paul, Paris, 1943

Manna, Paul, P.I.M.E., and Maestrini, Nichlas, P.I.M.E., *Forward with Christ*, Newman, Westminster, Md., 1954

Mitchell, Walter, *Vocation*, translation of *Le Discerement des Vocations de Religieuses*, Newman, Westminster, Md., 1952

Myers, Rawley, *The Greatest Calling*, Macmillan, New York, 1951

—— *This Is the Seminary*, Bruce, Milwaukee, 1953

Nilles, N., *Commentarius de Vocatione ad Statum Ecclesiasticum*, Oeniponte: Pustet, Cincinnati, 1892

Olier, J. J., *Traite des Saints Ordres*, Migne, Oeuvres Completes, Paris, 1856

Pinault, Joseph, *Discerement et Culture des Vocations*, Desclee, Paris, 1934

Poage, Godfrey, C.P., *Recruiting for Christ*, Bruce, Milwaukee, 1950

—— *Your Opportunity in Catholic Religious Vocations*, Vocational Guidance Manuals, New York, 1952

Reilly, Sr. Mary Paul, O.S.B., *What Must I Do?*, Bruce, Milwaukee, 1950

Religious Sisters, translation of *Directoire des Superieures* and *Les Adaptations de la Vie Religieuse*, Newman, Westminster, Md., 1952

Stockums, W., *Vocation to the Priesthood*, translated by J. W. Grundner, Herder, St. Louis, 1937

Suhard, Cardinal, *Priests Among Men*, Fides, Chicago, 1950

Vermeersch, A., *Religious and Ecclesiastical Vocation*, translated by Joseph Kempf, Herder, St. Louis, 1925

BOOKLETS, BROCHURES, AND ARTICLES

August, Brother, *Catechism Lessons on Vocations*, La Salle Bureau, New York, 1950

Caliri, Fortunata, "Religious Vocations — For Parents," *Catholic World*, December, 1950

Digna, Sister M., O.S.B., "A Tentative Testing Program for Religious Life," *Review for Religious*, 1951

Finn, Lyman, S.S., *Vocations to the Priesthood*, Paulist Press, New York, 1945

Follow Christ, Vocational Magazine Series, Grail Press, St. Meinrad, Ind., 1945 —

Frederick, Brother, F.S.C., editor of *Findings of Vocational Workshop of Christian Brothers*, Glencoe, Mo., 1953; and editor of *Proceedings of National Conference of Brother Vocational Directors*, Christian Brothers College, St. Louis, Mo., 1954

Garrigou-Lagrange, Reginald, O.P., *De Sanctificatione Sacerdotum*, Taurini, Marietti, 1946

Griffin, Bishop, "The Family, Nursery of Vocations," *Follow Christ*, 1945

Harrison, J., O.P., "St. Thomas and Religious Life," *Irish Ecclesiastical Review*, Vol. I, 1913

Henry, Brother, C.F.X., editor of Xaverian Brothers' *Handbook for Vocation Moderators*, Xaverian Provincialate, Baltimore, Md., 1954

Herbst, W., S.D.S., "Doubts About Vocation," *Ecclesiastical Review*, 86, I, 1932

Lelen, J. M., *Towards the Altar*, St. Anthony Guild, Paterson, N. J., 1952

McCarthy, E. J., "The Obligation of Priests to Foster Vocations," *Ecclesiastical Review*, 84, I, 1931

McDonnell, Msgr., "The Vineyard of Christ at Home and Abroad Needs More Servants of Christ," *Missionary Union of Clergy Bulletin*, New York, 1945

Nimeth, Albert, O.F.M., *The Spiritual Life and Vocations*, Seraphic Society for Vocations, Westmont, Ill., 1954

Nutting, Willis, *Parents Are Teachers*, Liturgical Press, Collegeville, Minn., 1950

O'Connor, John, "Too Young To Live," *Sign*, Union City, N. J., July, 1951

Plus, R., "Vocation," *Dictionnaire Apologetique de La Foi Catholique*, Vol. IV, col. 1895 ff.

Poage, Godfrey, C.P., *Follow Me*, Grail Press, St. Meinrad, Ind., 1941

——— *Follow Him*, Grail Press, St. Meinrad, Ind., 1942

——— *Christ Calls Today*, Catholic Information Society, New York, 1950

——— *Have You Heard Christ's Call?*, Catholic Information Society, New York, 1948

——— *St. John Bosco Club Handbook*, Vocational Clubs, 5700 N. Harlem, Chicago, Ill., 1943

——— *Life at the Prep*, Paluch Press, Chicago, 1947

Ralenkotter, Howard, C.P., *Our Lady of Good Counsel Club Handbook*, Vocational Clubs, 5700 N. Harlem, Chicago, Ill., 1944

——— *What Others Have Done*, Paluch Press, Chicago, 1946

——— *What Other Parents Have Done*, Paluch Press, Chicago, 1947

Rose Agnes, Sister M., O.S.F., *How to Be an Instrument of Grace in Fostering Religious Vocations*, Seraphic Society, Westmont, Ill., 1950

Sempe, L., "Vocation," *Dictionnaire Theol. Cath.*, t. 14, col. 3148 ff.

Senieur, Jude, O.F.M.Cap., *Vocational Notes for Sisters*, St. Anthony Vocational Club, Pittsburgh 1, Pa., 1950

——— *Our Lady's Friends*, St. Anthony Vocational Club, Pittsburgh 1, Pa., 1949

——— *Why Do My Parents Object?*, St. Anthony Vocational Club, Pittsburgh 1, Pa., 1951

Sophronia, Sister M., O.S.F., *Notes on Fostering Vocations*, Serra International, 38 S. Dearborn, Chicago, Ill., 1952
Stocker, Leonard P., O.M.I., *Admission to Minor Seminaries of the United States: Policies and Practices*, Catholic University Press, Washington, D. C., 1952
Wilson, John, C.S.C., editor of *Vocational Digest*, Notre Dame, 1945–1954
Wunschel, E., C.SS.R., "The Traditional Notion of Vocation," *Missionary Union of Clergy Bulletin*, 1945
Zoffoli, E., C.P., "L'Obbligo di Corrispondere alla Vocazione," *Vita Cristiana*, Vol. 17, 1949

LECTURES AND ADDRESSES

Barth, Pius, O.F.M., *Teaching Through Teaching*, Proceedings of Third Vocation Institute, Notre Dame, 1949
Bergh, E., S.J., *Canonical Impediments*, translated by W. Mitchell, Newman, Westminster, Md., 1952
Bernice, Sister M., O.S.B., *Vocations in Colleges*, Proceedings of the Third Vocation Institute, Notre Dame, 1949
Bonduelle, A., O.P., *The Recognition of Vocation*, translated by W. Mitchell, Newman, Westminster, Md., 1952
Columba, Mother Mary, *Qualifications of Candidates for Foreign Missions*, Proceedings of First National Congress of Religious Women in U. S., Paulist Press, New York, 1952
Coogan, Aloysius, "The Need for Vocations," *Missionary Union of Clergy Bulletin*, New York, 1946
Corbett, Mother M. Killian, C.S.J., *Crusading for Christ, How to Attract Vocations*, Proceedings of First National Congress of Religious Women in U. S., Paulist Press, New York, 1952
Denise, Sister M., O.S.F., *Vocations in High School*, Proceedings of Third Vocation Institute, Notre Dame, 1949
Esser, Ignatius, O.S.B., *Development of Qualities Required in Lay Brothers in Clerical Institutes*, Proceedings of First National Congress of Religious Men in U. S., Paulist Press, New York, 1952
Estelle, Sister Mary, S.S.N.D., *Psychological Procedures in Guidance and Counseling*, Proceedings of National Catholic Educational Association, 1954
Fox, Dom M. James, O.C.S.O., *The Contemplative Life in the United States*, Proceedings of the First National Congress of Religious Men in U. S., Paulist Press, New York, 1952
Francois de Sainte-Marie, O.C.D., *The Recognition of a Contemplative Vocation*, translated by W. Mitchell, Newman, Westminster, Md., 1952
Gerty, Francis E., *The Natural Background for the Religious Life*, Proceedings of the Third Vocation Institute, Notre Dame, 1949
Healey, Kilian, O.Carm., *The Intellectual Formation of Religious Seminarians in America*, Proceedings of First National Congress of Religious Men in U. S., Paulist Press, New York, 1952
Hoflich, James E., *Lay Organizations and Their Help in Vocations*, Proceedings of National Catholic Educational Association, 1954
Hug, Pacific L., O.F.M., *Proceedings of Vocational Institutes*, Quincy College, Quincy, Ill., 1943 –

Joanne, Sister Mary, C.S.J., *Our Lady of Good Counsel Clubs,* Proceedings of National Catholic Educational Association, 1954

Kennelly, John P., *The Priest's Role in Fostering Vocations,* Proceedings of Second Vocation Institute, Notre Dame, 1948

—— *Discovering and Guiding Vocations,* Proceedings of Second Vocation Institute, Notre Dame, 1948

Maura, Sister, S.L., *The Modern Girl and Religious Vocation,* Proceedings of Third Vocation Institute, Notre Dame, 1949

McAuliffe, Clarence, S.J., *The Theology of Vocation,* Proceedings of National Catholic Educational Association, 1954

McCarthy, Charles F., M.M., *Vocational Literature, Publicity, and Public Relations,* Proceedings of National Catholic Educational Association, 1954

Motte, A., O.P., *The Obligation to Follow a Vocation,* translated by W. Mitchell, Newman, Westminster, Md., 1952

Omez, Reginald, O.P., *Negative Criteria of Vocation,* translated by W. Mitchell, Newman, Westminster, Md., 1952

O'Neill, Dennis, *Vocation Advertising,* Proceedings of Third Vocation Institute, Notre Dame, 1949

Philippe, Paul, O.P., *Discerning of Vocation,* notes given at Institute of Spiritual Theology, River Forest, Ill., 1953

Ple, Albert, O.P., *Unconscious Attraction to the Religious Life,* translated by W. Mitchell, Newman, Westminster, Md., 1952

Poage, Godfrey, C.P., *Vocational Guidance for Teenagers,* six lectures in 1949 Blue Book, Summer School of Catholic Action, Queen's Work, St. Louis, Mo.

—— *How to Promote Vocations,* six lectures in 1949 Blue Book, Summer School of Catholic Action, Queen's Work, St. Louis, Mo.

—— *How to Hear Christ's Call,* twelve lectures in 1950 and 1951 Blue Books, Summer School of Catholic Action, Queen's Work, St. Louis, Mo.

—— *Discovering and Guiding Vocations,* twelve lectures in 1950 and 1951 Blue Books, Summer School of Catholic Action, Queen's Work, St. Louis, Mo.

—— *How to be Successful in Recruiting for Christ,* six lectures in 1952 Blue Book, Summer School of Catholic Action, Queen's Work, St. Louis, Mo.

—— *Discovering and Fostering Vocations,* Proceedings of National Liturgical Week, 1951

—— *Meeting the Objections to Minor Seminaries,* Proceedings of National Catholic Educational Association, 1953

—— *The Harvest is Ripe: Vocations,* Proceedings of National Catholic Hospital Association Convention, Kansas City, 1953

—— *The Fundamentals of Recruiting,* Proceedings of the National Catholic Educational Association, 1952

—— *What's Being Done for Vocations,* Fourth Vocation Institute Proceedings, Notre Dame, 1950

—— *Practical Methods of Stimulating Religious Vocations,* Proceedings of First National Congress of Religious Men in U. S., Paulist Press, 1952

Ralenkotter, Howard, C.P., *Good Counsel Clubs,* Proceedings of Third Vocation Institute, Notre Dame, 1949

—— *Winning Parents,* Proceedings of National Catholic Educational Association, 1954

Riedel, Louis, *The Priest in the High School,* Proceedings of the Third Vocation Institute, Notre Dame, 1949

Robinson, W. M., C.S.C., *Theology of Religious Vocations,* Proceedings of the Third Vocation Institute, Notre Dame, 1949

Rousseau, Dom O., *The Call to Perfection in Patristic Tradition,* translated by W. Mitchell, Newman, Westminster, Md., 1952

Secondo, Louis, T.O.R., *Development of Qualities Required in Religious Seminarians: Their Spiritual Life,* Proceedings of the First National Congress of Religious Men in U. S., Paulist Press, New York, 1952

Senieur, Jude, O.F.M.Cap., *Education of Parents Concerning Vocations,* Proceedings of Third Vocation Institute, Notre Dame, 1949

Stabb, Giles, O.F.M.Cap., *Qualities Required in Candidates for Admission to Religious Life,* Proceedings of First National Congress of Religious Men in U. S., Paulist Press, New York, 1952

Vocational Conferences, Proceedings of the Conventions of the Missionary Union of the Clergy, Society for Propagation of Faith, New York

Weissler, Victor, O.F.M., *Making the School Vocation Conscious,* Proceedings of Second Vocation Institute, Notre Dame, 1948

Wulstan, Mother Mary, S.H.C.J., *Overcoming the Prejudice to Vocation Clubs,* Proceedings of the National Catholic Educational Association, 1954

Index

CREATIVE RECREATION FOR THE MENTALLY RETARDED

CREATIVE RECREATION
FOR THE
MENTALLY RETARDED

By

ISSAM B. AMARY, M.S.E.
Recreation Therapist
Marshall State School and Hospital
Marshall, Missouri

CHARLES C THOMAS · PUBLISHER
Springfield · Illinois · U.S.A.

Published and Distributed Throughout the World by
CHARLES C THOMAS • PUBLISHER
Bannerstone House
301-327 East Lawrence Avenue, Springfield, Illinois, U.S.A.

© *1975, by* CHARLES C THOMAS • PUBLISHER
ISBN 0-398-03292-0
Library of Congress Catalog Card Number: 74-11390

Printed in the United States of America
W-2

Library of Congress Cataloging in Publication Data

Amary, Issam B
    Creative recreation for the mentally retarded.

    1. Mentally handicapped—Recreation. I. Title.
[DNLM: 1. Mental retardation—Rehabilitation.
2. Occupational therapy. 3. Recreation. WM300 A485c]
GV183.7.A43   790.19'6   74-11390
ISBN 0-398-03292-0

To You, For Your Contribution To The Mentally Retarded

and

To The Healthy Children . . . So They May

Think Of The Retarded

PREFACE

THIS MANUAL IS designed primarily for use by recreation therapists and activity aides working in institutions or other facilities housing mentally retarded individuals. It is also meant to give the student of recreation an idea of actual concepts and work with the retarded, thus, preparing him for a career in recreation services, as well as equipping him with ideas that might assist him in designing a recreational program for the mentally retarded.

For the past several decades, mental retardation, as a profession, has taken great strides forward, and due to the interest and effort of countless dedicated people ranging from highly skilled professionals to attendants working directly on the ward, retardation is now in the proper prospective and society has realized the need for rehabilitation. Any student of retardation is undoubtedly familiar with the various eras that brought retardation from extermination to today's sophisticated programming and rehabilitation to which this manual is devoted. It might be worth the reader's time to take another look at these eras and see the development that took place since the earliest time from which consistent records are available.

1. Era of Extermination: During this time, the strong survived, and nature took care of the weak. Mentally retarded and handicapped children were abandoned, and nature took its toll.

2. Era of Ridicule: This was more apparent during the Middle Ages, particularly in royal courts where weak kings, in order to prove their own strength, ridiculed mentally retarded individuals such as the court jesters. Also during this era, people believed that God spoke directly to the fool, and that the mentally retarded possessed supernatural powers. Needless to say, very little, if anything, was done during this era to improve the well being of the retarded; however, it was one step above extermination.

3. Era of Asylum: After Christianity, people felt that they were obligated to help; however, they did not wish to be too involved in the retarded life. They constructed asylums, and all who seemed to be retarded or deviated from the normal were housed there—sometimes in the same ward, without discrimination between incompetent, deviant or mentally ill. Asylums became overloaded, and many escaped.

4. Era of Education: Special education classes were started in the early 1900's, and Chicago was the first major United States city to introduce them. During World War I, the mentally retarded were needed to assist in factory assembly lines, as well as in other capacities.

5. Era of Vocational Rehabilitation or Occupational Adequacy: Started shortly after the Second World War and in the early 1960's, research was accelerated, and retardation was on its way to being put in the proper prospective.

Obviously, the normal person did not have to endure such eras. His life cycle was established, and the value of education and recreation for him was generally accepted without argument. This simple fact violates the constitutional rights of the retarded individual and gives rise to discrimination which is one of the most destructive injustices that can be imposed upon the retarded and handicapped individuals. This is precisely what we would be doing if we did not make every effort to provide them with all possible opportunities to take part in as many well developed recreational and physical activities as essential to their positive development.

If, or when, a retarded individual supersedes the world's record in the 100 meters dash, the mile run, the shot put or any other competitive activity, should he be banned from competition due to his retardation or handicap? It is this author's opinion that the responsibilities for providing these opportunities lie with those people who, regardless of profession, work directly with the retarded and are involved in his daily life. These same people must also realize that the retarded individual needs their guidance and understanding so that he may meet the challenge of existence and live a fruitful life.

ACKNOWLEDGMENTS

I AM PARTICULARLY grateful to Mrs. Bettye Trimble Potter, secretary, for the many tedious hours she spent deciphering my handwriting, correcting my spelling and, finally, typing the manual in an acceptable form.

Special appreciation is expressed to Mr. E. Patrick Baker, Jr., Therapist Aide, who created the illustrations and contributed some of the activities included in this manual.

Community Center photographs are reproduced with the permission of the Marshall State School and Hospital, Marshall, Missouri.

Finally, I wish to express my deepest appreciation to my wife, Wilma, two children, Jason and Jarred, for their patience, assistance, love and understanding.

INTRODUCTION

ALTHOUGH RECREATION has been a major ingredient in the physical and mental health of us all in our complex and pressurized society, it has been sadly neglected in the lives of the educably and trainably mentally retarded.

With the recent normalization philosophy coupled with vastly successful workstudy programs for both the educably and trainable youngster, more and more retarded persons have proven themselves to be competent workers, taxpayers, and contributing members of society. Those of us involved in such work placement and follow up have found that these youngsters do not learn how to use their free time. They have not been conscientiously taught how to use their leisure time for release and recreation.

Creative Recreation for the Mentally Retarded has been carefully designed, developed, and scoped according to the learning characteristics, the interest, and abilities of retarded youngsters. As such, this book will be a major aid to educators, therapists, and recreational personnel, who have foreseen the need for such a program but were unable to find an appropriate resource.

The author's valued experience as recreational director of a program for the trainable retarded, his years of study, and his devotion to the needs of the mentally retarded youngsters he serves are exemplified in this exceptionally useful book.

Although this text will contribute much to the program success of the professional worker, it will be of even greater value to ultimate beneficiary retarded youngster and his future.

PATRICK COONLEY, Ed.D.
Assistant Professor of Special Education
Central Missouri State University
Warrensburg, Missouri

INTRODUCTION

RECREATION HAS BEEN a key stone in an institutional setting for many years. In years past, when either education or vocational education programs were virtually nonexistent, recreation was left with the task of providing activities for basically all institutional residents.

With current trends and philosophy leaning towards a deinstitutionalization approach to return patients to community based living arrangements, more emphasis will be placed on recreation for the mentally retarded. Making worthy use of leisure time through recreational activities is certainly one of the most important aspects of community living in our complex society of today.

It is felt that *Creative Recreation for the Mentally Retarded* has been written on the basis of thorough research along with several years of first-hand experience in the area of recreation with an institutionalized mentally retarded population. Our society is beginning to address itself more and more to the recreational needs of the mentally retarded as exhibited through our habilitation training programs. This book should be a valuable tool and lend positive assistance to physical educators and recreational personnel in an institution or school setting.

The author's sincerity and dedication to the cause of mental retardation gives him a keener perspective and awareness to their recreational needs, as exemplified in this book, and should benefit all levels of mentally retarded individuals.

CHARLES A. COOPER, M.A.
Assistant Superintendent, Treatment
Marshall State School & Hospital
Marshall, Missouri

INTRODUCTION

T HIS BOOK IS the result of the varied experiences the author
has had in assisting the institutionalized mentally retarded to
grow and develop to their fullest potential. With the change of
population within institutions for the retarded, it becomes more
apparent that the recreation and activity therapy personnel must
play a major role in assisting the severe and profoundly retarded
who frequently have multiple physical handicaps. Work with
this group of residents requires attention to activities that provide
sensory stimulation.

The long term institutionalized resident must be made fully
aware and interested in their environment before they can
develop and learn. Activity therapy plays a major role in stimulating the individual, both physically and mentally. Many of the
activities described in this book are designed to meet the needs
of the severe to the profound physically handicapped retarded
individual. Other activities can be readily adjusted to the needs
with minimal imaginative changes.

ADRIENNE D. McKENNA, MSN
Superintendent
Marshall State School and Hospital
Marshall, Missouri

CONTENTS

CREATIVE RECREATION FOR THE MENTALLY RETARDED

RECREATION,

WHO NEEDS IT?

SINCE THE BEGINNING of time, man has participated in some type of recreational activity. He discovered that along with his daily chores and routine of hunting and providing food and shelter for himself and his family, he must devote some time for play. He realized that participating in various simple games did not only contribute to healthy, physical living, but it was also a form of relaxation for his mind, when he could relax and enjoy life.

Through the ages, man became more sophisticated in his approach to recreational activities. Throughout the Egyptian civilization, the pharaohs devoted time for recreation and play activities that ranged from palace dancing to swimming competitions on the Nile River. The Romans introduced chariot racing and built arenas for sports competitions. The Greek civilization, more than any other, encouraged sports competition and recreational games. They were responsible for what may be termed as the most inspiring and effective recreational development of all times: from a handful of barefoot message carriers racing between cities, they developed and perfected a competitive spirit that met recreational needs to the nth degree with the end result being today's Olympic Games. Today, throughout the world, millions of people participate in thousands of different forms of recreation, and, needless to say, billions of dollars are being spent to build sophisticated recreational facilities ranging from massive sports complexes to small community swimming pools, and in the process, modern man spends approximately one third of his time participating in recreation.

At this point, it should be of interest to the reader to consider the consequences of withdrawing recreation from man's daily life. The twenty-four-hour day of work and sleep would become an unbearable routine; no reading for pleasure, no television, swimming, skiing, attending movies, plays, and sports games, boating, fishing, hunting, camping, hiking, stamp collecting, and countless other activities and hobbies. Only work and sleep— man obviously would not survive, particularly in today's highly sophisticated, pressurized and industrialized world, and as a result, nervous breakdowns, suicides, broken families would become inevitable. The very structure and survival of modern society would be jeopardized.

In view of the above facts, we believe that recreation is just as vital for physical and mental health as food is vital for the body nourishment. Constructive recreation fulfills man's inborn desire of self-enjoyment, pleasure and accomplishment.

It is of the utmost importance, however, to realize that what may be recreation for one person is hard and strenuous work for others. Wood chopping, for instance, is a means of earning a living for a woodchopper, but it is a competitive sport at the county fair, where the participant has the opportunity to exhibit his masculinity and receive applause for his perfected art. Thus, each individual must choose the activity that will naturally best suit his needs and desires. On the other hand, recreation will be of no apparent value if it were mandatory. Each individual must have the desire to take part in order to derive maximum benefits. Who needs recreation? I do! You do! We all do!

Chapter II

RECREATION AND THE
MENTALLY RETARDED

THE RETARDED INDIVIDUAL has the same basic needs for mental, spiritual, social and emotional growth as the nonretarded and because their handicap has isolated them, their needs are even greater. The mentally retarded, as any other person, will learn only as much as he is emotionally ready to learn, and this fact makes recreation of vital importance to him.

The term "recreation" applies to any activity which revitalizes the individual's interest and helps him create and feel refreshed; however, recreation must be an activity that is different from the individual's daily routine. It must provide a change for the individual to enjoy the break from his regular daily activities. This point is of particular interest when working with mentally retarded individuals in an institutional environment. If recreation does not provide an activity that is different than the daily ward routine, participation and interest will be very low, thereby jeopardizing the entire recreational program for that particular area. For an institutional recreation program to be effective and successful, it requires a good deal of precise planning and organization.

The exact amount of time an individual needs for recreation is an unsettled question; however, it is generally agreed that a minimum of two and one-half hours per day is necessary for the younger person. Four hours would be better. Half of this time should be spent in active, outdoor activities, and the balance of the time may be spent in inside or quieter activities. In an institutional environment where opportunities for individual achievement are rather limited, the time for recreation and free play is very important. This may be the only time an individual will have the opportunity to develop his independence and resourcefulness.

For many years, it was an accepted fact that the institutionalized mentally retarded only needed to be clothed, fed and protected from danger or harm. In addition to basic nursing needs, there was very little programming, and the existing programming was geared toward making the attendant's job easier, rather than improving the well-being of the retarded person. Of course, this type of treatment was due to several factors. Lack of funds and qualified staff ranked as the number one reason. Public awareness of institutions and the retarded was at a minimum. Today this concept has changed tremendously. The entire concept of institutions providing basic care has moved to that of intensive programming. The U.S. courts have upheld the right of the retarded for treatment and ordered institutions to implement programs geared to develop each retarded individual to his maximum potential. Some of the court decisions went as far as spelling out the ratio of professional staff to institutionalized patients. The Federal government awarded grants to implement hospital improvement programs, physical therapy and recreational therapy improvement projects. The public became more cognizant of the needs of the retarded and accepted the fact that their needs are the same as any other normal individual. Thus, society has taken another step in favor of the retarded individual.

Under the new concept of intensive programming, recreation plays a major role. It is through recreation that the retarded develops physical stamina and body awareness. The promotion of muscular control, balance, eye and hand coordination through individual and group participation in recreation is quite apparent.

Through experience in working with the retarded in an institutional environment, the author has found that bowling, skating, music and dance are very effective means in reaching the retarded and teaching him social skills, discrimination, balance, independence and, above all, instill in him the sense of competition, achievement and accomplishment. As the retarded improves his performance in the recreation hall or gymnasium, he will also improve his performance in the classroom, home, community and, eventually, on the job.

Recreation provides the individual with an opportunity for creativity. Other than this objective, it assists in developing the individual socially, physically, mentally and emotionally. It constitutes an outlet for many needs such as aggressiveness. It provides the individual with a sense of accomplishment, to gain confidence and trust in himself, as well as others, to enable him to take part in community recreational facilities and to learn to use leisure time effectively.

The value of recreation and sports competition for the retarded cannot be overemphasized. A history of failures in a retarded's life may cause him to look upon himself as a failure. His first real accomplishment may come in recreation. Here, he can succeed and build a positive attitude, gain confidence and understanding, as well as physical training and development. In many cases, the recreational skills achieved by the retarded will become their most valuable asset. The development of these skills, however, lies with those who are responsible for providing opportunities where the retarded can participate and achieve.

Chapter III

ORGANIZING A

RECREATIONAL PROGRAM

AN EFFECTIVE RECREATIONAL program includes a variety of activities designed specifically to meet the needs of the mentally retarded and conducted by a qualified recreation therapist assisted by activity aides who have undergone basic training in providing recreation for the retarded. A recreation program includes but is not limited to the following:

Acting	Organized Sports
Arts and Crafts	Physical Training
Bingo Games	Picnics and Parties
Bowling	Photography
Calisthenics	Scouting
Competitive Games	Skating
Dances	Social Mixtures
Free Play	Special Events
Group Recreation Activity	Special Olympics
Hikes	Storytelling
Hobbies	Swimming
Movies	Table Games
Music Therapy	Track

A recreation program must be designed to fit the needs of the individual rather than the individual fitting the program; therefore, before setting up a recreational program, the therapist should take into consideration several points:

1. Type of facilities available for recreational activity (indoor and outdoor areas).

2. Screening—meet with each retarded individual to understand and evaluate his particular needs in order to provide him with a beneficial program.
3. Coordinate the recreation program with the overall daily routine of the individual. Avoid conflict with other scheduled programs.
4. Attendance—every effort should be made to make the recreation session a pleasant experience so that each individual will look forward to attending.
5. All equipment should be checked to see that it is in proper working condition before an activity is conducted.
6. Safety precautions should be taken at all times, regardless of the simplicity of the activity.
7. Periodic evaluations should be made to see how effective a program has been in improving the skills of the individual.

Procedure

In introducing an activity, the therapist should:
1. Give the name of the activity.
2. Clearly explain the directions and how an activity is to be carried out.
3. Clearly explain the functions of all equipment to be used in a particular activity.
4. State the rules and guidelines for each activity.
5. In group activity, demonstrate himself, or ask a few people to demonstrate, the activity so the others will have a good idea of what is expected.

Discipline in Recreation

In all walks of life, people have to comply with a set of rules that is designed to protect them, as well as others. In this area, recreation is no exception. Each individual has to adhere to a set of rules and values designed to increase the recreational benefits derived by the individual. When an individual deviates and refuses to comply by the rules, then he should be taught the difference between right and wrong, and the recreation therapist has the responsibility to teach these values and instill in the individual the ideas of respecting the law and other people's properties.

The therapist should also be prepared with a specific discipline plan to be utilized as needed. This plan may include such things as counseling the offender, restriction of activities, reduction of some privileges and change of the individual role within the group. Other measures may be used as required by a particular incident.

Special Activities

The mentally retarded, just as all people, need to be kept aware of their heritage and environment. Being confined to an institution does not mean a complete isolation from society. The life of the retarded must include those activities that put in proper prospective such events as Christmas, Independence Day, Valentine's Day, Easter, Thanksgiving, state fairs, circuses, horse shows and picnics. Professional and amateur ball games, theatre, music hall and other activities that may be available in the community should also be included. The retarded should learn to participate in community activities, since the ultimate goal for 80 percent of institutionalized retardeds is to return them to the community to lead as normal a life as possible.

Preparation for Special Activities

In making preparations for special events both within and without the facility, the therapist must be aware of many factors governing the overall operation of the facility. These factors range from state laws to institution policies to department procedures, and, since these special events are conducted for the sole benefit and enjoyment of the retarded individuals, a specific procedure outlining the duties and responsibilities must be followed. For a field trip, this outline may include:

1. Obtain permission of the proper institutional officials to conduct the trip.
2. Contact the concerned outside agency or group and make proper arrangements for the trip.
3. Inform supervisors and unit directors of the date and

time of the upcoming trip and the desired number of people to participate from each unit (based on tickets, seats, etc.).

4. For individuals whose names were submitted, medical approval must be obtained allowing them to attend.
5. Arrange for spending money for participant's use.
6. Some participants may need medication. A qualified person (R.N. or L.P.N.) should obtain adequate medication to last the duration of the trip and must accompany the group to administer the medication.
7. Arrange for food and transportation.
8. Meet with all aides, volunteers, chaperones and others expected to assist to explain specific assignments, details.
9. Prepare an interoffice communication informing supervisors, unit directors, aides and all concerned of the following:
   A. Name and location of each person attending.
   B. Expected time of departure and where to board the bus.
   C. Proper attire to wear or bring along.
   D. Approximate time of return.
10. Check the name of each person as he boards the bus and obtain a total count. (Same procedure should be followed before leaving the trip site.)
11. The ranking therapist should assume the leadership role during the trip. All volunteers, chaperones and other personnel will be expected to follow his or her instructions.

Preparation for special activities within the institution are not so complicated as field trips; however, to be successful they require precise and detailed planning. This may include the preparation of an interoffice communication announcing the type of activity, date, location and duration of an institutional special activity. The therapist must make plans for refreshments, decorations, supervision and games to be utilized. If the activity is to celebrate Independence Day, arrangements must be made for a parade where a theme may be selected and each building may enter a float, with a carnival, fireworks and a dance. Even though preparations for special events may be long and tedious, they are a source of tremendous enjoyment and benefit to the mentally retarded. They should not be slighted, neglected or inadequately prepared.

The Game Room

In a residential facility for the mentally retarded, the game room usually is the center of attraction, particularly when it is well-equipped with new and innovative games. Any person will be delighted to take time out from the regular daily routine to spend an hour or more in the game room. For the mentally retarded, this may be an unsurpassed treat. On the other hand, a poorly located and equipped room will not serve as a good incentive for participation. In preparing a game room, the therapist must look for a well ventilated, centrally located large or medium size room with adequate lighting, heat and restroom facilities. Before placing games and equipment, the room should be painted with bright colors and decorated with pictures, posters and colorful curtains. The equipment to be used will depend on the ability of the user. An ideal game room may include a juke box, pin ball machines, table tennis, pool table, foosball game, table shuffleboard, card tables and a variety of table games. Adequate supervision should be provided at all times when the room is open, and it should be made accessible to all those wishing to utilize it.

The Arts and Crafts Room

The right to creativity does not belong to the normal person alone. Every person, regardless of his ability, has certain creative potential. This potential can be reached only through training and motivation. In a residential environment for the retarded, it is the facility's responsibility to provide the opportunity, equipment and staff to encourage creativity among its mentally retarded clients and to channel their creative urge into art products which are both acceptable to society and beneficial to the individual. These products, however, need not be masterpieces of art—they simply need to be an art form.

In preparing an arts and crafts room, the therapist should be particular as to its location; it should be spacious, well venti-

Figure 1.
Community Center Games Room

Figure 2.
Ceramic Molding

Figure 3.
Ceramic Greenware

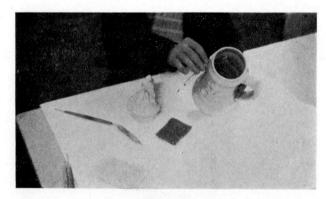

Figure 4.
Ceramic Finishing

lated, accessible to ambulatory and nonambulatory individuals and equipped with adequate toilet facilities. The arts and crafts instructor should be a qualified person who is familiar with program planning for the mentally retarded and can provide a variety of art activities such as picture making, design, ceramics, candle making, painting, lettering, modeling, paper mache, clear casting, model building, mobiles, sculpture, photography, sewing, and mosiacs. Equipment needed may include but is not limited to, standard furnishings, tables, chairs, desks, and office supplies. For ceramics, kiln and accessories, clay, underglaze, glaze, overglaze, decals, slip, stain, molds, brushes, cleaning tools, specialty tools, gleaners, sponges, pyrometric cones, decorating wheel, potter's wheel, kiln wash, felt pads, air brush, compressor, air compressor, sieve, slip mixer, wedging board, and a spray booth should be provided. For art work, glue, construction paper, crepe paper, tempera paint, finger paint, funnels, trash containers, tongue depressors, leather, leather working tools, lacing, and scissors are needed.

Additional equipment, such as plaster casting molds, plaster, basket-making kits, glass staining (fired on) china paints, mosaic tiles, tile giftware, decoupage plaques, decoupage paints, decoupage finishes, decals, decoupage prints, woodburning kits, candle-

Figure 5.
Candlemaking

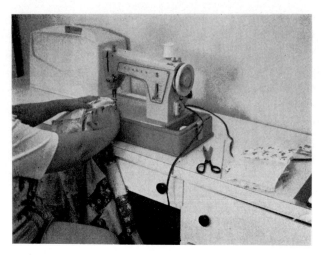

Figure 6.
Sewing

Figure 7.
Handicraft

wax, steric acid, candlewicks, candle colors, candle molds, dipping pots, hot plates, hot gloves, candle releasing spray, bottle cutter, saber saw, ¼ inch drill, circular saw, orbital sander, router, wood, jewelry findings, needles, thread, transfers, pillow cases, towels (hand and dish), view camera, film, chemicals, dryer, enlarger, print washer, safelights, film dryer, easel, trays, photographic paper, lens, photo oil colors, timers, darkroom clock, darkroom ventilator, chalk, jigsaw puzzles, iron, ironing board, sewing machine, measuring tape, adding machine, typewriter, loopers, looms, jewelry kits, jewelry tools, crewel hooks, arts and crafts books, opaque projector, color filters for enlarger, color chemicals could also be available. The room itself should be divided into several sections, with each section devoted to a specific activity. Periodic evaluations should be made by the instructor to determine the effectiveness of a particular program and the benefits derived by the individuals involved in it.

The Music Room

Music is one of the most effective means of reaching the mentally retarded. It plays an important role in taking him away from himself and his problems. In an institutional environment where access to music-oriented programs is rather limited, music therapy programs are of vital importance, particularly in the area of socialization. The music therapist is not only concerned with how the retarded responds to the music activity, but how he relates to others in the group. The major goal of a music therapy program is to bring about changes of behavior in the retarded and to better enable him to adapt and function within his own environment, making a major contribution to the retarded's rehabilitation that may result in his leaving the institution and becoming a productive member of the community.

In establishing a music room, the therapist should take into consideration such items as location, lighting, electrical outlets, restroom facilities, proper ventilation, adequate temperature controls and comfortable furnishings. As to equipment, the music room may include a piano, record players, tape recorders, assorted records, assorted rhythm instruments, drum set, two trumpets, two alto saxophones, one tenor saxophone and other assortments of music instruments.

A small practice room adjacent to the main music room should be utilized to allow for practice and private lessons. The

Figures 8 and 9.   Community Center Music Room

utilization of a music listening center where a record library may be housed will be the highlight of the music room. The center should be equipped with tape recorders, record and tape players, as well as earphones so that each individual may listen to his own type of music without disturbing others who may be using the library at the same time.

The Community Center

The skill of managing money and purchasing various goods from a store is generally taken for granted by a nonretarded individual. For the retarded, an opportunity to manage money, whether it is U.S. currency or affiliated with some type of a token economy system, is a learning experience that assists in preparing him for community living. This opportunity may be provided in the classrom where the instructor teaches the retarded the difference between each monetary denomination, as well as explaining its purchasing power. The instructor may go to the extent of using "play money" and "play goods" to demonstrate the lesson. This may get a point across, but it is not real, and the mentally retarded individual knows it. If I needed a haircut, a loaf of bread and a good book to read, I automatically know where to go to obtain these services. I am also aware of how much must be paid for them. How about the retarded?

Should he stand in line for a uniform haircut? Get bread in the cafeteria during meal time? A book; where can he get that?

The resident community center will serve many purposes in a residential facility for the mentally retarded. A properly located and managed center will provide a true life experience where each retarded individual will be able to learn money management, decision making and socialization. The community center should be open to render services seven days and evenings per week. A reasonable number of hours may be 8 A.M. to 12:00 P.M., 1:00 P.M. to 4:00 P.M. and 5:00 P.M. to 9:00 P.M. On Fridays and Saturdays, the hours may be extended to accommodate various weekend functions.

The location of the center should be easily accessible to both ambulatory and nonambulatory individuals and may include a variety of rooms such as a Library, Recreation Games Room, Ice Cream Parlor, General Store, Music Listening Room, Barber Shop, Beauty Salon, Bank and City Hall. The outside decor of these rooms may be tied together in a "Mall" form, depicting a particular theme such as "Around the World" or "Early American." For example, the Bank and City Hall may have a brick front depicting an old Western building. Inside, it may house a teller's alcove to disperse token money or be utilized for other banking services. A visiting lounge and the center manager may be housed here as well.

The Ice Cream Parlor may have a Parisian theme, with tables and chairs inside and outside in the hall, depicting a French sidewalk cafe. It should be colorful with paintings on the walls. The parlor may have a bar or sales counter, a soda fountain to dispense soft drinks and also equipped with popcorn, snow cone and cotton candy machines. Additional consumable goods may be sold at the parlor as deemed necessary by the facility.

Decor for the General Store may depict an early American log cabin. It may be stocked with soft goods such as the latest styles in clothing, grooming aids, radios, cassette recorders, records, guitars, crochet and needlepoint items, toys, games, hats, purses and countless additional items such as those found in a

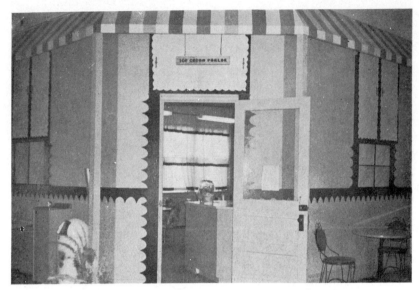

Figure 10.   Community Center Ice Cream Parlor Exterior

Figures 11 and 12.   Community Center Ice Cream Parlor Interior

Figure 13.   Community Center General Store Exterior

Figure 14.   Community Center General Store Interior

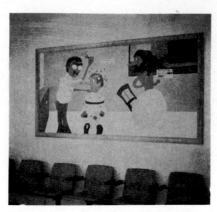

Figure 15.   Community Center Barber Shop Interior

local community department store. These items should be displayed in the same manner as found at a department store where each customer will have an opportunity to browse around, shop for the items he needs, then bring them up to the sales clerk for payment. A lay-away plan may be utilized at the General Store.

The Recreation Games Room, complete with table tennis, pool, pin ball and table games, may have the exterior of a shingled house. The Barber Shop and Beauty Salon may have a Spanish motif with a wrought iron gate at the entrance and a barber pole. A Swiss decor with window casements and flower boxes filled with red geraniums may be incorporated in the Library. In the center of the area, a large square or round planter filled with live green plants may be placed.

In addition to the learning experience, the center will provide a place for recreation on holidays, weekends and week days, as well as a visiting area where parents may visit with their children.

For the mentally retarded, the Community Center will be a place where they may enjoy recreation and where they may find a distinct, stimulating change from the areas where they spend the greater part of their time.

Establishing a Community Center

A successful and operational Community Center requires specific and detailed planning. The recreation therapist should take several points into consideration:

Figure 16.   Community Center Beauty Shop Exterior

Figure 17.   Community Center Beauty Shop Interior

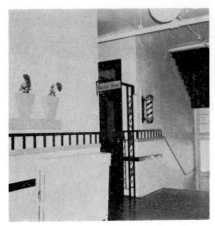

Figure 18.   Community Center Barber Shop Exterior

Figure 19.   Community Center Bank Interior

Figure 20.   Community Center Bank Exterior

1. Location and accessibility.
2. Safety features, fire escapes and toilet facilities.
3. Adequate personnel to provide proper supervision and operate the various sections.
4. Utilization of a sound accounting sytem.
5. Recruiting reliable venders to stock the Ice Cream Parlor and the General Store.
6. Determine capacity of each room.
7. Adequate lighting and electrical outlets.
8. Adequate pricing systems (markup, etc.).
9. Compliance with the rules and regulations outlined by the state health division.
10. Compliance with institutional policies pertaining to dissemination of food.
11. Establishing a sound financial backing to stock and replenish merchandise.

Chapter IV

ACTIVITIES FOR THE

MENTALLY RETARDED

U SUALLY, RECREATIONAL ACTIVITIES are looked upon as a means of relaxation and enjoyment. For the mentally retarded, it consists of much more. It is through recreational activities that the retarded is given an opportunity to develop a positive self image and generate enough interest and desire to be successful. The therapist may modify and adapt an activity so that it may aid in developing the individual physically, socially, emotionally and mentally, as well as providing him with time for relaxation and enjoyment. Recreation may also be utilized to reinforce or modify certain physical and social behaviors. In making a specified recreational program for a particular individual, the therapist must decide which aspects of development he wishes to focus on; then he plans the activities considering the selected goals. In making these plans, the following objectives for each phase of activities should be taken into consideration:

A. Competitive Games
   1. To cooperate with others
   2. To develop endurance
   3. To listen to and follow directions
B. Calisthenics
   1. To increase one's stamina and breath control
   2. To improve one's posture
   3. To develop self-discipline
   4. To know parts of the body by command

C. Activities for Healthy Physical Development
 1. To develop arm, neck, stomach muscles for good posture
 2. To gain a better sense of timing
 3. To overcome any awkward body movements
 4. To gain better gross and fine muscle coordination
 5. To increase one's coordination
D. Gross Motor Skills
 1. To develop gross motor skills and coordination through
  a. running
  b. throwing
  c. jumping
  d. kicking
  e. racing
  f. catching
  g. bouncing
  h. pulling
  i. walking
  j. marching
  k. bending
  l. twisting
  m. rolling
  n. sliding
  o. hopping
E. Fine Motor Skills
 1. To develop fine motor skills and coordination through
  a. grasping
  b. releasing
  c. holding
  d. catching
  e. finger exercises
  f. hand exercises
  g. foot and leg exercises
  h. toe exercises
 2. To develop eye, hand and finger coordination through the use of
  a. pencils
  b. crayons

    c. scissors
    d. paint brushes
    e. ceramics
  3. To develop coordination of body movements through rhythm and tempo
    a. clapping
    b. stamping
    c. swaying
    d. walking
    e. dancing (square, ballroom)
    f. running (trot, gallop)
    g. marching

F. Mental Health Skills
  1. To derive satisfaction and relaxation through the use of
    a. crayons, paints, clay, puzzles, books
    b. group games with participation with others

G. Communication Skills
  1. To become aware of one's own voice
  2. To learn to listen to others
  3. To learn to respond to verbal command
  4. To learn to distinguish different sounds

H. Sensory Skills
  1. To learn to discriminate between objects with colors, shapes, sizes and figures
  2. To be able to identify hot, cold, soft and hard
  3. To be able to identify directions—left, right, up and down

I. Social Skills
  1. To develop acceptable social behaviors
  2. To respect the property of others
  3. To respect other people
  4. To cooperate with others
  5. To develop acceptable social relationships with the opposite sex

The following pages are devoted exclusively to games and activities that may be utilized in a residential facility, school, home or any other area where a mentally retarded individual may be found. These activities are not listed according to importance, difficulty or level of the participant's ability. Also, since each activity may contribute to the development of more than one aspect of the individual's well being, they are not listed under subheadings such as "Activities to Develop Fine Motor Coordination." It is felt that the therapist is capable of determining the individual's need and selecting the activity best suited for that particular need. With interest, creativity and imagination, the majority of these activities may be adapted to suit any ability level.

Apple Bobbing

Equipment
   One medium-sized livestock water tank ¾ full of water
   Apples

Area Required
   Indoors or outdoors

Participants
   Any number

Procedure
   Place the apples in the water tank. Each player may have a chance to bite an apple and take it out of the water with his hands behind his back.

NOTE: Ideal for a carnival game. Good for nonambulatory wheelchair participants.

Apple Pick

Equipment
   One 30 feet rope clothesline
   Knitting yarn
   Apples

Area Required
   Indoors or outdoors

Participants
    Any number

Procedure
    Stretch rope between two walls (inside) or two trees (outside) at the desired height. Cut the yarn into 12 inch-long pieces. Tie each apple with one piece of yarn and tie the other end of the yarn to the stretched rope at two-feet intervals. Each player takes a position in front of one apple with his hands behind his back. At a given signal, each player tries to pick the apple by biting it. First player to get an apple is the winner.
NOTE: Good for nonambulatory wheelchair participants.

Backward Wheelchair Race

Equipment
    None

Area Required
    Indoor large room or outdoors

Participants
    Four per race

Procedure
    Make a four-lane, 25-yard race track. Establish a starting and a finish line. Players take positions with their backs to the finish line. At a given signal, each wheelchair, powered by its own occupant, proceeds to the finish line. The first player to reach the finish line is the winner.

Ball in the Jug

Equipment
    One wide mouth jug
    Six table tennis balls

Area Required
    Medium size room

Participants
    Six to twelve

Procedure

Place the jug at one end of the room. Divide the players into two teams. From a six-feet distance, each player will have three chances to throw the ball into the jug. One point is awarded for each ball going into the jug. The team with the most points is the winner.

Balloon Bust

Figure 21.   Balloon Bust

Equipment
    Multi-colored balloons
    Thumbtacks
    String to tie balloons
    One 4 x 8 x ½ inch sheet of plywood
    Six steel tip darts

Area Required
    Large room or outdoors

Participants
    Any number

Procedure

Place the sheet of plywood next to the wall, six feet from the throwing line. Inflate 25 balloons and tack them to the board with at least a five-inch diameter around each one. Each player may have three chances to throw the darts at the balloons. Points or prizes are awarded according to the number of balloons burst. NOTE: Ideal for a carnival game.

Barrel Roll

Equipment
40 gallon clear, fiber barrel

Area Required
Outdoors

Participants
Two per barrel

Procedure
Lay the barrel on its side. One player sits inside, and the second player rolls the barrel a certain distance (25 yards). Players exchange places, and so on.

Variations
The player may lie inside the barrel.
Have a barrel roll race.

Basketball Race

Equipment
Official size basketball

Area Required
Large room or basketball court

Participants
Six to twelve

Procedure
Divide group into two teams and line in two columns. A player from each team dribbles the ball to the other end of the room and back to the starting point where he passes it to the second member of his team, and so on.

Variations

Basketball relay

Players can dribble the ball, then shoot at the basket.

Basketball Shoot

Equipment

Portable or permanent basketball goal

Two official size basketballs

Area Required

Large room, gym or outdoors

Participants

Any number

Procedure

Establish a shooting line at least twelve feet from the basketball goal. Each player may have three tries to make a basket. Prizes or points are awarded according to the number of baskets made.

Variation

Divide group into two teams and have competitive basket shooting.

NOTE: Ideal for a carnival game.

Be Like Me

Equipment

Color pictures of many different people and objects, for example policeman, mailman, soldier, boat, airplane.

Area Required

Any size room

Participants

Any number

Procedure

The leader chooses a picture and shows it to the players. The players take turns in giving their impressions (pantomime) of the functions of the person or object pictured.

Figure 22.   Bean Bag Board

Be Your Buddy

Equipment

Polaroid camera   Glue

Polaroid film and flash bulbs   Scissors

Posterboard

Area Required

A room accommodating a table and four chairs

Participants

Two or more

Procedure

Take a full length Polaroid picture of each participant and allow him to cut around his body. Separate the face and exchange it with other participants. Place your buddy's face on your body.

Bean Bag Pitch

Equipment

Six light weight bean bags

Area Required

Indoors or outdoors

Participants

Two to six

Procedure

Draw two lines on the ground six to ten feet apart (depending on need). Players take positions at one line and pitch the bean bags to the other line. The player whose bag lands closest to the line without touching or crossing it is the winner.

NOTE: Ideal for a wheelchair activity.

Bean Bag Toss

Equipment

Two bean bag boards (Fig. 22)

Twelve bean bags

Area Required

Medium size room or outdoors

Participants
Six to twelve players

Procedure
Place board at one side and draw a line approximately twenty feet away. Divide players into two teams. Each team takes six bean bags. Each player throws one bag at the board. If bag goes into lower holes, one point is awarded. If bag goes into top holes, two points are awarded. If bag goes into middle holes, three points are awarded. Team with most points wins.

Figure 23.   Rear View of Bean Bag Board

Bicycle-Go-Round

Equipment
One bicycle welded to a barrel (Fig. 24)
Barrel of sand

Area Required
Large room or outdoors

Participants
Any number

Procedure

Players take turns riding the bicycle.

Figure 24.   Bicycle-Go-Round

Bingo

Equipment

25 to 30 official Bingo cards

50 Bingo prizes (candy bars, toys, etc.)

Area Required

Medium sized room

Participants

25 to 30

Procedure

Distribute Bingo cards, one per player. Determine the type of Bingo game to be played (four corners, regular bingo, cross bingo, blackout). The leader will call the number. Ten winners are allowed per game.

Variations

A member of the group may be allowed to do the calling. Substitute pictures for numbers.

Use homemade cards and use beans or corn to cover the called numbers.

NOTE: Ideal for a carnival game.

Block Stacking Race

Equipment
    48 stacking blocks

Area Required
    Any place with a smooth surface

Participants
    Two

Procedure
    The blocks are divided between players with 24 blocks each. Upon a given signal, each player begins to stack the blocks, one on top of the other. The player who stacks his blocks first without a spill is the winner.

Bowling

Equipment
    Two plastic bowling sets

Area Required
    Large room

Participants
    Six to twelve

Procedure
    Place pins in U-shape close to a wall. Divide group into two teams. Players take turns rolling the ball and trying to hit the pins from a specified distance (20 feet), one point awarded for each pin hit. Team with most points wins.

Variation
    Use for nonambulatory.

Button Pitch

Equipment

4 foot square of ¾ inch sheet of plywood, divided with a paint brush and black paint into an equal number of one inch squares (similar to a Penny Pitch Board) (Fig. 25)

50 buttons of various sizes with the largest being an inch square

Area Required

Medium sized room or outside

Participants

Any number

Procedure

Place the board on the floor. Each player will have three tries to pitch the buttons from a distance of four feet. A winning button is the one falling on a one inch square without touching the black lines. Prizes may be awarded according to the number of perfect buttons pitched.

NOTE: Ideal for a carnival game.

Figure 25.   Button Pitch

Camel Fight

Equipment
None

Area Required
Grassy area

Participants
Six

Procedure
Divide participants into two teams. Each team constructs a human camel as follows: Player A stands erect. Player B in a bending position places his head in the middle of Player A's back with his hands placed firmly around Player A's waist. Player C climbs on Player B's back. The camels take positions facing each other. At a given signal, the riders maneuver their camels and try to make the opposing camel retreat at least 25 feet.

Figure 26. Camel Fight

Candle Shoot

Equipment
  Two chairs
  One 2 x 4 piece of wood, 8 feet long
  Twelve candles
  Six water guns

Area Required
  Indoor or outdoors

Participants
  Any number

Procedure
  Secure each end of the 2 x 4 on each chair and place it at a distance of four feet from the shooting line. Place six lighted candles at certain intervals on the 2 x 4. Each player may empty contents of one full water gun and try to put out as many candles as possible. Prizes or points are awarded according to how many candles were put out. Relight candles, and the next player may have a chance to shoot.

NOTE: Ideal for a carnival game.

Cards in the Hat

Equipment
  One deck of playing cards
  One hat

Area Required
  Large or medium size room

Participants
  Any even number between two and twelve

Procedure
  Divide participants into two teams. Each player tries to throw three cards into the hat from a distance of six feet. One point is awarded for each card that falls in the hat. Team with the most points wins the game.

Variation

Cards may be replaced by marbles, beans or something similar.

Cat and Mouse

Equipment

Stepping apparatus with a tunnel opening under the steps

Area Required

Indoors or outdoors

Participants

Two

Procedure

One player is labeled the Cat and the second is labeled the Mouse. At a given signal, the Mouse climbs one side of the steps, descends the other and then crawls through the tunnel. The Cat chases the Mouse and tries to catch him. When the cat succeeds, the players exchange positions.

Chain Race

Equipment

None

Area Required

Indoors or outdoors

Participants

Any even number

Procedure

Establish a starting and finish line. Every two players stand back to back and clasp arms and palms. In that condition, they take positions at the starting line. At a given signal, they proceed, walking sideways to the finish line. The team who reaches the finish line without breaking the chain is the winning team.

Chopperball

Equipment
One basketball or playground ball

Area Required
Large recreation room or outdoors

Participants
Any number

Procedure
One player is chosen to be the leader. The other players form a circle with the leader in its middle. The leader throws the ball to each player, one at a time. The player must catch the ball with both hands and return it to the leader. If he misses the ball, he must catch it the second time with one hand. If he misses, he must return it with his feet. If he misses with both feet, he must return it with his head. If he misses, he is out of the game. Every time a player successfully returns the ball, he gains back a limb and so on.

NOTE: The ball is only thrown one time per player per turn. If he loses a limb, he must wait for the second turn to gain it back.

Crawdad Race

Equipment
None

Area Required
Wading pool

Participants
Four to six

Procedure
Participants take positions at one end of the pool in the following manner: Facing the starting end, feet touching the starting wall and resting on the palm of their hands with their back touching the water, they crawl backward toward the finish line at a given signal. The player who reaches the finish line first, without turning over, is declared the winner.

Crawling Race

Equipment
    None

Area Required
    Grassy area

Participants
    Four per race

Procedure
    Establish a four-lane, 25 yard long track, with a starting and a finish line. Players take positions on hands and knees at the starting line. At a given signal, the players crawl to the finish line. The players may be timed.

Crawling Tag

Equipment
    None

Area Required
    Grassy area

Participants
    Any number

Procedure
    All players get into a crawling position. One player is chosen to be "it." At a given signal, all players disperse. When "it" tags a player, they exchange places, and so on.

Crawl Through the Hoop

Equipment
    One Hoola® Hoop

Area Required
    Indoors or outdoors

Participants
    Three per hoop

Procedure

Two players hold the hoop at each side with the bottom edge touching the ground. The third player crawls through the hoop, first forward, then backward. Players take turns crawling through the hoop.

Variations

Lift the hoop about six inches off the ground, and the players hop through it. Several players may form a human train and go through the hoop.

Crib Car Race

Equipment
One 1 x 10 piece of wood 18 inches long
One 2 x 4 piece of wood 10 inches long

Area Required
Crib or table top

Participants
One or two players

Procedure

Elevate the 1 x 10 piece of wood by using the 2 x 4 piece of wood to form a downhill race track. Place the track in the crib close to the player. The players place the cars at the top of the track and see which one wins.

Variation

If a player cannot place his own car, it could be placed for him.

Deep Sea Treasure Hunt

Equipment
A medium sized livestock water tank ¾ full of water
Many waterproof prizes
Stones and other false prizes

Area Required
Inside recreation room or outside

Participants
    Any number

Procedure
    Muddy the water so no one can see the bottom of the tank. Throw in a few real prizes and a few false ones. Each player will have one try to reach in and hunt a prize.
NOTE: Good for nonambulatory, wheelchair participants.

Doll Throw

Equipment
    12 pieces of wood cut in the form of small dolls 6 inches high
    12 door hinges and nails
    1 8 foot 2 x 4 piece of wood
    1 canvas backstop
    Two saw horses
    Six softballs

Area Required
    Outdoors

Participants
    Any number

Procedure
    Using the door hinges, fasten the dolls at equal intervals to the 2 x 4 allowing them to fall backward when hit by a ball. Nail each end of the 2 x 4 to one saw horse. Using the canvas for a backstop, place the doll apparatus at a distance of 15 feet from the throwing line. Each player may be allowed three chances to hit the dolls with a softball. Prizes may be awarded according to the number of dolls hit.
NOTE: Ideal for a carnival game.

Duck Walk

Equipment
    None

Area Required
    Large room or outdoors

Participants
Any number

Procedure
Establish a starting and finish line. The players line up at the starting line in a deep knee bend position. At a given signal, players proceed in a duck walk fashion to the finish line. The player who reaches it first without a spill is the winner.

Variations
Divide players into two teams and have a team duck walk race.
Have a duck walk relay race.

Filler-Up-Cup

Equipment
2 chairs
1 8 foot 2 x 4 piece of wood
12 9 oz. paper cups
Thumbtacks
6 water guns

Area Required
Indoors or outdoors

Participants
Any number

Procedure
Secure each end of the 2 x 4 on each chair and place it at a distance of four feet from the shooting line. At certain intervals, tack the cups by their rims at an angle to the 2 x 4 with the opening facing the shooting line. Each player may empty the contents of one water gun trying to fill at least one paper cup. Prizes or points are awarded for the amount of water contained in a single cup.

NOTE: Ideal for a carnival game.

Fish Pond

Equipment

Medium sized livestock water tank

12 pieces of wood cut in the shape of fish, painted different colors, number from one to twelve, with an eye hook on their backs

3 broomstick handles, with a 4 foot string and a hook attached to one end

Several prizes

Area Required

Outdoors or recreation room

Participants

Any number

Procedure

Fill the tank ¾ full of water. Each player is given three chances to catch a fish by using the broomstick. Prizes are awarded according to the number of fish hooked.

NOTE: Ideal for a carnival game.

Fly a Kite

Equipment

Kite and kite string

Area Required

Outdoors

Participants

Any number

Procedure

Each player ties the string to the proper position on the kite. At a given signal, all of the players fly their kites at the same time.

NOTE: May be adapted for wheelchairs and nonambulatory individuals.

Follow Me

Equipment
None

Area Required
Indoors or outdoors

Participants
Any number

Procedure
Divide the players into two teams, with a leader chosen for each team. The players line up behind the leader. At a given signal, both leaders start moving forward, each deciding which path to take. They may crawl, hop, turn at a right angle, go up and down a hill. All of the time the players must remain in a straight line behind the leader. The player who gets out of line is out of the game. The team with the most players left in line is the winning team.

Guess Who I Am

Equipment
One face mask for each participant

Area Required
Large room or playground

Participants
Any number

Procedure
Each participant wears a face mask and, at the same time, tries to identify the real person hiding behind the other face masks. The winner will be the participant left with the un-identified real face.

Variations
One participant may wear the mask while all others take turns to identify him.

Divide participants into two teams.

Participants identify the face mask rather than the real person.

Hand Numbers

Equipment
   Table and chairs

Area Required
   Indoors or outdoors

Participants
   Two or more

Procedure
   Each player makes a hand fist and lightly hits the table while the opponent counts to three. When the player hits the table for the third time, he extends one or more fingers, trying to match the number of fingers that may be extended by the opponent. When the match occurs, the first player does the counting, and the opponent tries to match him.

Hand Pool

Equipment
   Regulation sized pool table and balls

Area Required
   Medium sized room accommodating a pool table

Participants
   Two or more

Procedure
   Stack balls in regular "8-ball" pool fashion. Each player uses his hand in place of a cue stick. One player shoots striped colored balls, and the second player shoots solid colored balls. The winner is determined in the same manner as in regular pool game.

NOTE: Good for nonambulatory, wheelchair participants.

Hide Your Color

Equipment
Various colored cloth discs

Area Required
Large room or outside

Participants
Two or more

Procedure
Pin one color on each participant's back. Each participant tries to hide his color from the others while, at the same time, he tries to identify their colors. The winner will be the participant left with the unidentified color.

Variation
One participant may select a color, and the others take turns to identify it.

Hoop-A-Ball

Equipment
One Hoola Hoop
One beach ball

Area Required
Wading pool

Participants
Two or more

Procedure
Place the Hoola Hoop at one end of the wading pool. Each player tries to throw the beach ball to make it land inside the hoop.

Variation
Divide participants into two teams and have a competition similar to basketball.

Ice Man Freeze

Equipment
    None

Area Required
    Outdoors

Participants
    Any number

Procedure
    One player is chosen to be Ice Man. At a given signal, all other players disperse. Ice Man tries to touch each of them. When a player is touched by the Ice Man, he freezes in that position and spot. When all players are touched, a new Ice Man is chosen.

Variation
    Frozen players may be released if touched by another player. Players may be divided into two teams. One team is ice men, and the second team dispersed. When all players of one team are frozen, they will become the ice men.

Inner Tube Race

Equipment
    Two large, inflated inner tubes

Area Required
    Wading pool

Participants
    Two players

Procedure
    Each player sits in the inner tube (as a lounge chair) and takes a position at one end of the pool. At a given signal, each player uses his hands to paddle to the other end of the pool. The player who reaches the opposite end first is declared the winner.

Figure 27.   Inner Tube Race

Let's Eat

Equipment
    Two cooking pans
    Two complete table settings
    Tablecloth and napkins
    One table
    (Pictures of the aforementioned items may be substituted.)

Area Required
    Indoors

Participants
    Any number
    (Players must wear large name tags.)

Procedure
    One player is declared the Cook, and he leaves the room.
One item or picture is assigned to each player left in the room.
The players must hide their items behind their backs. When
this is completed, the Cook is called in. The object is for him
to set the table complete with one pan, one table place setting,
tablecloth and napkins. He accomplishes this by choosing a

player and calling his name; the player then hands the Cook the item in his possession. If a duplicate item is called, the meal is declared "burned," and a new Cook is chosen.

Marble Shoot

Equipment
    4 large 1 inch marbles

Area Required
    Medium sized room or outdoors

Participants
    Two or more

Procedure
    The first player places his marble on the floor three feet from the shooting line. The second player tries to hit the first player's marble.

Variation
    Hold the marble between the thumb knuckle and the tip of the index finger, and when ready to shoot, hit the marble with the thumbnail—causing it to roll in the direction desired.

Match Box Cars

Equipment
    Empty match boxes
    Toothpicks
    Buttons

Area Required
    Any place

Participants
    Any number

Procedure
    In each match box, insert two toothpicks to serve as front and rear car axles. On each toothpick, place two buttons, forming four wheels. Players may line their cars on a slanted ground,

and at a given signal, the cars may be given a slight push, and the race begins.

Miniature Boat Race

Equipment

    4 small plastic, wooden or paper sailboats.
    1 large portable wash basin
    Water

Area Required

    A room where a table accommodating at least four wheelchairs may be placed.

Participants

    Four or more depending on accommodations

Procedure

    Fill up basin with water. Each participant places his boat in the water at the starting line. At a given signal, the participants blow their boats to the opposite end. The first boat to reach the finish line is the winner.

Variation

    Nut shells, feathers or something similar may be substituted for boats.

Figure 28.   Miniature Boat Race

Miniature Wind Ball

Equipment
    Table tennis ball
    Large portable wash basin
    Water
    Card table

Area Required
    Medium size room

Participants
    Two to six

Procedure
Fill basin with water. Divide participants into two teams. Each team takes up its position at one end of the basin. Place the table tennis ball in the center of the basin. At a given signal, each team (with their hands behind their backs or off the table) tries to blow the ball to the opposite end.

Variations
    Obstacle may be placed in the basin.
    Feather may be substituted for a table tennis ball.

Monkey Roll

Equipment
    None

Area Required
    Indoors on mats or outdoors on grass

Participants
    Three players

Procedure
Players line up side by side on hands and knees. Player A jumps over Players B and C and takes a position to the right of Player C. Player B jumps over Players C and A and takes a

position to the right of Player A. Player C jumps over Players A and B and takes a position to the right of Player B, and so on. See how fast the monkeys can roll.

Figure 29.   Monkey Roll

Music Freeze

Equipment
   Records and a record player

Area Required
   Indoors or outdoors

Participants
   Any number

Procedure
   The leader starts a record, and the participants may dance or do any other self expressions according to the music played. Every once in awhile, the leader stops the music, and the players must freeze in the position he is in at that time. Any player who moves is out of the game. The player who successfully freezes through all the stops after all other players are out is declared the winner.

Musical Rugs

Equipment
Twelve throw rugs, one must be red

Area Required
Large recreation room

Participants
Twelve

Procedure
Place the rugs on the floor at twelve different locations in the room. The players take positions at least ten feet away from the closest rug. The leader starts the music, and the players begin moving in the room around the rugs. They cannot stop while the music is playing. When the music stops, each player must stand on one rug. The player who happens to stop on the red rug must tell a humorous short story or make a funny movement of some type, and so on.

Variation
The player standing on the red rug is out of the game, and one other rug is removed until only one player remains.

Name Game

Equipment
None

Area Required
Any place

Participants
Two to six

Procedure
One player starts off by saying a name of a state. The second player, using the last letter, must say the name of another state. Example: If the first player said "Missouri," the second player may say "Illinois," the third may say "South Dakota," and so on.

Variation

Names of cars, people, objects, food may be substituted for names of states.

Obstacle Course

Equipment

Walking board, stepping ladder, tumbleslide

Area Required

Medium room or outdoors

Participants

Any number

Procedure

Use the equipment to form a circle. Participants start with the slide, then walking board, then the stepping ladder.

Variations

Use any combination of two equipment.

Go through backward.

Pass the Apple

Equipment

Many apples

Area Required

Indoors or outdoors

Participants

Six to twelve

Procedure

Divide the players into two teams, and the teams line up facing each other. The leader of each team holds an apple between his chin and chest. At a given signal, the players, with their hands behind their backs, begin passing the apple from one end of the line to the other. Each player must receive the apple between his chin and chest and pass it to the second player in the same form. The first team to pass the apple to the end of the line without a spill is the winning team.

Pass the Ball

Equipment
Two official size basketballs

Area Required
Large room or outdoors

Participants
Ten to twenty

Procedure
Divide group into two teams. Each team lines up in vertical fashion. First player passes the ball between his legs to the player behind him, then player runs to the back of the line. Team whose players finish passing the ball first is the winner.

Variations
Pass the ball over head.
Line up side by side and pass the ball.
Make a complete turn about and give the ball to person directly behind.

Pony-Go-Round

Equipment
Pony-Go-Round apparatus
Four to six properly saddled Shetland ponies

Area Required
Outdoors

Participants
Four to six

Procedure
Properly hitch the ponies to the apparatus. The participants take turns in riding the ponies. A maximum of five minutes per participant should be sufficient. (This activity must be adequately supervised.)

NOTE: Ideal for a carnival ride.

Record Break

Equipment
>100 45 RPM records
>100 33 RPM records
>12 softballs
>1 large canvas backstop
>2 saw horses

2 wooden rectangles (made of 2 x 4) with ¼ inch grooves on the inside, one to accommodate two large records and the second to accommodate three small records

1 8 foot 2 x 4 piece of wood

Area Required
>Outdoors

Participants
>Any number

Procedure

Firmly nail the rectangles on the 2 x 4. Nail each end of the 2 x 4 on a saw horse using the canvas for a backstop. Place the record apparatus at a distance of fifteen feet from the throwing line. Place records in their respective rectangles. Each player will have three chances to break the records by throwing the softball. Prizes may be awarded according to the number of records broken.

NOTE: Ideal for a carnival game.

Remember

Equipment

Several small objects, such as a comb, brush, pencil, note pad, ashtray

Area Required
>Indoors or outdoors

Participants
>Any number

Procedure

Mix the objects, then expose them for one minute in order for all the players to see them. One at a time, the players recall the objects. The player who recalls the most objects is the winner.

Variation

Exposure time may be increased or decreased to make the game harder or easier.

Ring Toss

Equipment

Six rings and one peg one foot long

Area Required

Large room or outdoors

Participants

Six to twelve

Procedure

Divide participants into two teams. Each player tries to hit the peg with the ring from six feet distance. One point awarded for each correct hit. Team with most points wins the game.

Variation

Game could be played by one or two participants.

Roll the Ball

Equipment

1 basketball or soccer ball or playground ball

Area Required

A large room or outdoors

Participants

Two or more

Procedure

Players take positions at least fifteen feet from each other.

Player A rolls the ball to Player B who rolls it to Player C. Then the ball is rolled in reverse or Player A to Player C.

Variations

Players kick the ball to each other.

The ball may be kicked to the player whose name is called by the therapist.

Shoulder Fight

Equipment

None

Area Required

Large room or outdoors

Participants

Two or more

Procedure

The participants, facing each other, stand on one foot with their arms crossed in front of their chests. On a given signal, each player tries to make the opposition lose their balance by hitting him lightly with his shoulder. Note: only shoulders make contact.

Variations

Form two teams.

Start on the left foot, then change to the right one.

Figure 30. Shoulder Fight

Skateboard Race

Equipment

   Two skating boards (see illustration)

Area Required

   Asphalt or concrete playground

Participants

   Two per race

Procedure

   Establish a starting and a finish line. Each player lies face down on his skating board and takes a position at the starting line. At a given signal, players proceed to the finish line, each player moves his own board as if it were a boat.

Variation

   Sit on the skating board and move it by using the feet.

Figure 31.   Skateboard Race

Skating

Equipment
A pair of skates with rubber stops for each player

Area Required
Large, empty room or, preferably, a skating rink

Participants
Any number

Procedure
Each player wears skates. Skate in circular fashion. Skate according to directions. Skate according to music. Skate under limbo stick. Skate in doubles.

Soccer Relay Race

Equipment
Two soccer balls

Area Required
Large room or outdoors

Participants
Any even number

Procedure
Divide players into four groups. Lined up in columns, place Group 1 and Group 2 at one end of the room and Group 3 and Group 4 at the opposite end. Give a soccer ball to the leaders of Groups 1 and 2 who will give it a small kick in a running fashion and pass it to the leader of the opposite group. The two groups that finish passing the ball first are the winning teams.

Softball Throw

Equipment
Six softballs
100 feet measuring tape

Area Required
Outdoor field

Participants
    Any number

Procedure
    At one end of the field, make two horizontal lime lines six feet apart and allow at least 150 feet of throwing area. Divide group into throwers and retrievers. Each player is allowed three throws, and the distance of the best throw is recorded. After all throwers are finished, the two groups exchange places. The player with the best distance is declared the winner.

Square Ball

Equipment
    Large playground ball

Area Required
    Outdoors

Participants
    Five

Procedure
    Draw a fifteen foot square on the ground. A leader is chosen, and he takes a position in the middle of the square. Each of the other players takes a position at one of the square corners. The leader throws, bounces or rolls the ball to the players. He may throw it to the same player twice; he may throw it in a routine turn or at random. Each player must catch the ball and return it to the leader. The player who misses three times is out of the game. When all four players are out, a new leader is chosen, and so on.

Stamp Decoupage

Equipment
    Many colorful, cancelled foreign and domestic postage stamps
    1 inch 8 x 10 inch piece of pine wood
    Glue
    Shellac and brush
    Stain and picture hook

Area Required
   Any room

Participants
   One or more

Procedure
   Chip the edges of the wood, then stain it. Place the chosen stamps in a particular design and glue them to the wood. Apply one coat of shellac; after it dries, apply three additional coats. Place the picture hook in the top center of the finished product.

Variation
   Use photographs or other pictures.

Stamp Mosaics

Equipment
   Many colorful, cancelled foreign and domestic postage stamps
   Posterboard
   Scissors, glue, pencil

Area Required
   Any room accommodating tables and chairs

Participants
   One or more

Procedure
   Glue postage stamps or posterboard until it is completely covered (no particular pattern to be followed). After glue is dry, draw a picture on the stamps. Cut the picture out and glue it on another posterboard. Fill in the background with other stamps.

Variations
   Draw the picture first, then glue stamps on it.
   Make "funny pages" mosaics.
   Make magazine mosaics.

Stepping Ladder

Equipment
One stepping ladder (Fig. 32)

Area Required
Medium size room or outdoors

Participants
Any number

Procedure
Stand at one end and walk forward to the other end. Walk backward. Hop on one foot forward from one end to the other. Hop forward on the second foot. Hop backward. Walk sideways. Hop sideways.

Variations
Use two ladders and have a team race.
Walk or hop according to verbal directions.

Squeeze a Picture

Equipment
Six empty rubber mustard containers
Six colors of tempera or finger paint
Posterboard

Area Required
Any room accommodating a table and chairs

Participants
Two to four per table

Procedure
Fill each mustard container with one color. Place the full containers and the posterboard on the table. Each participant chooses his own colors and squeezes the paint onto the board forming shapes or paintings. Participants should be allowed to keep their drawings after they dry.
NOTE: Ideal for a carnival game.

Figure 32. Stepping Ladder

Swinging Football Target

Equipment
    One official size football
    One large car tire
    30 foot rope

Area Required
    Outdoors

Participants
    Any number

Procedure
    Tie one end of the rope to the tire and the other end to a large tree limb, allowing the tire to swing at least 10 feet above the ground. From a distance of 25 feet, each player may have a chance to throw the football and make it go through the swinging tire.

Figure 33.   Swinging Football Target

Table Tennis Ball Race

Equipment
Six table tennis balls
Six table tennis paddles

Area Required
Medium size room or outdoors

Participants
Three to six

Procedure
Draw a starting line at one end of the room and a finish line at the other end. Each player receives a paddle and a ball. At a given signal, the players begin bouncing the ball on the paddle and walking with it to the other end. The player who reaches the finish line first without a spill is the winner.

Target Fish Casting

Equipment
Fishing rod and reel
Fishing line and weights
Four different sized hoops

Area Required
Large room or outside

Participants
Any number

Procedure
Establish a starting line. Place hoops at different angles at least 20 yards from the starting line. Each participant will have three chances to cast at the hoops.

Variation
Use bamboo poles with string.

Figure 34.   Target Fish Casting

Tennis Ball Dribble

Equipment
One tennis ball

Area Required
Indoors or outdoors on asphalt or concrete playground

Participants
Any number

Procedure
Players form a complete circle. With players spaced at two-feet intervals, one player starts the game by dribbling the ball three times, then passes it under his own leg to the player to his left, who in turn dribbles it 3 times and passes it under his left leg to the next player, and so on.

Variations
Pass the ball to the player at his right.
Pass the ball according to specific directions.

Thumb Competition

Equipment
   None

Area Required
   Any place

Participants
   Two

Procedure
   Competitors clasp the right or the left hands with the thumb in an erect position. Upon a given signal, each player tries to pin down the opposing thumb.

Tiger Hunt

Equipment
   One set of playing cards
   Table and chairs

Area Required
   Indoors

Participants
   Any number

Procedure
   Scatter the deck of cards on the table face down. At a given signal, players begin turning cards right side up. When a player turns over an Ace, he shouts "Tiger." Points may be awarded as follows:
   4 for the first Ace
   3 for the second Ace
   2 for the third Ace
   1 for the fourth Ace

Variation
   Use animal pictures instead of playing cards.

Tiptoe Race

Equipment
  None

Area Required
  Indoors or outdoors

Participants
  Any number

Procedure
  Establish a starting line and a finish line (25 feet). Players take their position on tiptoe at the starting line. At a given signal, they proceed to the finish line. The player who reaches the finish line without a spill or without losing his balance is declared the winner.

Tiptoe Tag

Equipment
  None

Area Required
  Small indoor or outdoor area

Participants
  Any number

Procedure
  One player is chosen to be "it." At a given signal, all players disperse. When chased by "it," players must move on tiptoe only; however, when they are not chased, they may rest on their feet. When "it" tags a player, they exchange places, and so on.

Tire Race

Equipment
  A short stick or rod
  A bicycle wheel for each player

Area Required
Outdoors or gym

Participants
Two or more

Procedure
Establish a starting and a finish line. Participants take positions at the starting line. At a given signal, each participant pushes his bicycle wheel with the use of the stick.

Figure 35. Tire Race

Tire Tunnel Crawl

Equipment
Six large used car tires
Six ropes, each 30 feet long
10 feet high horizontal bar

Area Required
Indoors or outdoors

Participants
Any number

Procedure

With the use of the ropes, tie each tire to the horizontal bar. Tires should be close together, forming a tunnel no more than 18 inches above ground level. At a given signal, one player crawls through the tire tunnel. When he reaches the other end, the second player starts crawling. Players may be timed, and the player with the best time is declared the winner.

Towel Wrestling

Equipment
  One bath towel

Area Required
  Indoors or outdoors

Participants
  Two

Procedure

Players take positions facing each other and holding one end of the towel. At a given signal, each player tries to make his opponent move his feet from the original position.

Treasure Dive

Equipment
  Wading pool
  Waterproof objects or prizes

Area Required
  Wading pool

Participants
  Any number

Procedure

Participants form a circle in the pool. An object is thrown in the circle. At a given signal, the players dive after the object. The player who comes up with the object may keep it.

Tumble Slide

Equipment

One tumble slide (Fig. 36). (Five steps on one side and slide on the other.)

Area Required

Medium size room or outdoors

Participants

Any number

Procedure

Participant walks up the steps without the use of rails and slides down the other side.

Variations

Climb two steps at one time.

Slide down in a standing position.

Use two slides and have a race.

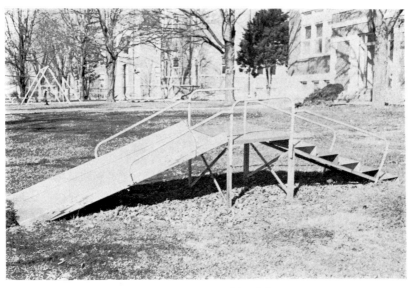

Figure 36. Tumble Slide

Up, Down and Crawl

Equipment
    A set of steps as illustrated (Fig. 37)

Area Required
    Recreation room

Participants
    Any number

Procedure
    The players form a line in front of the steps. At a given signal, each player climbs up the steps at one side and descends on the other side, turns to his right, goes around the steps and crawls under them, and so on.

Figure 37.   Up, Down and Crawl

Volleyball Toss

Equipment
    Two volleyballs
    Volleyball net

Area Required
Large room, gym or outdoors

Participants
Any number

Procedure
Outline a volleyball field and place the net appropriately. Divide the group into servers and retrievers. The servers take turns at serving the ball. The retrievers return it for the second player. When the servers are finished, the two groups exchange places.

Walk a Tight Rope

Equipment
A piece of chalk

Area Required
Medium size room or outdoor hard surface

Participants
Any number

Procedure
Draw a straight line 25 feet long and ask each player to walk on it without deviating from it.

Variation
Walks backward, sideways, walk a crooked line or a circle.

Walking Board

Equipment
One walking board 8 feet long (a 2 x 4 built as in Fig. 38) and 6 inches high

Area Required
Medium sized room or outdoors

Participants
Any number

Procedure

Step on the walking board and walk forward. Walk backward. Walk sideways.

Variations

Use two walking boards and have a race.

Walk according to directions called by the therapist.

Figure 38.   Walking Board

Wall Baseball

Equipment

One tennis ball

Area Required

Large recreation room or gym

Participants

Any number

Procedure

Players take turns in throwing the tennis ball. The ball must first hit the floor, then the wall. The player must make an attempt to catch the ball when it bounces back in his direction. One point is awarded for each catch.

Variation

Players may be divided into two teams, and a score may be kept.

Water Volleyball

Equipment
A volleyball or beach ball
Volleyball net

Area Required
Wading pool

Participants
Six to twelve

Procedure
Fasten the volleyball net to the pool's edge, dividing the pool into two equal parts. Divide the players into two teams. Each team takes a position at one side of the pool, and the game proceeds as in regular volleyball.

What Is It?

Equipment
A room containing furniture and many other miscellaneous objects

Area Required
Recreation room

Participants
Any number

Procedure
One player is declared a leader, and he looks about the room and picks an object. He gives the other players three clues as

to what the object may be. Players begin looking for the object. The first player to find it is declared the leader and picks his own object.

What Is My Color?

Equipment
    10 inch square patches of various colors

Area Required
    Any size room

Participants
    Any number

Procedure
    The leader chooses one color and asks the players to identify it by name. The first player to identify the color may hold the second color.

What Is My Name?

Equipment
    Colored pictures of different people and objects

Area Required
    Any size room

Participants
    Any number

Procedure
    The leader chooses a picture and asks each of the players to identify the person or object by name. The first player to identify the name may hold the second picture.

Wheelbarrow

Equipment
    Two people

Area Required
    Large room or outside

Participants
   Two people per wheelbarrow

Procedure
   First player lays face down on the ground. The second player holds him by the ankles and gives him support while the first player walks on his hands imitating a wheelbarrow.

Variation
   A wheelbarrow race.

Figure 39.   Wheelbarrow

Wheelchair Badminton

Equipment
   Badminton net
   Rackets
   Shuttlecock

Area Required
   Outdoor badminton court, a large room or a gym

Participants
   Two teams consisting of one to nine players each

Procedure

Modify court layout to coincide with number of participants. Each team's members take their positions on the court with each chair occupant covering a certain area. The first shuttlecock round determines which team serves first. The regular badminton rules are followed for scoring.

Variation

Each player may be allowed two hits before the shuttlecock is passed on.

Figure 40.   Wheelchair Badminton

Wheelchair Relay Race

Equipment
   Stop watch
   Whistle
   Starting gun
   Five relay objects

Area Required
　　Outdoor asphalt or cinder track

Participants
　　Twenty per race

Procedure
　　Outline a 100-yard, five-lane track and line up the wheelchairs at 25 yard intervals, with the first five at the starting line. At a given signal, the race starts with each chair powered by its own occupant and carrying the relay object to the second player who carries it to the third. The third takes it to the finish line. The first team who reaches the finish line with the relay object is the winning team.

Wheelchair Spoon Race

Equipment
　　Tablespoons
　　Table tennis balls

Area Required
　　Large room or rubberized track

Participants
　　Any number

Procedure
　　Establish a starting and finish line. Participants take positions at the starting line. In each participant's mouth, place a spoon with a ball in it. At a given signal, participants proceed to the finish line. The first to reach it without spilling the ball is declared the winner.

Variation
　　Develop a relay race.

Wheelchair Tag

Equipment
None

Area Required
Large recreation room or outdoor asphalt or concrete playground

Participants
Eight maximum

Procedure
One wheelchair occupant is chosen to be "it." At a given signal, all other wheelchairs disperse, powered by their own occupants. When "it" touches the back of a chair, they exchange places, and so on.

Wheel of Fortune

Equipment
A standard Wheel of Fortune (May be homemade)
Prizes

Area Required
Indoors or outdoors

Participants
Any number

Procedure
Place the Wheel of Fortune on a table where it can be reached by players. Place various prizes by the numbers. Each player may have one chance to spin the wheel. The player receives the prize on which the needle stops.

NOTE: Ideal for a carnival game.

Whisper

Equipment
None

Area Required
Indoors or outdors

Participants
Any number

Procedure
The players form a complete circle. One player starts off by whispering a word to the player to his right, who in turn whispers it to the player on his right, and so on, until the word returns to its originator who says it out loud. If it is the original word, then he whispers a new one. If it is not the original word, the next player whispers a word, and so on.

Who Is in the Bag?

Equipment
Twelve medium size paper grocery bags

Area Required
Indoors or outdoors

Participants
Any number up to twelve

Procedure
One player is asked to take a good look at all the players, then leaves the room. In his absence, all players cover their heads with the paper bags. The player is called in. He must identify who is in each bag without looking at the faces. If he makes four correct identifications, a new player is chosen to leave the room, and so on.

Who Is Lost?

Equipment
None

Area Required
Recreation room

Participants
    Four to twelve

Procedure
    One player is asked to leave the room. While he is out, another player hides some place inside the room. The first player has three chances to identify the "lost" player.

Wood Is Safety

Equipment
    None

Area Required
    Outdoors, close to many wooden objects

Participants
    Any number

Procedure
    Divide the players into two teams. One team will be the woodchoppers, and the second team will be the woodpeckers. At a given signal, the woodchoppers disperse, and the woodpeckers try to catch them. When the woodpecker gets close, the woodchopper may touch any wooden object which, automatically, makes him safe. When a woodchopper is caught, a member of the woodpecker team stands guard. The woodchoppers may release their teammate by touching him without being caught themselves. When all woodchoppers are caught, they exchange places with the woodpeckers, and so on.

Variation
    Wooden objects may be substituted with higher grounds so that safety comes when the person is on ground at least three inches higher than the original ground.

Chapter V

SUMMARY

P UBLIC RESIDENTIAL FACILITIES in the United States are providing services for over 200,000 mentally retarded individuals. The trend of these services has changed by evolution from basic custodial care to that of intensive programming where recreational therapy plays a major role. Throughout this manual, we pointed out the importance and the objectives of recreation as related to the development of the mentally retarded, not only in a residential facility but in any facility where a retarded may be found.

We provided ideas and guidelines that may assist in establishing a comprehensive recreational therapy program; however, it is left up to the therapist or aide to choose from this material and utilize those activities that will be of maximum benefit to his retarded clients.

In order to derive maximum benefit, it is recommended that the recreation program designed for a particular individual should be geared to improve a specific disability and, consequently, substituting a stronger function for it. When planning the program, the ability of the retarded should never be underestimated; designing an activity that is slightly above his ability level may prove to be both challenging and effective.

In implementing the recreation program, the therapist or aide should pay particular attention to the time of day or week the activity is to be conducted. Evenings and weekends seem to be the most effective, since not too many other programs are conducted during these hours, and the retarded individual will be receptive to recreation. In a residential facility, nursing personnel should never be slighted since they can influence the success of a recreation program to a great extent. The therapist should make every attempt to involve them in the planning, preparation and implementation of the activities. Finally, it is not an understatement to say that a dynamic and enthusiastic recreation worker who possesses leadership qualities and enjoys participation in various activities may make the real difference between the success and failure of a recreation program.

Appendix 1

SOURCES OF RECREATIONAL EQUIPMENT, MATERIALS AND SUPPLIES

American Handicraft
2101 W. Broadway
Crossroads West Shopping Center
Columbia, Missouri 65201

Atlas Athletic Equipment Co.
2115 Locust Street
St. Louis, Missouri 63103

Audiotronics, Inc.
7428 Bellaire Avenue
P.O. Box 151
North Hollywood, California 91603

Beckley-Cardy Company
1900 N. Narragansett Avenue
Chicago, Illinois 60639

Bergfeld Recreation, Inc.
12025 Manchester
St. Louis, Missouri 63131

"Bingo King" Co., Inc.
P.O. Box 1178
Englewood, Colorado

"Chicago" Skate Supply, Inc.
P.O. Box 356
Plattsburg, Missouri 64477

Chicago Roller Skate Co.
Hardie Building
14th & Smallman Streets
Pittsburgh, Pennsylvania 15222

Childplay of New York, Inc.
43 East 19th Street
New York, New York 10003

Collegiate Specialty Co.
427 River Street
Troy, New York 12181

Creative Playthings, Inc.
Princeton, New Jersey

Dealer's Warehouse
1102-1106 Kenmore Boulevard
P.O. Box 3786
Akron, Ohio

Dick Blick
P.O. Box 1267
Galesburg, Illinois 61401

Educational Record Sales
157 Chambers Street
New York, New York 10007

E. R. Moore Co.
7230 N. Caldwell Avenue
Niles (Chicago), Illinois 60648

Everlast Sporting Goods Mfg. Co., Inc.
175 Walnut Avenue
New York, New York

Fischer Price
East Aurora, New York 14052

Garrison-Wagner Company
2018 Washington Avenue
St. Louis, Missouri 63103

Giant Manufacturing Company
South 6th St. at 12th Avenue
Council Bluffs, Iowa 51501

Hewig-Marvic
861 Manhattan
Brooklyn, New York 11222

Hicks-Ashby Company
1610 Baltimore Street
Kansas City, Missouri 64108

Hoover Brothers, Inc.
1511 Baltimore Avenue
Kansas City, Missouri 64108

Jayfro Corp.
1 Bridge Street
P.O. Box 50
Montville, Connecticut 06353

J. E. Burke Company
1016 Baltimore
Room 322 Dept. B
Kansas City, Missouri 64105

Kansas City Audio-Visual
3242 Holmes
Kansas City, Missouri 64109

Lee Wards
Creative Crafts Center
Elgin, Illinois 60120

Lowe & Campbell Athletic Goods
6601 Troost
Kansas City, Missouri

Lyons
688 Industrial Drive
Elmhurst, Illinois 60126

MacGregor Company
4861 Spring Grove Avenue
Cincinnati, Ohio

Milton Bradley
Springfield, Massachusetts 01101

Miracle Equipment Company
Grinnell, Iowa 50112

North America Recreation Convertibles,
    Inc.
P.O. Box 668
Westport, Connecticut 06880

Novo Educational Toy & Equipment
    Corp.
585 Avenue of the Americans
    (Sixth Ave.)
New York, New York 10011

Passon's, Inc.
824 Arch Street
Philadelphia, Pennsylvania 19107

Peripole, Inc.
P.O. Box 146
Lewistown Road
Browns Mills, New Jersey 08015

Program Aids Co., Inc.
550 Garden Ave.
Mount Vernon, New York

Playground Equipment
The Mexico Forge, Inc.
Mexico, Pennsylvania

Playtime Products, Inc.
Warsaw, Indiana

Recreation Equipment Corp.
Department 970M
724 W. 8th Street
Anderson, Indiana 46011

Rhythm Band, Inc.
P.O. Box 126
Fort Worth, Texas 76101

Russell Records, Inc.
P.O. Box 3318
1403 Callens Road
Ventura, California 93003

Salsich Recreation, Inc.
13222 Manchester
St. Louis, Missouri 63131

Sears, Roebuck and Company
Kansas City, Missouri

Skil-Crafts
Division of Brown Leather Co.
309 Virginia Avenue
Joplin, Missouri

Skill Development Equipment Co.
P.O. Box 6497
Anaheim, California 92806

S & M Athletic Goods Co.
2113 West Broadway
Sedalia, Missouri 65301

S & S Arts & Crafts
Division of S & S Leather
Colchester, Conn. 06415

Tandy Leather Company
3333 Manchester Rd.
Coventry Plaza
Akron, Ohio 44319

Montgomery Ward
Kansas City, Missouri

Wilson Sporting Goods Co.
2233 West Street
River Grove, Illinois 60171

Appendix 2

PROFESSIONAL, PRIVATE AND PUBLIC ORGANIZATIONS PROVIDING SERVICES FOR THE MENTALLY RETARDED

American Association Health, Physical
Education and Recreation
1201 Sixteenth Street N.W.
Washington, D.C. 20036

American Association on Mental
Deficiency
5201 Connecticut Ave. N.W.
Washington, D.C. 20015

Association for Exceptional Children
1411 S. Jefferson Davis Highway
Suite 900
Arlington, Virginia 22202

Bureau of Education for the
Handicapped
Washington, D.C. 20201

Council for Exceptional Children
Washington, D.C.

Joseph P. Kennedy, Jr., Foundation
1701 K Street, N.W.
Washington, D.C. 20006

National Association for Mental Health
1800 N. Kent Street
Rosslyn, Virginia 22209

National Association for Retarded
Children
New York, New York

National Association for Retarded
Citizens
2709 Avenue "E" East
Arlington, Texas 76011

National Institute of Mental Health
5600 Fishers Lane
Rockville, Maryland 20852

National Recreation and Park
Association
1601 North Kent Street
Arlington, Virginia

National Therapeutic Recreation
Society
1601 North Kent Street
Arlington, Virginia 22209

President's Committee on Mental
Retardation
Washington, D.C. 20201

President's Council on Physical Fitness
and Sports
Washington, D.C. 20202

Special Olympics, Inc.
1701 K Street, N.W.
Washington, D.C. 20006

REFERENCES

O'Morrow, Gerald S.: *Administration of Activity Therapy Service*. Springfield, Thomas, 1966.

Kolstoe, Oliver P.: *A High School Work-Study Program for Mentally Subnormal Students*. Carbondale, Southern Illinois University Press, 1965.

SREB Recreation Committee: *Recreation for the Mentally Retarded*. 1964.

INDEX